IT'S ALL ABOUT THE KINGDOM

IT'S ALL ABOUT THE KINGDOM

Godly Steps and Instructions for Successful Kingdom Living

(Apostolic, Spiritual, and Kingdom Protocol for Fivefold Leaders, Ministers, and Laypersons)

Session I-III

Dr. J. G. Rice
Chief Apostle

Library of Congress Control Number:		2010911155
ISBN:	Hardcover	978-1-4500-6479-8
	Softcover	978-1-4500-6478-1
	Ebook	978-1-4500-6480-4

This book was printed in the United States of America.

To order additional copies of this book, contact:
Xlibris Corporation
1-888-795-4274
www.Xlibris.com
Orders@Xlibris.com
www.greaterharvestworldwide.com
ghccstaff@yahoo.com
66843

Contents

Dedication

To my beloved husband,
Archbishop James Rice Jr.
It is with you I also live, breathe, and have my being
for God has graced me to be with you, and it is with you that we
accomplish our ***Kingdom*** task.
You cause it to be so, and it is.
I appreciate you, and I know that God gave you to me;
I forever praise Him for this.
Our lives have just begun to reach the sky and beyond,
to experience untapped and unlimited overflow in his favor.
We embrace it because it is the will of God for us.

My bishop, my love, unlimited blessings I speak into your life as you have blessed me with the same. Your strength and confidence have been a blessing to me and an example of true manhood to men all around the world. I can share it with everyone and declare it as a point of victory. You have *never* tried to take away what God has put in me or to overshadow the anointing in my life. You have never put me down or undermined my calling or appointment. Nor have you neglected the gift in yourself.

As you embrace who you are, you have allowed me to be who I am, without condemnation, fear or intimidation, or persuasion. It has allowed me to flow into spheres of clouds and unseen places of peace, undeveloped by others . . . It has allowed me to see Jesus! And experience the Holy Spirit in riches untold. Wow! I thank you; because of you, this work can be read by others and people of faith all across the globe will grow in "grace and glory."

You are truly the man, the "Bishop Himself," the rock of Greater Harvest Christian Center and all the churches worldwide. I salute you, my king and my priest! May God favor you forever and add to you long life and prosperity!

Loving you always, our archbishop James Rice II,
the "Bishop Himself"
PS I wish every day that every "woman of God" had a set man of God in her life, like God has given me.
This world will be better because you have been in it.
Your "wife-e for life-e"
Chief Apostle Dr. J. G. Rice.

Bishop and Apostle Rice

Founders and CEOs
Greater Harvest Christian Center Churches Worldwide

Judah Praise Ministries
Circle of Power—Circle '59
Wealthy Place Empowerment InterGlobal Ministries
Rice Ministries InterGlobal
InterGlobal Association of Christian Churches Worldwide—IGACCW

Headquarters (Fort Lauderdale, Florida)

Bishop James R. Rice and Dr. J. GraceLyn Rice are business and spiritual gurus from Columbia, South Carolina, with over thirty-six years of ministry and business development. The Rices are a gift to the church and the business world, and you will enjoy their works of love and grow in your faith as you embrace the spirit of empowerment and grace.

Our Thanks

To Our Parents
Mr. and Mrs. (Deacon and Deaconess) Calvin and Ara Moore
Mother Bishop Doris C. Rice
International Mother Martha T. Ruff

Our godmothers, church mothers, spiritual parents, and spiritual children (present and the ones to come).

To Our Biological Children
Candace, Ara, Calvin, James III, Amanda, Jessica, and Ashley. To all our grandchildren and grands to come.

To Our Churches Interglobally
The Greater Harvest Christian Center Churches Worldwide (family)

To Our Association and Sister Churches
InterGlobal Association of Christian Churches worldwide

To Our Partners
To our partners and spiritual-support team, all intercessors (globally), and all Eagle and Elephant partners

To Our Covenant Partners
The prophetic chamber partners and the Women in Worship *power* team.

To all our family and friends.

With you, we can do all things . . . You have pushed us to fly, and we thank you!

Chief Apostle Dr. J. G. Rice
The Queen Lady
"Lady J GraceLyn Rice"
God's General
God's Ambassador
God's Prophet

It's All about the *Kingdom*

Godly Steps and Instructions for Successful *Kingdom* Living

Apostolic, Spiritual, and *Kingdom* Protocol for Fivefold Leaders, Ministers, and Laypersons

SESSION I-III

Introduction

The *Kingdom* Mind-Set

A ***Kingdom*** mind-set must be established within our spirits, and our lives, before we can understand value; and to take authority in a ***Kingdom*** lifestyle, *we* must change our mind-set and our ***Kingdom*** language. This will happen only when we press into understanding what the enemy is really trying to do to us.

He, the "*trickster,*" is not only after our stuff. He is after our relationship of faith and hope in our *King.* He wants to make us doubt Him, curse Him, and then perish. But our King wants to use us to set the unprecedented glory in our lives. He wants to develop in us something special to make a record in earth and in heaven.

I visited Columbia, South Carolina (my hometown), on a ***Kingdom*** assignment to minister at the spiritual house of our friends, pastors (Bishop-elect John and Pastor-elect Sally) Lakin. And our Father God, the King, spoke to me these words for their house, which is in fact a *rhema* (***Kingdom***), "word" for ***Kingdom*** citizens. It is a word that will cause you to "rethink and embrace why you are going through, what you were selected to go through, and to what you have been selected to set a 'precedent' for."

A Set "Precedent"

This term may be new to you, so let it soak in. What does this mean? *"A PRECEDENT"? It means that you and I have been selected to "set" or establish a direction or a way of expectation by our going through a certain set of circumstances or events that has provoked the hand of God on our behalf and caused a pattern of faith to become relevant to this particular event. This causes a metaphor or allegory to be used forever more in the lives of the believers and within the* ***Kingdom*** *of God. It is like God has used our lives to set an edict for* ***Kingdom*** *rules.* Now think, "A precedent for something in my walk with God to benefit the learning life of myself and another ***Kingdom*** citizen. What is it that I am supposed to set a precedent in, or for?" Only you can establish that with the

King, as you understand "what your orders of ***Kingdom*** dimension are, then you understand your precedent." It is only when you learn what it is; then you will begin to understand your path and what you call your struggles, and you can change your sorrows into joy. You will then laugh at the enemy for trying to get you to change your course. Your life then will bring joy to you, and not sorrow. So then the number one task in your life, and rule of the ***Kingdom***, is to *seek to learn what your precedent is.*

The "Thumbprint" of the King

Let's search the thumbprint of the King (in this noted example of faith); the thumbprint of the King is just like our thumbprint or fingerprint. It denotes that we have been there and that there is no mistake about it. It is our DNA and there is no other like it. So it is with our King's thumbprint; it will let us know that this is his pattern and his DNA, a example for us to follow, a character of his, to get to know, a method to observe, and something for us to adhere to: a precedent that was set for us to follow and learn from, and so it is in the short *dilemma of Job.* Now don't get ahead of me, for there is a principal point that has been overlooked for years. Let us see the *thumbprint of God.*

The enemy still wants to break you off from the COVENANT with GOD!

Job had a relationship with God that the enemy wanted to break. He used several areas to try to break Job's "*spiritual protocol* of faith" and his established covenant.

When the *trickster* could not move the relationship by *death, stuff, family, social problems, finances*, **and** *marital* **crisis,** he took another route of destruction; he felt that if he would afflict him physically. This powerful ***Kingdom*** relationship would fail, crumble, forfeit, that Job would break rank, and covenant, with God.

The ***Kingdom*** relationship of *trusting God,* his faithful King and Lord, would be destroyed, diminished, and derailed. But Job overcame all these smoke screen obstacles, outside stimuli, and *pressure* of the demonic influences *by knowing God,* by knowing his character, and by TRUSTING him. "Yes, they may slay me, but yet will I trust Him." *This has got to be your mind-set* if you are to win the battle of covenant keeping. When the trickster comes your way, you have to really trust GOD. So many times we forget to TRUST

God, we fail to TRUST God, or "our talk does not make it through our test." In other words, we talk a lot; but in times of the test, can you talk it out, your convictions, and keep the faith while walking through your test?

We fail to keep the *language of the* ***Kingdom*** flowing in our hearts and minds; we let go our grip. We begin to allow our minds to go with what we see, instead of what God's Word has spoken to us. *We look at the wind* and see the billowing of the sea, and we begin to sink. Why? Because we really *do NOT believe GOD!* We really think God is like us and will not hold up to his end of the bargain!

Do not sink. Keep the faith if you are called to walk on the water; God knows you can! That's why your feet are different! You have webbed feet for water walking; you just did not know what they were for until you had to spread them out on the water. Now you understand why you and your feet were different all your life

Trust God to know what he is bringing you into. Do not doubt in your heart. Do not let the enemy into your conversation because he will trick you and you will be the one sinking . . . sinking . . . sinking . . . *Because the enemy is after your COVENANT* and he knows you have to be the one to break it. God will not break it with us. NEVER will he break his word, bond, agreement, or covenant with us.

God is not a covenant breaker;
what he says he will do, he will do!

We have to break the covenant with him. He will never leave or forsake us; we will always be the one to walk out the marriage with God. This groom will never leave us. So it is then that if the enemy can get you to flee from the promise, He can laugh and say "another one bites the dust." Then he goes back to God and says, "See, I told you. They don't trust you either. They don't really believe your Word. See, I told you they could not hang in there. They would not make it past five years." God is depending on us to hang in there, and the enemy of our soul is betting against us. Don't let him win, not on your watch!

When examining this *thumbprint,* we must understand that God has made a way of escape for us, that he will not tempt us beyond what we can bear or overcome. He addresses all these issues in this example of faith that we can overcome all spiritual and natural pressures of life and hold on strong to our faith.

Let's learn these nine ways to overcome the spiritual pressures of life as we grow in the ***Kingdom****.*

Introduction Part 2

Nine Areas of Spiritual Pressures

These are some areas that the enemy will try to attack to put the pressure on you just so they (these oppressions) do not get lost in this overview; let us list them:

Stuff—all property/houses/cars/land
Family members—and their opinions and their problems
Death of loved ones—children, family members
Physical affliction—health issues and pains
Spouse—unsaved and unbelieving copartners/spouses
Physical—ongoing worsening condition
Finances—all money and resources
Mental affliction—the attack of your mind
Accusation—from society, peers, and others

Nine Ways to Overcoming Spiritual Pressures

Point # 1
You must learn and know that you will be tested in one or more areas of your faith in your life. Make up your mind to stay pure in your mind!

Overcoming Takes a Made-up Mind!

After these *spiritual pressure points* and areas of disaster were all thrust at him, he (Job), kept his mind, mouth, motives, and spiritual manifestation *pure*. He held on to his ***Kingdom*** covenant and his beliefs—"The Lord giveth and the Lord taketh away, Blessed be the name of the Lord." Job is saying "No matter what, I will still give God the glory in my life, for all that he has done, or has chosen to do. Yes, I will still trust Him." Will you be able to say and do the same things as this spiritual giant does? This takes ultimate ***Kingdom*** purity and trust.

I don't want to labor on the obvious points that we have all been blessed to know and somewhat understand. I do, however, seek to point out three facts within point # 2.

Point # 2
You must learn and know the Enemy has no new tricks; learn his three simple tricks to survive and overcome.

Three Facts to Overcome Spiritual Pressures

Fact One: The *trickster* always begins with simple tricks, but that's not what he is really after.

Fact Two: Don't be so quick to give up at the same junction of pressure every time. You will find out that there is more on the other side of your stumble, if you will keep going and refuse to stay down. *Just don't fall into a pity party. Get up*!

Fact Three: God does *not* get the *glory* out of your life, and *the **Kingdom** does not grow in statue if you abandon your **Kingdom** principles.* We give him, the enemy, another opportunity to brag about our defeat when we abandon our confession. So fight to the end, but don't quit.

Find out what the devil is really after, and then you can **STOP him!** Know that when the enemy starts his battle with you, it can be fast and furious; however, at this point, you must ask yourself, *What is the trickster after? That is the main question you must ask yourself before, during and after any battle. What were they (the oppressors) really after?*

*I watch a lot of Western movies. I like them, I always have; but I learned early, any time there was a battle, the people—good guys or bad guys (or girls)—were after something. For example, if strangers came to town and seemed to be all right, they might be befriended. Until the town knew that they were really out to rob the bank. Now sometimes they caught them in advance and sometimes they caught them after the bank was robbed. Sometimes the enemy got away because they were to slow figuring out what the strangers were really after. This is how the enemy moves. When he comes in your life, he knows what he is really after. It's up to us to be smart enough to know his plan before the attack and be ready to whip him down, handcuff him, and throw him in jail. That's what smart **Kingdom** citizens do: they protect their town, space, and place in the **Kingdom**.*

Guard your mind at all cost! It is vital to your survival!

Point # 3
You must learn and know the trickster is after your mind-set and that you have been given enough power to stop him from getting it!

What is he (the trickster) really after?

The answer: your mind—not just your mind, but your ***Kingdom mind-set****. The devil knows if he can take your mind-set from you, he will steal your covenant promises and finally your victory! Your mind-set is "that what you have set your mind to do and not to change from." It is your covenant promise to God, yourself, your ministry, and your family. That is what the enemy wants to destroy, your mind-set!*

God gave me this word to prophesy to the body of Christ and tell them, in 2009. It is an end-time word of revelation and *rhema* to the ear of the **Kingdom**.

. . . *"You have something very important to offer to this earth and the* ***Kingdom*** *of God. The enemy must defeat you before you deposit your gifting and anointing into the atmosphere and begin to change lives. The unprecedented pathway has to be juggled up to get you to miss the oasis on the other side of the jungle. The battle is to stop you from reaching the living water, and you are just a few feet away. You will then be able to lead others through the jungle of life to the spring of living water. The enemy must get you to give up before you reach the* realm of experiencing the *joy of your salvation, your precedented glory. Just know that the glory that God (the King of every king), the* ***Kingdom*** *(heaven), and the body of Christ (the church) and everybody else (people on the earth) will be illuminated* by and taught of the faith in *the 'unprecedented glory' through you if you can just hold on to and press into your established faith, your* ***Kingdom*** *mind-set!"*

WOW, what a word, learning what we are really put here on this earth for and getting it done, to bring our God the glory. Not letting anyone steal, kill, or destroy this mind-set is the matured place in God. We must all reach this place.

Don't quit now; you are too close to the glory!

The unprecedented ***Kingdom*** *glory will never be set or established in the earth realm in you if you quit, give up, or curse God! You must understand why you have been selected to go through what you have gone through; God trusted that He could use you to set a precedent. He wanted to use you as an example; He knew you could go through the trial and test and hold on. He never thought you could not take it. He trusted to make the case a fact.*

In past times, **you did** *not understand* that *God chose you* and your life; your ***Kingdom*** destiny was selected to "*show up the trickster as a liar,*" to expose him, and to let others know that truly in Him (the

Father and in the Son and in the Holy Spirit) we have the ultimate victory: And that you could stand against the wiles of the devil *and be a trophy in the showcase of the* ***Kingdom*** *of God.* That you could fight the battle and win a touchdown for God through his son Christ Jesus! Glory Hallelujah!

If I was preaching right here, I would say, "Grab your head and scream, 'I have to keep my mind right!'" Somebody Say AMEN !

On with the Revelation

Let's get to a *major revelation, Job 3:38.* This is really where I want to reveal these special truths and **Kingdom** revelations.

Job had "problems" for three chapters (chapters 1-3)—yes, yes! Major BAD happenings! That was enough to shake anybody's faith. But Job held on.

Then for the next thirty-four chapters, his biggest problems *were his friends* (or so-called friends), who were operating on an assignment from the devil himself, *to work on Job's mind!* Minister Joyce Myers wrote a book, *The Battlefield of the Mind,* exposing the fact that the enemy wants to operate in the realm of our subconscious. The enemy, however, has to have a way in; and with Job, the devil himself sent three demons in the form of people (called friends) to work on Job's mind!

Point # 4

You must learn and know how to guard your space. **Do not let** *unanointed, unassigned, unauthorized, undeputized, uninvited people speak to you, especially in your time of crisis.*

Unanointed friends will kill you in your time of crisis

They (friends of Job) came on an assignment from Satan. They may or may not have been in agreement with Satan when they came to visit, but they surely did the work of the enemy. *They did not come to speak faith to Job*; they came to rain poison and disbelieve. They came to work on his peace and to break the covenant with him and God. These "friends" did not come to build up Job. They came to take his *mind-set*; they wanted his real promise; they wanted his testimony; they wanted his confession to waiver; and they wanted to demolish his peace, his faith, and his ***Kingdom*** place in God. *They wanted to see him FALL* from GRACE and FAITH, to see him DIE and miss a place of promise and hope.

Let's look at the word *mind-set again.* Remember, a *mind-set is* "that what you have set your mind to do, with purpose, passion, tenacity, grace, and glory assigned to you and with everything within you." Combined with this definition and my understanding, *mind-set* (as *I define it)* is simply "what you have made up, within yourself, to *not* take down from"; mind-set is the practical application of *daily principles* that are not wavered on, and that you are *not willing to change* from or about, *no matter what.*

Kingdom *mind-set (as I define it with this above definition in reflection) is what you will not change in yourself because you have made a promise to God. It is a way of "Christian lifestyle or living" that you will not take down from your principles in; a mental agreement, which becomes personal and public; a deep convicting way of living, expecting, and believing for yourself and others that create a glorious presence in your life. It is our "firm foundation."*

For *thirty-four chapters* (how did we miss this important point for so long?) *thirty-four chapters* (I cannot stress this enough), *thirty-four chapters,* the enemy set demons to try and take that which was most important to him (Job) and us today.

What is the most important thing we have in the **Kingdom**?—*our minds* and our *mind-set,* what we truly stand for and believe. The devil wanted Job's ***Kingdom*** mind-set, just as he wants ours today! Nothing is new under the sun. He is still after the ***Kingdom*** covenant that we have made with God. He is still after our testimony and our faith!

Yes, please believe it; the devil today wants our ***Kingdom*** mind-set. *That is why we must strengthen our* ***Kingdom*** *beliefs and what we stand for, strengthen our mind and set it toward the* ***Kingdom*** *so we will not be moved in testing time. These demon-sent tormentor friends of Job "sat around Job's bed and tormented him night and day trying to get him to forfeit his "unprecedented glory."*

They wanted him to fulfill the plan of Satan and "curse God and die" (perish).

I would like to use *perish* because as my bishop (*Archbishop James Rice)* says, "*When we first pluck a fruit from the tree, it begins to die, as well when we are first* **disconnected** *from the vine, tree, as the fruit (consider yourself as the fruit), we begin to perish, 'die.' It may not look like it is dying, but the process has already begun."*

It may take days, weeks, or even years to finish the perishing process. *But the fruit began to die the moment it was plucked. This is why the enemy wants to disconnect you from the vine of life through your relationship with the father God, the ministry you are in, or the leader you are under. A disconnected fruit is a dead fruit.*

The fruit also once disconnected can never be reconnected in its original state and in fact is a "*dead* item." Really, it is *not a produce* because it is *not "producing" anymore.* It is a perishable (dying) item.

Point # 5
You must learn and know that the enemy will use those closest to us (sometimes) to throw us off guard.
Be prepared to separate yourself (if necessary) when necessary from unbelieving family and friends.

Mrs. Job (The dear wife)

Let's talk about Mrs. Job. In my mind, Mrs. Job represents those people (family and friends mainly) who say they want the best for you but do not know what is really best for you and often cause you who walk in destruction and death, promoting you to curse God and die. They do not understand your promise or God's plan for you.

When Job's wife said "Curse God and die," she was not meaning "drop dead." She meant *"Give up on what you believe in, and disconnect from this covenant. Do not hold us accountable to this King anymore."*

Give it up—*stop talking* **Kingdom** *talk; stop talking FAITH*; and stop saying God is faithful, good, and good to you. *Stop trusting*; disconnect from this source. Mrs. Job (the good wife or, should I say, the good "knife") wanted Job to "change his ***Kingdom*** contract, to forfeit his ***Kingdom*** covenant.

When the devil can't get you one way, he often goes another way. You must watch who opens a crack in the door of doubt and unbelief in your life, they often leave it cracked for others to come in, and take a seat. Although this lack of faith, when she presented it to her husband, it did not work for her, *it opened up the door to other "verbal demons"* to be sanctioned and assigned on the same assignment.

This is why we must be in control when others speak into our ear gates and spiritual atmosphere. Block them out, and do not let them open the door for other demon spirits to enter on the wings of their negative energy and assignment.

Yes, the devil will try to work on you through your so-called *loved ones.* I could give you at least one hundred examples of how *I have personally seen family members with an assignment from hell come to disconnect someone who was now finally doing good after they had become planted in a ministry of sound doctrine and teaching.*

They were doing better than they have ever done in their lives, clean, sober, having hope, leaving the life of negativity and despair. Only then do they (these loved ones) now want them out of and disconnected from the church, the ***Kingdom***, and finally from the assignment of God. To go back to being the laughing matter of the family and the joke of the friends.

They will not tell you these things; however, *you will know when someone is trying to disconnect you when they say stupid things* like "You are going to church to much," "That must be a cult," "Why are you going to church again?" "How much money are you putting in that church?" "Do you really have to go on a fast?" "Why do you have to read the Bible all the time?" "I don't like your pastor. I think they are controlling," "I think you are being controlled by the 'church people,'" "Why do you pay so much money in the church?" "All they want is your money," "God understands you're not perfect," "You don't really have to do it that way."

If they (the people who claim they love you) say anything other than "I am so glad you found the Lord," "You are doing great, keep it up," "I love to see and know that you are doing well," "I am proud of you as you get stronger in God!"

If they can't encourage you to keep going higher and higher in the Lord, then they are after your covenant promise.

In all their selfish sayings, remember that they are only sent to throw you off your course to success.

Don't let the enemy interrupt your destiny

This kind of stuff and crazy words are interruptions to your destiny. *RUN* from them because these people, whether they know it or not, are trying hard to get you disconnected.

People (no matter how lovely), a lot of them do not want you to change and outgrow them! That's the bottom line. Ask yourself, "Am I growing?" If the answer is yes, you can believe that someone is jealous and in envy over your life of change. They want to change but do not want to sacrifice, so instead of change, they will just pull you back in the crab barrel. *RUN!* I also tell our members and leaders when going through this with people who say they want the best for them, "Listen closely and think about it.

"Did they, the people now so concerned about you and your Love for Christ and the church, *do you ever remember them telling you* that you '*were going to parties so much, smoking too many cigarettes, drinking too much beer, that you had too many boyfriends or girlfriends?*

"Do you ever remember them telling you to stop living in sin or adultery or fornication? Did they tell you to stop playing lotto or bingo or any other habits you had that you were spending all your money on or spending your time doing?

"Before you came to Christ, *Did they tell you to turn the TV off, and stop wasting your entire day on courtroom saga, and bad habits of others?* To stop sitting on the porch, cursing your children out or being negative! Did they tell you that you gave too much money to the 'dope lady or the crack man'?"

Did they add up the money you spent on clothes, for parties, special outfits, and had-to-have shoes? How about the money you gave to strippers or one-night stands! Tell them to add up the money they are now spending for beer, wine, or lotto tickets. Since most of the time they are so concerned about the money you invest in the ***Kingdom***, ask them where were they when you gave your money to negative behavior and antics.

Where were they when you really needed them to tell you to stop *bad behavior*? And now that you are serving God, they say you are doing too much . That's CRAZY, and these people can only come as an assignment from the devil, whether they know it or not!

Who has the dagger in their hand?

Now that you are embracing the truth of the ***Kingdom***, *the enemy has to use someone to get you off track*, and guess who that someone is—yes, the people who you think love you, the people you love, the people that you see every day, the people in your circles, the people whom you talk to, the people whom you care about. Those are the ones who sometimes have the biggest daggers. Why? Because the people you don't know about or care about cannot influence you, their opinions really do not matter. The enemy, he knows who can influence you and he is trying his best to make that happen. DO NOT fall for this trick.

You must *get bold in Christ*; it must begin in you and resound around the world. You must get a comeback language for the enemy. Don't keep quiet; SAY something! Prepare to stop the negative behavior quickly, or they will keep coming back at you, another day, another time, another word, to wear you out.

The scriptures say, the enemy is trying to wear out the saints! Don't let him wear you out; prepare to fight back!

Tell them that you are all good now, baby, so don't sweat the righteous living. Let them know to "stop drinking hater-aid," and get with the GOD-aid. Tell them "only what you do for God will last" and that you are on the "G-Train now" and "No ticket, no ride, so get off the train!"

They obviously don't have a ticket because if they did, they would understand the journey you are now on and where your train is going. "NO ticket, NO ride!"

WOW, I know that feels good already. I told you; you have to get ready to stump all negative in advance, NO matter WHOM it may come from!

Let's get back to Mrs. Job

*Another revealed word God showed me about the need for **Kingdom** relationships. You must have **Kingdom** people around you to protect you when you are weak. Real **Kingdom** people, real faith talkers.*

Think back on the *houses* in those days. This "wife" *had to hear the men attacking her husband's mind—day in and day out;* this wife was always around. Let's think. *Who fed them for seven days? Who gave them water? Who went in the room to check on Job? She was very much aware of Job being tormented.*

However, because *she had become disconnected from her covenant,* she had lost *hope.* Her ***Kingdom*** mind-set was gone. She allowed her pride to work, and it was working overtime. When this attack did not work *through* her, she was more open to allow this attack to happen *around* her so she would not feel convicted by her actions.

How many times can you remember when one of your family/friend/spouse or social members tried to attack your faith and then they called others in to help them out with this assignment? Or a coworker attacked you and then the entire staff turned on you or your ministry turned on you because you spoke truth to them and they were convicted? They needed to feel right, so to make you feel wrong, they all "ganged" up on you to try to change your confession of the truth.

Well, they were like Job's wife. She justified these actions and called them love. How many people have tried to distract you off your ***Kingdom*** assignment and called it *love*? They want you to disconnect from your promise from God? In fact, the problem is often people around you will *lose* their *faith,* and when they see you still holding on, they get *mad* because you speak the truth. They do not want you to *hold* on when they have *let go.* Let's face it; there are times when we should *let go.* Let me give you some examples of these times!

When to let go!

Now there are the people like the lady that went to our church with somebody else's husband, who wanted me to pray for her to *get this man,* who was married to his wife for seventeen years and has a child with the outside woman and five with his wife but was playing house with both women.

After hearing this story, I told her to "let go, and give the other woman her husband back." Her reply was "Oh no, I have come too far with this man, and I am still holding on." This type of holding on is not a ***Kingdom*** promise; it is foolishness.

I am not talking about coveting something that is not yours, or that you think is supposed to be yours, and asking God to bless your selfish desires.

I am talking about those of us who are truly living a "***Kingdom*** lifestyle" and are under unsolicited attack from the enemy.

He is not after your stuff; really, don't believe this for a minute. The truth is he is after your *mind!* He wants to cause you to "break down" mentally and then he knows everything else will follow, but he has to get your *mind* first.

So Job's wife did not know that her husband had been selected for an assignment of *unprecedented glory.* Job, like many of us, was on an unprecedented assignment to bring back the glory to his house, life, and ***Kingdom*** of God.

Point # 6
You must learn and know to guard your mind.
Know that you are charting "unprecedented territory" to get the glory!

Don't Let the Enemy Take Your Mind off Christ

This mental attack almost worked; Job, after being beaten down for days, finally begins to question God. This negative behavior caused doubt in Job, and it created a conversation between God and Job, which has created a precedent for today's believers. Understanding "who God really is" is always an eye-opener. Job said, *"I have heard of thee, now I see you for myself."* What a wonderful place to be in, where we can finally see the King of glory for ourselves!

This mantle of *grace* can never be described; once you know why you went through something and you see the plan of the enemy to take you away from the relationship with your King, you will get angry that the devil could think you would not be able to hold on. What a jerk! *You will begin to fight back.*

When you see the plan of the enemy to take you out of the game of life and hope, when you see the plan of the trickster to take you out of your ***Kingdom*** assignment, and then when you see the hand of God that reaches out and takes you out, then when you truly see this *King* in action for you and on your behalf, finally you are on your way to fulfilling and charting the *"unprecedented glory"* to encamp everything you do.

Your life will take you from when you have doubt to where you have set examples on what God can do (testimonies) and knowing what the King can do. You will learn on the journey how the King really cares for you, and when it is finished, the precedent will be set for others to follow. You will be entered into the *spiritual hall of faith.* You'll get to have your story placed in the ***Kingdom*** trophy case for all to see your touchdown!

My question for you as we begin our journey in *It's All about the* ***Kingdom*** is

> *What have you come through that others can follow? What in your life have you overcome victoriously and that will give strength to them to use for an example to follow? It is the "unprecedented glory" in your life that is supposed to give to the* ***Kingdom*** *of God.*

"Zion, put on your strength," for the glory of the Lord has risen among us. Stop whining and complaining and *go* through with faith.

Point # 7
You must learn how to "get bold enough to put the devil out of your ear gate"! Do not be tormented by the enemy of negativity! Not today and not tomorrow, this is *not meekness.* This is self-destruction and distraction to your purpose.

Put the Negative Out of Your Life

Put those *"no-no and nay-nay"* sayings out. *Change those who are around you* causing you to fall into the spirit of depression. *Change those lying people*—not sent by God to speak into your life.

Let me pause and say, while studying, *I asked the Lord, "Why didn't you stop the 'bedside bogeymen demons' [assigned "friends"] that were trying to cause Job to have a mental breakdown?*

"And why did you wait to chapter 42 to let Job know they were not sent by you? *Lord, you could have stopped them* in chapter 12, 9, 15, 19, or 30. Why did *you let them* torment Job so long?" *He (the Spirit of the Lord) spoke to me and said, "I didn't let them do anything."*

Job had enough strength to tell them to get out! He did not have to endure this foolishness. He had enough strength to have extensive conversations with them, to debate with them for so long (thirty-four chapters). *So he had enough strength to take his **Kingdom** authority and put the enemy out. Job had the authority to put the enemy out of his room, life, business, and destiny—and so do we!*

We Have the Authority

We choose, like Job does, to talk to these negative spirits, to justify with them, and to let them hinder and hammer away at us. *We choose* to let them steal our peace and chop away our faith and our souls. ***We choose** to let them take our mind-set!* All we really have to do is to take ***Kingdom*** authority and put them out! *No* excuses or pity—just put the demons out! Because they had a familiar face—"familiar spirit" called friend—we think we owe people to have to listen to their opinions without being cocky. When it is not going anywhere (their lame advice), stop listening to them and put them out of your mental space.

If you can't put them out, find your *"spiritual patrol"* and tap into their strength, along with the Holy Spirit, and put the devil out. The enemy is a trickster; he wants your ***Kingdom*** vision! Put him out!

Put the devil out! Don't let them bring the *"three stooges—the cousins of despair"* in your life. You have to know the enemy and his cousins to win this war.

Point # 8
*You must learn to know your enemy and his tricks in **advance!***

Know your enemy and his cousin
The Three Stooges of despair
*The three cousins are against the **Kingdom***

The "three cousins"—the spirits of depression, oppression, and possession—they will creep into your life and have your mind gone; they will go in to your room. *Your rooms, in this sense, are your "head, heart, mind, spirit, soul, and finally, your mouth."* This is where the enemy wants to really get into your *mouth because if it comes out of your mouth, it is in your heart!* And then he knows you are on a pathway of death because you have become disconnected from the ***Kingdom*** promises and faith in your King. You are on the road to perishing.

Anybody remember the show *The Hee-Haw Show*? They had a section where they would sing a song; in it were the lyrics "Deep down depression, excessive misery, if it were not for bad luck I have no luck at all."

That's how some Christians talk, always singing the blues. We must watch our mouths. Give me thirty minutes with you and I can tell your faith level by what is coming out of your mouth! I can tell if you are living with the cousins of despair *because faith comes by hearing*. If your faith level is that bad, then you are not pumping enough faith materials into your spiritual pipeline. If you fill your spiritual line with crap and crude materials, eventually it will take on the pattern of what has traveled through it.

Free yourself *now* (start in your mind); be free from people not sent to speak into or about your ***Kingdom*** destiny. Stop it today! These people will cause you to miss it.

That is the true story of J*ob*; the enemy wanted him to *miss it.* He, the devil (the trickster), his trick was that he was *not after the stuff.* He was after the *relationship. Know what he is up to; ask the Holy Spirit to reveal to you what he is doing concerning you and your loved ones.*

Yes, he wanted Job's relationship to be separated from God. After all, it worked with Adam and Eve, why not Job? But Job was committed to the ***Kingdom*** *and the King! Are you committed to the* ***Kingdom*** *and the king today?*

The *Kingdom* is calling and You must learn how to hear the call.

The **"*Kingdom* call"** is one that only ***Kingdom*** citizens can truly hear! It is a call that will set you on your road to your ***Kingdom*** destiny. It is a call that will allow you to finally know who you are in Christ Jesus. It will free you from fear, as you walk out the mandate of avoiding the spirit of meritocracy, trading it for excellence into an excited life: a life filled with joy abundance, hope, laughter, rest, and glory.

Can you hear the "***Kingdom*** call" to be better? The call to have a more excellent spiritual presence and to show the unprecedented glory in your life, this is the ***Kingdom*** call. Do you hear it? Do you seek to answer it? If you can hear the call, then you (we) are on our way to living the ***Kingdom*** life. This is the beginning of a graceful walk in Christ. If you cannot hear the call, take time to pray and "seek" his face; he will answer you.

How do you seek the face of God? You lay aside everything that will distract you; get quiet and ask the Spirit of the Lord to speak to you, in clear, plain language, and you sit quietly until he speaks.

Apostolic and Spiritual Protocol
Sets a Precedent for the "*Kingdom* Order."

Finally Job sets an "apostolic and spiritual protocol." This protocol is with how to deal with those not sent to speak in your life, ending in chapter 42 (Job 42). It will bring you to an area in your life that will grant you recovery; *you will have a process of recovering all* and receiving a financial, physical, material, familial, physical, marital, and social recovery.

Apostolic and spiritual protocol brings recovery in area of your life.

Point # 9
You must learn and know (with a plan of victory) how to gain restitution for what you have lost and keep a mind-set of recovery: never give up, for in the end, you shall recover all.

IF you hang in there, you will RECOVER ALL

What I like about our God is, if you let him use your life for a short time of (what is thought to be) suffering, there will be an established place in your going and your coming. He will give you *"hind feet,"* and those who thought you would fall *will watch you climb.*

You will be able to laugh as you get to the top of the mountain of life, then you will see straighter and farther than ever. You will see what God has in store for you when you change your attitude, an altitude; *your view will change*. Then you will see another mountain and know that you can speak to it or climb it. It will not matter; you will know that God will be faithful in allowing you to see other horizons that others will only read about.

Setting these *apostolic and spiritual protocols* will help you reach the top quicker and quicker, faster and faster, with fewer bumps, and allow you to rest in the journey.

I encourage you to use these experiences of life (mine and many other "spiritual generals" of the ***Kingdom*** that God will bless you to know and experience their ministries). Our life's lessons of faith, pressure, and perseverance are only an example of what God has done for us and for you to see what God will do, as well, for you.

Refer back to this book and life manual often, and grow in God . . .

This is my ***Kingdom*** *destiny*, and I now realize that everything I have gone through in life has been to set my own ***Kingdom*** *precedents*, to say to all "*Oh yes, God can!*"

The King of kings—He can take a *little girl from South Carolina.* Yes, I have a story, but God has given me the glory; I was adopted, sexually abused, had broken marriages. I have been rejected, put down, and kicked over. I have had spiritual disappointment and failed hopes, to name a little bit of my story and his glory that kept my life balanced through it all and made me to be prosperous, wealthy, whole, and healthy. I have become a Proverbs 31 woman, a phenomenal woman, who is extraordinary, unique, remarkable, and strong by His grace.

However, in the face of it all, I kept the faith and sought to hold on to the promises and *positive of this life God has selected for me.* Truly, through this life of "bouncing back" I have been purified by the fire of life, and now I am and going through the ***Kingdom*** of God, saying, "Oh yes, he can . . . and yes, you can!"

From South Carolina to the world—only God can set this precedence, and only God get the *glory!*

I hope and pray, as it is my assignment to challenge you—tremendously to move into a ***Kingdom*** *covenant and contract* with the *King* of kings with our god (Jehovah, El, the Great "I Am") and His Son, Christ Jesus, our Savior and Lord—the Messiah. To be taught by the "teacher, the comforter, the guide, Holy Spirit" in all truth to ***Kingdom*** living, being guided by the power of the Holy Ghost in every manner of ***Kingdom*** living, and joining in submission and order with His earthly spiritual patrols sent to help and guide you in daily ***Kingdom*** walk.

Get to know the fivefold ministry team under local leadership who has been assigned to help usher you into your "unprecedented glory" and fulfill your ***Kingdom*** purpose on this earth.

This is my "***Kingdom*** destiny": to know, grow, and show the love of God. Join me in the ***Kingdom*** as we focus on successful ***Kingdom*** living and apostolic and spiritual protocol.

Brought by his blood,
Chief Apostle Dr. J. G. Rice

SESSION

1

Chapter 1

Understanding ***Kingdom*** Protocol

Nine Major Rules of the ***Kingdom***

Learning the Ways of the ***Kingdom***

2 Chronicles 7:14

The ***Kingdom*** ways are not so different from our moral compass to do what's right; there is a pendulum on the inside of us that swings to the righteousness of God. Even in the hardest decision, that inner compass tells us whether what we are doing is right or wrong. Even if it goes against our feelings, it will speak!

Now having said that, how do we get so out of order, out of ***Kingdom*** connection, and out of spiritual balance? Simple—we *don't listen* to the ***Kingdom*** pendulum. We *push it back* the opposite way and say *"Oh, it's OK if I do this or that. God knows my heart."*

This has been one way not to deal with our ***Kingdom***: disobedience in our lives.

Picture this—you live in a country; let's call it Eden. God = "the King" gives you specific instructions, "Don't eat of this tree." You decide one day, it's hot and you are a long way from any other food; you are hungry now, so you decide, "God knows my heart." And you sit down and eat the fruit; you were told "not to do this." Along comes the King and catches you. What would you say? "Oh, well, King, you know my heart." Well, by biblical example, the King would say, "Depart from this. You are not in my ***Kingdom****, and by the way, I do know your heart—I've seen it before—it's a heart of disobedience!"*

You see, *you have a choice,* to believe God for who he truly is or make excuses. Bishop Rice and *I have heard thousands of excuses* for everything concerning ***Kingdom*** commitment and ***Kingdom*** accountability; sometimes, we try to speak truth to help those Christians become true ***Kingdom*** citizens. Sometimes, we are aware that *they have convinced themselves* that God will make a "special pass" for their sin, indiscretions, pain, disobedience, rebellion, evil ways, and awful attitudes. However, this will not happen, for he spared not his own son, but delivered him up. How shall he then, and will, judge us for all sins?

These *excuses* have come from both lay and lead members, fivefold ministry persons, priests, and kings of this world. Everyone has an excuse not to believe the ***Kingdom*** constitution, which is the "Word" of God. But we must STOP the excuses and become true ***Kingdom*** citizens, ones that Our King, the most high God, can truly trust and believe in to keep the constitution.

Are You a True Believer?

This is what makes the difference in "churchdom" and ***Kingdom***. We must elevate to the order of the ***Kingdom***. To learn the ways of the ***Kingdom***, one must adhere to the biblical passages found in *2 Chronicles 7:14*. In reading it, it says, "If my people whom are called by my name would humble, themselves and pray and turn from their wicked ways, . . . I will heal their land." Let us review the part of the passage that denotes what our part must be: we pray, be humble, and especially, turn from our *wicked* ways. Let us all say "*We must turn from our wicked ways* to expect *God the King to heal* the land. We do something, turn, and then He does something: heal, us and our land."

When we truly receive this, our churches will have more prayer meetings than board meetings, more praise than war, and more love than hate. The healing will breed healing, and we will draw all men unto him.

Our King and ***Kingdom*** have a pattern; our King would not leave us without something to follow and observe, something to help us along our ***Kingdom*** path. It is simple and direct and often overlooked because it is so simple and direct, so very clear, even a child could follow it.

There are nine major rules of the ***Kingdom*** for practical application; let's review and grow in them.

Nine Rules of the *Kingdom*

The Patterns of the King and the *Kingdom*

Kingdom Rule # 1
You must follow the edicts of the King

This is the pattern of the King. "We do, then He does." This is how we learn the ways of the King and the ***Kingdom***. As parents, we would hope that our children follow our good patterns. We might have a family recipe for great cake, for good macaroni and cheese, or some other favorite dish we want others to follow and keep the dish going, and so we share the secret to make their dish great. So it is with our King; the secret is spoken to us in a parable to help us grow and understand our ***Kingdom***. The King says to those to have "a hear let them hear" what the Spirit (the instructor) is saying to the ***Kingdom*** (the citizens).

So here he gives us a perfect pattern for ***Kingdom*** communication.

We Pray — He responds
We Praise — He responds
We Worship — He responds

We get our instructions from reading and meditating on the Word of truth, our ***Kingdom*** constitution; through this we get divine answers and clarity for life.

He speaks = We respond = He blesses.

A very simple pattern that, if followed, will bring about a communication with our King and give us godly, golden instructions that will bring about manifested glory in our lives.

***Kingdom* Rule # 2**
You must say only what the King says!

In our learning to say what God says *only and to respond as He would by His Word,* doing as he says, no matter what, is the true response of a ***Kingdom*** citizen.

We must learn ***Kingdom*** talk! Any other language does not represent the ***Kingdom*** of God. We must ask ourselves, why seek to be a part of a country and not learn the language?

WE must learn the language of the *Kingdom*

It often perplexes me to hear those who are supposed to be in the ***Kingdom*** and *do not* know the language. Those are pitiful citizens. If I wanted to live in France or in Africa or Cuba, I must learn the language; it is so as well in the ***Kingdom*** of God. If this is the case, learning the language of ***Kingdom*** communication is necessary to flow well with the land that we are to possess. When we refuse to learn the language of the ***Kingdom*** of God, we do the King an injustice because we cannot hear our King when he speaks to us, because he speaks in his own language. He will not change his language for another who inhabits his domain; he will speak only in his tongue of choice, his language. I have never heard anyone say that Queen Elizabeth speaks anything other than the King's English, even when she is visiting another country; however, she has an interpreter to decipher what is being said to her and what she is saying. Even in this, some words are lost and missed because there is a language barrier.

I once watched a service of the Catholic pope speaking a mass. It was like the pope was speaking in a foreign country but in his native language only and others did not understand; there is no translator, and it was of no bearing to us. We did not understand a word spoken, and even though we attended the services, they were foreign to us. We just moved with the flow of the people trying to be in the mist, but with no revelation. I quickly learned that communication without understanding brings no revelation. To understand, both parties must have a revelation of the language used.

When the King of glory speaks the ***Kingdom*** language, it is "foreign" to those persons who do not know the King's words, and brings no revelation. It is fought over because people do not want to change or adhere to the king's language. It is even rejected, and people say I want to talk in my own language. Now do not get too far ahead of me as I continue to talk about the king's language. WE do not hear the king, our ears are closed to his language, and we treat it as foreign words and gibberish.

However, when the enemy speaks, because we (they, us, and you) are familiar with his voice, we respond. We will always respond to what is familiar to us. That is why we must become more familiar with the voice of the King. Our King does not want us to be disconnected from his voice; this is not how our King sought to raise a nation that does not know his voice. We can only come to know his voice by communication with him. So let's talk to the King and create a familiar sound in our spirit for our Creator, Savior, and Lord.

Kingdom Rule # 3
You must seek to understand the language of the King

We must learn how to hear and understand ***Kingdom*** language. This is an easy task. When you learn these three basic signs, you will be on your way to discern the voice of the King and will be speaking ***Kingdom*** language.

Three Basic Signs to Hear the King

How to discern the voice of God and learn to speak the language of the ***Kingdom***

Sign # 1 The "Judgment Test" to know if it is the King

- Judging what is from God can be simple or very hard. Many of us fail to know and pass the *"judgment test"* because we do not know His Word, His character, or what the King or the ***Kingdom*** stands for. We still believe that the ***Kingdom*** of God can be contained within four walls or a building. This great Spirit cannot be contained in any one location, person, or place. "God, our god, is an awesome God. He reigns from heaven above with wisdom, power, and love. We serve an awesome god!" So no one person is the only person that hears from God or receives his Word. Not one group of people who assemble themselves together or one family of believers. When you know him and his Word better, you will know his voice better. And you will hear his voice in many places and through many people: daily, weekly, hourly. When we begin to know his character, we then can began to judge if it is his Word.

Sign # 2 Is it in the Kingdom Constitution?

- The second reason we fail the test is we do not know our constitution or the rules of the ***Kingdom***. The ***Kingdom*** constitution is the holy Word of God; therefore, we do not really know what is an illusion or what an illusion is or what the truth or the lie is. We call the right wrong and the wrong right; so when truth comes, we call it a lie, and when a lie comes, we call it truth. We believe lies over the truth. *The King wants us to understand the* ***Kingdom*** so the twists of the enemy can be dissolved and disputed and truth can really prevail. We must seek to understand what our rights and privileges are in the ***Kingdom***. We must seek to read out constitution in its entirety and dwell on our possession as those engrafted into the ***Kingdom*** of God

Sign # 3 *Does it validate his Lordship in our Lives?*
For we must make him LORD!

- Some people are Christians. (They are believers that Christ died and have made *Him their Savior*!) Great! However . . . *but* they have not embraced their ***Kingdom*** citizenship *because they have not made Him (Jesus) Lord!* The Lord is not the "Divine Provider" of their lives.
  Yes, we have made Him Savior, but not Lord; and there is a big difference. We refuse to recognize Him as the King of our lives! We need to accept the fact that we are brought with a price, *we are not our own, and we belong to the KING OF KINGS* and the Lord of lords! When we make him Lord, or Supreme Being in our lives, we will retract from a lot of ungodly-behavior land, stop doing things on our own, without his direction, guidance, permission, or oversight; we must embrace his lordship in our lives and ask for his daily instruction, direction, and guidance.
  We will then begin to receive a word from him in every aspect of our lives; this would validate him as the Lord of our lives. It will line us up with his Word, and make him, our King, look good.
  If the "word" you receive from anyone does not place him Jesus the Christ and his Father Jehovah, God, the I-Am, in supreme control, it should be weighted as a "word" of shallow quality and thrown out of your life and your spirit.

WE SPEAK THE LANGUAGE

To access this relationship, we must understand the ***Kingdom*** *has a true language.* The King has given us a language just like any other country, a way of communication that people (true ***Kingdom*** citizens) really do understand.

Kingdom Rule # 4
You must conquer the language barrier and speak faith

Every ***Kingdom*** has a king, a language, rules, and other things the king does and things the citizens are responsible for. Every land and country rules and way of communications methods is respected and understood. So we must also learn to speak the *language of this* ***Kingdom****;* to our surprise, **this language is not *tongues***! And it is definitely not "cursing" or bad language, as some Christians must think, because that's the language they speak frequently.

I am often amazed at the number of people who wear crosses and curse, "no CUSS" as well as say amen. This is not the ***Kingdom*** language!

If you have not tamed your tongue to eliminate cussing from your speech, do so today. You are blocking the flow of the Holy Spirit with foul behavior, and you need to be Holy, give your tongue over to the Lordship of Jesus. This is not only for lay people but for leaders as well. I have a friend, Apostle C, who is gifted and anointed, believes in apostolic rule, but cannot tame his tongue from cussing. I have even spoken with him and tried to pray for his deliverance; however, he has firmly withstood against me and said he is not ready to be delivered from cursing. At this I shake my head, because he will tell women to put a hat on their heads, however he will curse at will.

This type of Ghost is not HOLY or the spirit of truth. So we must tame our tongues and speak the ***Kingdom*** language if we are to see great moves of God. *If it is not "tongues," what is it?*

The language of our *Kingdom* is *faith*! We speak *faith* today, tomorrow, and forever; **God only responds to our *faith***! That's our language, *faith;* nothing less will be accepted as the language of the ***Kingdom***. It is unwavering and full of hope. This is the language that we speak. *This is **Kingdom** talk.* **This is our language, *faith*.**

Kingdom Rule # 5
You must have a conversation of faith

This is how I know *who is not and who is* in the ***Kingdom***: listen to them. Do they **have *faith* in their conversation**? Do they constantly speak the Word of the King and the *faith* of His Word? Are they in spiritual yo-yo with their conversation, meaning they speak faith until problems arise and then they speak the problem, over and over? Then they are not in the ***Kingdom***, as yet. Yes, they are in church—DUMB, but not in ***Kingdom***!

When our faith is constant, not depending on circumstances, then and only then are they ***Kingdom*** citizens; and then and only then are we speaking the language of the ***Kingdom***. When we see a sign of language change is how we will know that they know the ***Kingdom*** language. When we pray (communicate with the King), if we go speaking any other language than *faith*, then He does not hear or reply to us.

Kingdom Rule # 6
You must know and discern the voice of the King

- **It Is Finally Time to Know Whether the Voices You Are Hearing are of God or Not.**

The test is simply to *apply these three principles* and you will be on your way to discovering if this is the voice of your King and if it fits in the ***Kingdom*** constitution.

Ask yourself these questions and then open your Bible to find out the answer.

(1) Does it fit His Word?
(2) Does it fit His character?
(3) Does it violate you, the body of Christ, or what the ***Kingdom*** *stands for?*

If the word you receive from yourself (in your spirit) or from others does not line up to this test, it is not of God. WE must control our fleshly desires and ungodly decrees when it comes to a real word from God! It does not matter *if you "like" the word or "hate" the word given to you or the person giving the word to you*; *your question must be, does* it line up with the voice of the King?

For example, someone tells you that *God is going to bless you* (e.g., you are going to get a million dollars—whatever the blessings, you fill in the blank).

On this type of prophecy, "*you are happy.*" You get excited, shout, and say "o*h yes*"! Even when you know that this word of "oh, happy day" does not line up for you right now in your life.

WHY! Because nowhere in his Word does he, God, Abba Father, say that "he will bless you in your mess." Where can you find it in the Word that "you can live like you want to and still be blessed"? *Where can you find that God does not judge*? Where have you ever seen in the Bible that you do not have to pay for your sins? Stop fooling yourselves. You will have to pay for your SINS; and GOD, who loves you, *will allow you the choice (by how you live now) to go to hell and burn as a repayment of your sins.*

This earth we now abide on is neither heaven nor hell; this is earth. Do not let people fool you that there is no heaven and that this earth is HELL or that there is no HELL. That is foolishness; WE will pay for not receiving Jesus and his suffering for our sins and not choosing him (Jesus) to follow as Lord and Savior! This is why we will pay the price, so make the choice today to live with God and Jesus forever when you leave this earth. Believe me and the Word of God, NO everyone will not choose Jesus. And for those persons, there, however, is a heaven and a hell to be set for the believers and the unbelievers, the righteous and the unrighteous, the holy and the unholy. We decide every day where we want to spend eternity. So let's make good conscious choices today for our soul's sake tomorrow.

We must understand that God is fair and has *a choice to cut us out of his will.* He observes our faith by our allegiance to him in our ***Kingdom*** walk here on earth. WE must follow the plan of God in all things to receive a spiritual BLESSING from our Father.

We cannot half do it and then believe that we will get the benefits of others who fully, faithfully, and consistently served the King. Now this would be an unfair king.

If you want the benefits of heaven, you must respond now as a ***Kingdom*** citizen and obey the laws of the ***Kingdom*** and the constitution. So we must not listen to anyone who dismisses the fact that God will judge according to his prewritten Word. They say God blesses everybody, no matter what. Yes, he does; he blesses you to have the time to make a godly decision where you want to be for the rest of your eternal life. Now this is the truth!

Reality Check to the Blessings of God!

How would God give us a million dollars, *if you are not even paying your tithes, are not faithful to the work of ministry, have a nasty attitude, and on and on . . . not living in the* ***Kingdom***. You may indeed get a million dollars, but who supplied it, is the question?

The church in its "infant mentality," however, will receive this and shout with excitement *because this FEELS good to us and makes us shout; we/you "cling to a lie" because it makes you feel good.*

What causes false prophesy and false prophets?

This spirit of needing a lie rather than the truth creates a problem, and the sad fact that is ***we who operate in this spirit then are the cause of false prophesy, and we pay or support this type of spirit and support the prophet to lie to us*** because we don't want the truth, which will really help us to grow and maybe get that *MDB* (million-dollar blessing). *How can you trick yourself to get excited*, shout, and say "O*h yes*!" when this word does not line up for you right now in your life?

How can you allow someone to prophesy to you that you are going to be married in three months and you are married to a secret spouse already and do not even have divorce papers filed? *Unless we want to be lied to*, as we desire to be tricked, the trickster comes to us with deceit that will lead to our defeat!

But on the other hand, when a *real prophet* calls you up and says "God said to you to 'get your life in order before you die in your sins' because you are living in fornication, you are not a tither, you are not keeping your life holy,'" then you get *angry, you refuse to hear the voice of God.*

The second violation is that you then invoke others to join your spirit of rebellion; you call everyone you know and try to get them to agree with you that you are all right, and stone the prophet with your words. This must be stopped if we are to move forward in ***Kingdom*** success and in ***Kingdom*** citizenship.

Kingdom Rule # 7
You must trade Church-Dom for ***Kingdom***

Let us define **church-dumb** or, shall I say, *churchdom.* This is "CHURCHDOM": *those who reject the truth of GOD and his Word.* For example, when you know that this is the "correct prophesy" that lines up with you at the time in your life, RECEIVE IT WITH JOY! *Yes, it is you,* just when you need a lifeline.

A true lifeline requires you to *balance with the Word of God.* Do not despise the true man and woman of GOD and God will send you help for your situation through the preached Word, the revealed Word, the Word of vocal prophecy, or the silent Word of God in your spirit. When God know you can receive the truth, he will send it.

Kingdom Rule # 8
You must Obey the "voice" of the King, NO matter what the cost

Do not "refuse" true prophetic word and seek "phony good feeling" prophesies that lead you farther away from GOD. *You cannot pick the good, prophesies, and refuse the truth* (the ones that bring you to balance) because the Lord of the land will judge your works and your rejection of his words, despite your excuse. *Matthew chapter 25* tells us what the ***Kingdom*** of heaven is like. Firm, fair, just, accountable, and of truth—this is what the voice of God is like; it supports His Word.

You must learn how to speak the language of the ***Kingdom***. You must leave "fear, family, failure, and other negative spirits out of the ***Kingdom***. Leave them and those other doubting inhabitants behind" who do not understand ***Kingdom*** talk!

You may even not at first be able to understand your own communication. Neither did I when I first began to speak Spanish. But as you continue to speak the language, you will begin to see more and understand more. Your change in your life will come as you become obedient to the King: You obey the king no matter what the cost. The King will reward all faithful and obedient servants and friends.

Faith really does come by hearing!

Negative associates and those who have been sent to plant negative seeds in your life must be silenced for your ***Kingdom*** talk to be developed. *Faith talk will produce the manifestation of events in your life that will let you know the King is favoring you* with His glory. Learn to speak the language of the ***Kingdom*** and know the voice of the King, as well as the constitution, and you will begin to see ***Kingdom*** results.

Put everything to the test: "THE WORD TEST"! And if it holds up, the *King will honor it. He honors His word,* his seal, and his edicts. We have a fair king who upholds His Word; speak His language and see Him work. Speak the constitution; it will prevail in court. You will hear the King rule in your favor.

Kingdom Rule # 9
You must Practice ***Kingdom*** Communication at all times

We must practice ***Kingdom*** communication. In other words, we must learn how to speak God's Word in every situation of our lives.

I often run in to seasonal Christians who can speak the Word in good season. When everything is going their way, boy, they do talk "good talk." They quote the constitution up and down, page by page, and line by line. However, when a little testing comes, they fail to "keep the faith."

They fail to continue to speak what they say they have. Some of them even start missing church and fall away from God personally. What happened to the talk? One of my spiritual daughters, *Minister Little* (Jacqueline E. B.), says, "Action talks." *Don't drop the constitution in time of despair; make your action talk!* I know people who can "outquote the scriptures when it is good." But when their boyfriend quits them, a job is lost, and a friend is mad, they miss their post in church, they forsake the assembly of the saints, and they lose the faith and forget their ***Kingdom*** language.

As we grow in the ***Kingdom***, we must find people and places to communicate our ***Kingdom*** language. In other words, if I wanted to be better in chess, I would join a chess club; better in acting, I would join the drama club; in golf, I would take golf lessons.

So to gain more knowledge in ***Kingdom*** communication, I must seek those speaking the language; I must "join the club." Let me please note that this may or may not be in your local assembly. I have met many pastors who do not speak ***Kingdom*** language. In fact, I know many pastors who are not saved or living in the ***Kingdom***!

There are even churches *that have more funerals than prayer meetings.* WOW! It seems like they would get a clue. However, if you ask the pastor to *have a healing service,* they try to scorn the believer. RUN from this place of death and never look back! God has called you to live a life of abundance and not death.

Do not worry about the size of the crowd; find, you, some ***Kingdom***-minded believers and find, you, some ***Kingdom***-minded people and live in the ***Kingdom*** of righteousness, peace, and joy in the Holy Ghost; that's the ***Kingdom*** of God: speaking the language, day in and out, increasing your ***Kingdom*** language. This will truly please the king.

Chapter 2

How the ***Kingdom*** Is Operated

*In the **Kingdom**, God has assigned, shall we say, spiritual patrols, or officers, of order and **Kingdom** government instruction for the assembly of faith. These officers I will call officers of protocol, or protocol officers that move in apostolic order.*

The Three Protocol Officers of the ***Kingdom***

The *Three Apostolic Protocol Officers* are
the Holy Spirit, the Apostle, and the Prophet.

For clarity, the office of the bishop is to oversee the orders as projected by these protocol officers as well because the bishop is the desired office (by one's own will) and not a directed office as the other parts of the fivefold ministry.

When these o*fficers are silenced,* the church has no authority of revealed discipline, order, and direction. It becomes as a "two-year-old *without* adult supervision."

We all know a two-year-old without discipline brings havoc to *everyone* (even to their parents). These undisciplined children, *they grow up to be five, seven, or even ten to twenty-one years olds who reject authority.*

*Let us further overview these offices as designated by God to be apostolic order officers to the **Kingdom** of God and its citizens.*

Kingdom **Protocol Officers**

Let's talk about the *three apostolic (**Kingdom**) protocol officers* that teach us the ways of the ***Kingdom***: the Holy Spirit, the office of the apostle, and the office of the prophet.

The First Protocol Officer

The Holy Spirit

The Holy Spirit, in some places, is still a "curse" word. I visited a service once in 2009 and said, "Praise the Lord." Everyone in the section turned toward one another as if I had cursed. I thought, how sad it is to go to a building (in this year and season) called church and not even be free to say "Praise the Lord!" (Of course, I was agreeing to a word that was being preached; I was not overly loud, and I was eyeballed like I were Satan.) This was supposed to be a prophetic conference on praise and worship and was supposed to be filled with excitement and joy, but the Holy Spirit was not welcome; the minister struggled and taught with great pain as she tried to break up the fallow ground. There were a few people there who finally got with the service, and finally, some deliverance took place after three days. The pastor was dead every time I looked at him; he was not responsive, did not praise, and had worshiped. This was a sad time in 2010, to not have the power of the Holy Spirit operating within the ministry. HOW SAD!

We Have Shut the Holy Spirit Out

We have shut the Holy Spirit out, we "sing" without his presence, we dance without his leading, and we speak without his anointing—this is dangerous because to learn about the ***Kingdom***, we need to tap into the chief ***Kingdom*** protocol officers, who were left to teach us all *things*! Yes, to *teach us* (all) things!

Envision this:

You are getting a new job, and they send you a person to teach you everything about the job. This job, by the way, has been done for over two thousand years by this family, and you have the best teacher available to teach you.

You have *unlimited time to prepare,* at least six months with this person (all expenses paid). But you never call this person; let us call him *Holy Spirit.* You never try to get to know him, you never ask any questions, and you never talk to him about the owner's company policy or anything. Now it's time to take the position; you go to the job, but you know nothing: Problem arises; you cannot handle and you totally fail your assignment because you fail to contact your best lead and access information, the information that will give you all the gain you need to learn the job you have been assigned to do, so you fail at learning your job. ***Who is to blame? YOU.***

This is how we treat the Holy Spirit, our ***Kingdom*** protocol officer, to give to us ***Kingdom*** training teaching and directions on how to increase in the job you are assigned to do. WOW, what a waste of good information.

I cannot stress this to you many times per day. I refer to "Holy Spirit" to lead, guide, direct, and teach us whatever we need, from business contacts to major decisions; God sent us a protocol officer to *teach* us *all things.* We must trust and use the Holy Spirit if we are to *learn the ways of the* ***Kingdom***.

In the ***Kingdom***, our Father has given the Holy Spirit an administrative assignment, and we must take full advantage of Him; learning from the Comforter for this assignment and tapping into his skills will only increase you and make you better in the ***Kingdom***.

It amazes me how we *call on the phone or e-mail them or fax them or telecommunicate with them "people"*—(Mom/Dad/friend BFF/sister/ other members) who all have limited knowledge to the divine destiny of our lives and fail to ask one of the device administrators (Holy Ghost) who knows our ***Kingdom***'s destiny to help us in our decision. Most of the people whom we call are frayed themselves and have problems that they cannot solve, yet we trust imperfect people and do not trust the perfected manifestation on the Holy Spirit. Because of this, we miss many things in our current lives and our upcoming future. Let's do better utilizing this wonderful resource.

Holy Spirit must be allowed back into our daily worship, our personal and corporate prayer time, and our ***Kingdom*** *growth. Holy Spirit will lead, guide, and direct you into all truth. If and when you allow him to speak, listen!*

Do not silence him; yield! He can always be checked with to see if this is the divine purpose for us by the Word. Any true protocol officer will never "*cross*" or disagree with the love, word, and truth of the ***Kingdom*** constitution. Holy Spirit will always speak *rhema,* "a word everlasting, fresh, and direct" that will cause ***Kingdom*** growth in your life. No matter when or how many times you hear it. This word will move you farther and take you deeper in your purpose and expected end."

The Second Protocol Officer

The Apostle

This is the voice of one sent to set in order *a "birther"* and a foundational builder, a church planter, a visionary. The apostle is the "grandmother or grandfather of the work"—the founder (whether male or female) and the one who has *heard the directing* from the Holy Spirit to start the ministry and word of faith in a specific area and continues to guide, direct, and influence us in ***Kingdom*** direction, order, and growth.

A person who leaves from under leadership out of order and starts a "*MAD ministry" is not an apostle* (MAD = minister/ministry against discipline) because they choose not to listen to their leader, to get mad, to leave, and to start a "work for God." This is not how the ***Kingdom*** works.

The Proper Way

One must be sent out as a pastor, breathed on by and *receive ministry life* from your "*apostle*" and your spiritual parent. Nothing starts from nothing. Even the beginning of man was birthed by God's breath, and God "*breathed*" on them and we became.

So the breath of life comes from those above us (when they *sent us out).* The orders of our work go on as extension of our ***Kingdom*** assignment from God, the Holy Spirit, and our apostle, in that order.

The Holy Bible, Our *Kingdom* Constitution

The Holy Bible: It is the "***Kingdom*** constitution and bylaw of ***Kingdom*** administration." It is the handbook and source of references and referrals for the ***Kingdom*** community and body of Christian believers.

The Holy Bible is our road map and moral compass for our Christian journey. Every protocol officer of the ***Kingdom*** should value the Word, and it should be the one true and living resource that all other resources must agree with. WE must now and always be true to its resources. In the Bible, God says he gives gifts to the body of Christ to EDIFY the body, to edify, as defined, means "to instruct and improve." Coming from the word base of *edit,* which means "to resize, assemble, and prepare, to direct revamp and rework, amend, correct and rectify."

The Office of the Apostle

The apostle understands this and uses this resource freely with Holy Spirit and godly interpretation to bring unity, clarity, judgment, and order to the perfected vision of the ***Kingdom***. To not have an *apostle* in your life,(that you are submitted to) limits your ***Kingdom*** understanding.

The apostle cannot be counted out of the *protocol offices,* as much as the *pastor* cannot be counted out of the edifying and training offices: Often, when a *pastor* gets or feels established, they feel "I don't need anyone *overseeing* me. I don't need a bishop, apostle, prophet, or anybody telling me how to run *my* church." To correct this, we must take the tone of this fact; this is still God's church and under his order, and he said he gives us these gifts until we come into the full unity of the faith. As of today in 2010, we in the faith are still not completely unified. (Would you agree?) Therefore, we would still be in need of the entire fivefold ministry today. Don't let people steal the word from you and cause you to miss your blessing. God gave us an order for a reason so we could abide by it and get in order.

I submit the order of the apostle is *not* as the office of the pastor, teacher on evangelism: It is a higher protocol officer in the ***Kingdom*** of God is a ***Kingdom*** *office of protocol.*

As with "in-house" ministry gifts, we have shepherds, lead minister, lay ministers, members, ushers, and overseers. Everyone has a place in ***Kingdom*** development. We, likewise, must seek to secure an apostolic gift in our lives.

The apostle should serve as a respected office in your life, whether male or female, preferably a joint and cohesive ministry team of wife and husband or husband and wife to give godly "birthing and spiritual parenting." Remember, no officer or office can reproduce when "homo," or alone; it takes "hetero," mutual contact, to have a divine encounter. While preaching in the Bahamas, I met a young man at the hotel where I stayed. This young man was about twenty-six years old and had had an experience with God, which he believed led him to his salvation. I was drafted into a conversation between him and the front desk personnel, who wanted to "ask me a question" while everybody was waiting for a ride in the lobby to go to noonday service, at which I was ministering. I was not seeking to be drafted into any conversation; I was seeking to be released to minister at church. The question, to my surprise, was "Can you be saved and still drink beer?" Immediately the young man went to justify and use scriptures (out of place) to defend himself. After ten minutes of bickering between themselves, I turned to leave, and was stopped again by them. I told them they did not want an answer; one wanted to justify, and the other wanted to prove the first one wrong. I ended this by saying "Does any of this help anybody get any closer to Christ? Does either one of your behavior draw anyone to God? And is God glorified by your lifestyle, now or in private? You answer these questions for me and I think you both will have your answer." I then took my seat. The young man went to me several minutes later and said thank you. He also went on to say some doubted his salvation, he had been saved for seven years now, and "people hated him." I asked him, "Where do you go to church?" He responded to me by saying, "Nowhere! I don't believe in NO church!" Right then I knew this young man's problems in a nutshell. He wanted to do what he wanted to do, he did not want to have spiritual authority, and he was operating in rebellion. I was so glad the Holy Spirit would not let me get into the mist of their folly. My ride honked and I left, but not before encouraging him to seek and find a local assembly to fellowship in.

People of God, you need a local fellowship to be accountable and have the gift speak into your life for direction and clarity. Yes, you need authority and someone to help you guide your life in the right direction and pathway of glory so you won't be caught up in flattering words and sound like an empty cymbal

I encourage you to seek those who "sets order, vision, and accountability"—not gender. And those who reproduce out of balanced relationships.

Rule of Protocol to the Office of the Apostle

Every apostle must have the Holy Spirit to function—they must be able to be bold, appointed, and anointed. They must love leading, working hard, and they must love teaching. They must understand ***Kingdom*** administration and understand their divine appointment as a protocol officer.

One needs the Holy Spirit deeply. Every apostle must want to help others avoid the pitfalls they have themselves encountered—this is through the ***Kingdom*** and spiritual life experiences and their failures and victories of faith. This is what will cause them to establish order in their lives: knowing through triumph what God is not pleased with and what makes the hand of God move in our behalf. EXPERIENCE AND SEASONING make one MATURED IN THE FAITH!

The Third Protocol Officer

The Prophet

It gives me joy to explain why the prophet is a ***Kingdom*** officer and finally put a place in the ***Kingdom*** to this highly misunderstood office. *The prophet* is a spiritual-patrol officer and a ***Kingdom*** administrator *of truth.* This is what this office was designed to be; however, because of *fear,* the prophet does not, in many cases, express the truth of what the Holy Spirit has assigned him (or her) to say.

Fear paralyzes many fivefold gifts from operating the spirit of truth (Holy Spirit). Therefore, false prophecies are influencing ***Kingdom*** dynamics. Whereas, the office of the prophet is one that should be the voice of *deliverance, order,* and respect for our Father, God, in holiness and divine order.

The Office of the "Prophet" Has Been Stripped

We have *reduced this office* to "houses and cars." "Oh, God is going to bless you. Turn around three times and get your millions."

We have stripped the office of the prophet to the entertainer; we want the prophet to "make me feel good or you will not be back to be a minister here." This fear has shut the mouth of the spiritual protocol officer because we want to please the people.

I have counseled hundreds of prophets who want to tell the truth to the pastor and the church, but they *fear "schedule suicide"* and being ousted from the church. The office of the prophet is not to stroke your sins, passions, or desires; it is the one that should help you prevent destruction and spiritual suicide.

The office of *the prophet should bless you with truth*; however, only ***Kingdom***-minded citizens can truly take the truth.

No one wants to receive a traffic ticket, but if you're driving drunk, *somebody* needs to stop you before you kill yourself or someone else. God does send a word to protect you, but if you cannot accept a real prophet—a "***Kingdom*** protocol officer"—then you are probably going to have a lot of bumps in your ***Kingdom*** growth.

The true prophet is not a "sugar fix" to pump you up but should cause you to examine, redirect, plant, seed, and uphold the ***Kingdom*** constitution (Bible). The prophetic voice has been locked down, distorted, and in some venues, silenced.

The Prophet's Office Has Been Limited!

In "churchdom," the prophet has a limited role and *sub-authority* to the pastor; therefore, the church has no judge and becomes lawless and fruitless. The voice of the prophet is rejected and made to "speak to be accepted versus speaking to bring repentance and repair."

I was at a church in Nassau, Bahamas, in 2010; and I was led to put a person who was actively involved in witchcraft in the service out of the worship experience. Not that I do this often, and I felt really bad about having to do it there, but I had to take authority over the service in apostolic power. These church witches had been sent to set on and damage the service. They had been out two nights in a row and, in fact, were so strong that I had to begin to teach on witchcraft in the pews and how not to let the witches create an atmosphere for the ***Kingdom*** not to praise God!

Anyway, this young girl refused to praise God, created a scene; and I had to ask her to leave church. The next night, because my heart was heavy, I wanted God to assure me he was with me. I prayed for God to send his witness of glory by the spirit of praise, and He did! WOW, what a service time of refreshing we had on Hospital Lane.

Many were confused and in stupor at what had actually happened the night before and had never seen order as such but were free the following night. We continue to teach there, and

God's power moved in might and power. Why could this happen? The pastor of the house was in agreement with the Spirit of God and yielded to the authority of the apostle. I, as the guest apostle, yielded to her authority as the pastor as well. I talked with her and knew her comfort zone, and we had a glorious time in building the body of Christ together. The prophetic spiritual patrol must have a powerful weapon to balance our lives. That weapon is *truth.* Without truth, a prophet has no spiritual authority and no weapon with which to "demand" respect.

Learning the ways of the ***Kingdom*** means to accept, respect, and honor the office of the *true prophet.*

"Who is a true prophet?"—one who speaks what God, through the Holy Spirit, has spoken under spiritual authority of the set apostle in their ***Kingdom*** assignment.

The Prophet is Stripped Naked; Who stripped the prophet?

Some prophets have made this office hard because of lack of order. Most of them feel as if they do not need a pastor, and run buck wild through the churches, wild with no guidance or submission! Some act as though they are apostles; however, they are not establishing any work as a general apostle would.

Because of this "renegade and sometimes "weird" spirit, some pastors shy away from allowing those who are prophetic inside their churches. Yes, to keep things balanced and in order, *prophets need accountability* and pastors and apostles over their lives. They, however, must be brought into order, but they cannot be silenced; this damages the church further. The people suffer from not hearing prophetically from God.

Therefore, let us establish, *every prophet without a local pastor "must" have a general apostle whom they are accountable to! (No exceptions.)* Why do we say this?

Let's look at the ***Kingdom*** again. A prophet says, "In a sense, I am an ambassador." Well, an ambassador *is still connected to a country and on assignment.* An ambassador is still under authority of a leader and is not on a wild tangent. These ambassadors return to their country after their assignment is finished. They do not just hang out/around for whatever reason. They are truly accountable; someone knows where they are and what they are doing at all times.

This must be the ***Kingdom*** assignment of the prophet, for accountability and the Holy Spirit to have accuracy, order, and truth in their lives. The overseeing of the apostle elected, selected, and set in their lives, as chosen by the prophet, must be done with great care and submission.

This apostle must be one who is *granted permission* or rein you in and even prove your ministry, at any time. A true prophet will allow *their set apostles* to speak, discipline, love, correction, reprove, rebuke, and speak reproof to them and their ministries. Without this, the prophet becomes (again) a wild horse, untamed and loose.

God expects this office of a prophet to submit to the house, and since a true prophet may have to have "stand-in house" accountability, they must retain a "set apostle."

This "set *apostle*" is often the *chief apostle or a person who is overseeing prophets and other local apostles and sometimes pastors, missionaries, and elders on assignment; these persons as well as* that the prophet pay tithes and offerings to their apostle. The set apostle visits with them at their location or in-house at least twice a year (so the ministry may continue to be proved) and continues to maintains contact with their leadership. This set apostle's number is posted on outreach materials and allowed to be contacted, if needed.

Gone are the days of people who do not have anyone to correct them and ensure they have not become poisonous to the stream that runs through the ***Kingdom***. If someone is speaking into your life (as a prophet), make sure he is a *set apostle (one that you see, visits your assembly and an apostle that acknowledges them, your leaders, as a mutual relationship in* **Kingdom** *work) and they are those* who are submitted to a church, overseeing them, and are faithful to the ***Kingdom***. Otherwise, "*shun this renegade*" (and give them a copy of this book).

We must *take the "harness" off the true prophet,* who, by the way, **does not have to be *weird* to be a prophet.** One thing I cannot stress enough is prophetic accountability. It is so easy to hear "voices" not *necessarily of God.* Our ministries must be accountable to others to remain balanced—not someone we never hear from or whom we have not submitted to, but someone who truly can *check us* and, if necessary, *sit down,* if it is their instruction.

Wow! *True accountability is a must for a true prophet!* I often *visit* those we cover at their events (most prophets travel a lot), ministries (if they have them), and even visiting their homes; and we minister to them the spirit of accountability and accuracy.

Some lift or leave from under our covering after being "parented," rebuked, and reproved. They felt that they *outgrew* the need for covering. And of course they want to be free to do whatever manner of evil and bring havoc to the local church. They get up and lie to the people why they left, and the people, being so gullible, believe every lie. Because they to want to be unaccountable. In fact, many of them obtained a spirit of rebellion, pride, and prophetic pimping. They knew that neither Bishop nor I would approve, and they ran to people who would (like others) let them *wreck* people and play the games of prophetic disrespect.

Others who we cover in grace and faith love the true caring and concern and mentorship and spiritual parenting we provide through Christ Jesus, and they grow and are blessed by our leadership for years and years to come.

For these "of the *prophetic connection,*" the *prophetic chamber* and the *InterGlobal Association of Christian Churches Worldwide,* we say, thank God!

When you are disconnected from authority, it is a dangerous thing, No community can operate without authority; no land, no country can operate without authority. When you do this, you are in grave danger. In fact, you must watch out for the *spirit of Joab.*

Out-of-order ministers of any kind, especially evangelist, prophets, and self-proclaimed apostles, are the worst if not in order.

You cannot fake it until you make it!

Some of these *have lost their anointing* and were counseled to move to other areas in ministry and submit to a local church pastor. (But they want to maintain the power they felt the prophetic order brings.) Others had fallen into weirdness (with male and females); others were "lying prophetically." *Others never dealt with peoples' real issues* but always had these "sweetie-pie prophecy," which came to people (members) who were in all kinds of sin and disarray. These type of prophets are "just a mess—not a messenger." You cannot fake it until you make it. You must wait on your calling. Lives are counting on you to be accurate and real; this is no time for on-the-job training. You cannot afford to have other people's blood on your hand for your sweetie-pie prophesy! You must sometimes cry loud and spare not! You must sometimes blow the trumpet and sound the alarm! Yes, God still speaks, and in his love, he still says "TELL them my whole GOSPEL! And tell my people the truth!"

Sometimes you cannot believe every "GO!"

These sweetie-pie "*prophets*" are *not* ***Kingdom*** *protocol officers.* They were like the prophets who told the kings to go into battle, people.

Prophets said "Go!" But *one* ***Kingdom*** protocol officer, *a true prophet, said, "No,* you will lose your life."

I pray God to maintain you in a level of prophetic maturity to receive the ***Kingdom*** protocol officer in the voice of the true prophet.

Operating as (being) a *"master prophet* (a *teacher, and set prophet to prophets*) and a *"chief apostle" (a teacher and set apostle to apostles) and sent to the body of Christ as a protocol officer,* I see many who need to go back in the local church, submit their gifts, be trained, and seek a set apostle to be accountable to receive instruction for their office and become a true prophet of the ***Kingdom***.

Kingdom Protocol Officers are Needed in the Ministry Today

When you operate correctly as *a **Kingdom** protocol officer,* then the body will become one, and the people will "*hear* from heaven, and turn *from their* ways, and receive ***Kingdom*** gifts—healing, deliverance, breakthrough, joy, peace, love, and order."

A Prophet is a Visual Officer, but Not a Show-Off!

The *Prophet is the visual* to the audible voice of God
that you can see in a person "a face" in front of you
as God speaks through a voice. So you will not be
frightened or spooked!

Everyone that goes up and speaks a word, once or twice or every now and then, is *not a prophet!* Do not mistake this office with a "high spiritual experience" or the ability to pray and make God speak a word to you. *Every Christian should have this ability.*

Just because you drive a car does not make you one!

Likewise, this does not make you a *prophet.* So many times I meet people who sometimes have a "word from God," and they think they are prophets. If all you ever have is a "feel-good word," you are *not* a prophet.

You are an exhorter and have the spirit of exhortation, and God may even use you to prophesy, but this is no ticket to leave your church and go around like you are "God's gift" and that you have the word for the nation! Stay in your place and make your calling and election sure!

Three Things a Prophet Must Have!

A "prophetic voice" must have *developed hearing, developed seeing, and developed understanding of the character, thoughts, and mind-set of the voice of God. Do you have these gifts in your life? Are you still missing simple things in God but trying to prophesy to others?*

Check your gift before you practice on others, to see if it is working for your life first. If not quite yet, WAIT until it matures before you practice on others.

The third of the three protocol officers *has a divine interpretation* (as does the apostle) between heaven and earth. God honors this office so much that he said, *"I will do nothing except that I first reveal it to my servant, the prophet."*

We must prevent the prophetic from being watered down because *if* the prophetic voice is *distorted,* watered *down,* operating in *fear, sin, or* unbelief, *the* ***Kingdom*** *has a problem. Because this limits the true voice of God and God uses this gift to speak through as a sign to his people. This is why we must require true prophetic accountability.*

Open your Hearts again to the PROPHETS OF GOD, NOT OF BAAL

We have made the prophet feel rejected, strange, and put out to satisfy our "feel-good" status.

Pastors! Do Not "Despise" Prophecy nor the Office of the Prophet.

Pastors have influenced this behavior *by not wanting their ungodly lifestyles exposed.*

To be truthful, within the "prophetic circle," the spirit of homosexuality has a rampant flavor that seems to go unchecked within this office. After all, who is going to check them? When they are put in place of accountability and exposed for these practices, they leave and go somewhere else to continue to operate without accountability. They tell their "circle"—group of their accepted friends—just what they want to hear. And they rob the people of God with fake lifestyles and words.

These "PCs" invite each other to speak at each other's events and supply each other with a herd of "commander cover."

Some have herds of women (or men) from town to town that they all share. *They don't invite the voice of God* to their church. For fear of exposure, they play "dumb-dumb in churchdom," not entering into ***Kingdom***; and so sad, the people suffer. I told you, we have our *Brokeback Mountain* in the church.

God will restore honor to the "true prophets," as ***Kingdom*** leaders and citizens cry out to learn more about the ways of the ***Kingdom*** and receive the protocol officers of the order of the prophet. We are entering into a season in the ***Kingdom*** where the prophet will be needed again. The office of the apostle will be embraced and sought out, and the Holy Spirit will be *reverenced,* respected, sought after, and spent time with.

We must *respect these three offices* when they operate under accountability and in order. And we must call them into accountability when they do not.

Please take note to embrace the *true officers of God* and personally address and pray mightily *for deliverance of those you know are not flowing in* ***Kingdom*** *order to get into the* ***Kingdom*** *order, and under protocol of a local assembly and pastor. Don't just accept and get junk food; require better food for your growth.*

Pastors, as well, make sure you are under protocol and a good apostle that you will *submit your ministry to,* become accountable to, and respect. Then you will see your ministry grow in a godly way. Do not mind so much the numbers. That is not so important in the ***Kingdom***; get quality verses quantity.

Finally, *relationship is important; no* church is an island (no pastor is an island), not even yours. We all need to connect to each other and build up our most holy faith.

Do not select people who will always agree with you or not tell you what you can improve on *to cover you.* This is not covering or connection; it is "whoredom." Truly, find someone who will call you in to accountability and increase your faithfulness in the ***Kingdom***.

A lot of local "independent" pastors (never found in the scriptures) stay that way because they truly do not want anybody to *tell them what to do.* How ridiculous! When you want to be able to tell other people what to do!

The anointing flows from the head down, but someone as well must be your head. Let's get over it and submit one to another so God can be glorified. If you have no one speak to in your life, then how can you be truly restored when you fall? Who can speak in your life, bridge the gap, and help you become stronger in your walk? "Physician, can you truly heal yourself?" *No*! So let's *humble ourselves and get true covering.*

Yes, I am saying that *"every pastor" needs a pastor!*

Please note that a pastor's pastor is an apostle or bishop; they are instructed to oversee the office of the pastor. No one "lateral" to you or equal to you can "birth" you or parent you. Find someone you consider to be a mother or father to you, and submit your ministry to their overseeing. The *bishop* is overseen by the office of the *apostle*: The *apostle* is overseen by the *chief apostle*, and the *chief apostle* is overseen by the *apostolic conclave of chief apostle*. This is why every chief apostle should belong to a conclave of sorts or an interglobal association or association of some sort.

This Is the *Kingdom* Order, so Let It Be Written, so Let It Be Known.

The local or senior pastor oversees the other "in-house gifts" or ministries and ministers of the house—all other local ministers *should submit to this local pastor*. This includes prophets, evangelist, ministers, elders (nonpastorate) shepherds, missionaries, and other in-house staff. I know you can see the order and circle of God's ***Kingdom*** and protocol for the ministerial gifts to the body of Christ. So together let's work on it to get better and come into divine order.

Chapter 3

Prophetic "Protocol"

The ***Kingdom***

Let's Set It in Order

What Is Prophetic Protocol?

"*Prophetic protocol*" is the gifting from the *apostolic mantle* to influence the church in the affirmed and distinct order of *spiritual discipline, life order,* and *divine-destiny direction.*

Protocol is when the office of the apostolic or prophetic *mantle is released to flow,* in an anointing, which is to *"set the church, body of Christ, individually, and spiritual families as it applies to an interglobal body of believers in a Christian social system on 'divine course,' as established by the Word of God or in* "order."

The spirit of "order" is one given to the apostle as a mantle of development and edifying that will bring change, correction, instruction, wisdom, peace, and growth. This mantel comes only with this apostolic assignment and this specific anointing, creating "*prophetic protocol.*" This anointing of protocol or apostolic order is truly given to maybe one in one hundred thousand. Although many take the "title" because they have started one church, *they are not really apostles, but are overseers and good pastors. They do not function as governmental ambassadors of order, ones sent to set order.*

We must embrace this time of change, when an apostle is in our midst, as a time of growth and true change. Therefore, an apostle is one "sent to set order or protocol" in the ***Kingdom*** of God.

To begin this order, the apostle themselves, the sent one, must have learned the order of God through trial, maturity, spiritual and life experience.

Some People Leave Ministries Wrongly Because They Do Not Understand Protocol

One who has *operated without* this spiritual order will often influence "ungodly and independently" ministries away from others with spiritual covering, "accountability."

This "independent and self-destructive spirit" is granted and accepted by persons following their ministries, and they feel sanctioned by the flock that follows them.

Sometimes these independent ministers (they are alone by their own choice), because of their own "unforgiveness, greed, or fear and pain that are residing in their spirits." This spirit of isolation and independence is created by hurt that is unresolved and unrepentant, the willingness to let go and walk in humbleness, and this equals to unforgiveness and more hurt, pain, and isolation.

I see this over and over where people start churches because they are hurt by someone else or their own interpretation of something that happened or did not happen as they think. Therefore, many ministries are birthed out of a person's pain or because a person has had an uncommitted, unloyal, and unforgiving attitude with those who have stewarded and shepherded them in the past. They left the fold with a "Burger King mentality"; these are those who move into ministry to have their "way."

Many are not blessed "in their going." And this spirit of having no spiritual parent (teaching, training on accountability) has caused the ***Kingdom*** of God to suffer and the "spiritual violence" to take by force the love, peace, and joy of the ***Kingdom***!

Some People Try to Leave Correctly When They Leave to Establish Other Ministries

Let's pause to say that some persons *seek* correct spiritual release from their leader that they wish to depart from, sensing a time of "***Kingdom*** maturity" and season of spiritual graduation have and are to come due to them, only to encase rejection and to be held back time after time from their God-given destiny;

Therefore, like abandoned children, they leave and start their ministries with much pain and sufferings; they as well, without parents, like in the natural, must learn through the school of "*spiritual hard knocks.*"

Because their "*spiritual parents*" do not understand their spiritual roles, harbor jealous thoughts, and envious attitudes, refusing to allow them, the spiritual children, to mature and develop, they reject their parents' rules and leave the house to grow up.

How sad to leave your spiritual home without the blessing, and more so without a spiritual blessing.

No Matter How You Leave, When you do leave, if you do not have a "Spiritual Parent" Get, Find, Adopt "Spiritual Parents" Quickly

However, there is always a *loss* when there is *no* "*spiritual parentage.*" I experienced initial *spiritual abandonment* when my ministry first started. However, I quickly received "spiritual adoption" from a wonderful spiritual parent and continued to grow under the direction of authority and grace.

One who is accountable (*truly accountable*) to someone of spiritual, "***Kingdom*** quality" will be humbly trained and ***Kingdom*** respected, which will birth forth in them, and they will have awesome "spiritual protocol" in their lives.

You can feel it, quality and training, when they go in the door; it's like a disciplined child, in public. What do people feel when you walk in the door? Do they know you are trained in the spirit of ***Kingdom*** excellence and spiritual protocol, or are you just a silly person bringing up bad kids in the ***Kingdom*** because you lack discipline in the ***Kingdom*** yourself? I was preaching a church in Miami, Florida, in 2000; and the pastor himself was chewing gum wildly on the pulpit; his kids were running up and down on the pulpit and jumping on the chairs; and to top it all, he took out the phone while I was preaching and begin to talk loudly on it. When I looked at him CRAZY like he was acting he had the nerve to put his finger up in the air (which I later was told meant "excuse me"), I thought it meant "hold on a minute," and he continued to talk on the phone. I had to openly rebuke him and tell him "Put the phone down, and please turn it off, Dr. Mc Bride." As you can see, out of orderness breeds out of orderness. No wonder the teens in his church were texting and playing around like it was a playground; there was no order. After church, I told him "If we were to serve them for the other two days, there must be order starting with him." We pointed out several things that were out of line with the spirit of Christ, things that hindered the move of God and was grieving the Holy Spirit.

He agreed, and now he is one of our best students and has a great congregation of order and excellence and the move of GOD! By the way, he was separated about a year before we met him; after one year of mentoring him and them, his family reunited and he is now happily married and a great pastor! To God be the glory! But he was willing to submit! He could have gotten prideful and this church would be no more and is not prosperous in ministry, but he heard us and God and reformed. When you are willing to submit, you can eat the fat of the land.

Know who you are in your authority and walk worthy!

Sometimes I try to hide in the rear when I go to a service because I just want to hear the Word and observe! I have had people stop preaching when I have even tried to slip through the door of a service. They have stopped and said things like "There is a spiritual general walking in among us," "The guards have just changed because your anointing walked in," "When you walked in, I saw two big angels walk in behind you," "I know you are a prophet. You are a woman of order. You are a powerful woman of God, a leader in the ***Kingdom***," "You are an apostle of order," "You are an apostle to the ***Kingdom***," "You are a spiritual mother," "You set the order of God. You have a governmental anointing," "You are a prophet of prophets [the list of words goes on. 'You really love the Lord,' however, is still my favorite!]" "My god, when you walked in, I say order all around you," "I see you in a general's uniform," "I see the cherubim on your shoulder," "I see you surrounded by white and gold, with an army behind you and a military force on both sides of you and you are setting order"—literally, people have stopped in the middle of preaching to recognize the gift in and on my life.

These people were all powerful men and women themselves, so I am humbled that God would speak to them about the gifts on my life.

Is your promotion Spiritually Legal?

Everyone knows if you have training. No matter what your gift is, if your gift has not received ***Kingdom*** discipline, apostolic protocol, and spiritual nourishment, it has not been ***Kingdom*** proved; and your promotion may not be spiritually legal. Many people have groups of people whom they minister to weekly and daily; however, they will not call themselves pastor because that will make them accountable. They are "bootlegging." They are not legal, and because they will not become legal in the spirit realm, they use spiritual attacks on the ones they serve and themselves. This is not right, and they will be arrested by the spiritual patrol and will have to serve time! Because they are operating without a license.

If you would not go to a unlicensed mechanic to do your car .(or maybe you would)
An unlicensed doctor to perform surgery on you .(or maybe you would)
An unlicensed barber to cut your hair (or maybe you would)
An un licensed chef or butcher to handle your meat and food (or maybe you would)
An unlicensed eye doctor to check your eyes (or maybe you would)

An unlicensed minister to practice on your soul (oops, maybe you have)

As you can see, your soul is just as important as your hair, your car, and your health; so go to people who at least are not "bootlegging," and then when things go wrong, you might have a leg to stand on with God!

Don't Look for GENDER; look for the Anointing and POWER *Spiritual authority is not "gender"* induced because contrary to popular belief, it takes a female and a male to reproduce, and "proper parentage" *denotes a mother and a father.*

So it must be recognized, it takes a *womb* to birth—a *seed* to fertilize and a womb to give life. Both seed (father) and womb (mother) must be received in the spirit to accomplish apostolic protocol. Some "ministries" like ours are graced to have "seed and womb" in our apostolic protocol, spiritual parentage, and ***Kingdom*** agenda. Therefore, we believe a true equal balance has been achieved that will cause balance between sons and daughters and ***Kingdom*** citizens.

Apostolic protocol can only be achieved when the ***Kingdom*** citizens receive true apostolic (foundational instructions) protocol (order) to help them succeed in ***Kingdom*** growth.

Why Apostolic Protocol?

Everyone in ***Kingdom*** ministry needs a "spiritual empowerment coach, an apostolic hand" to be mentored within the faith. You need quality ***Kingdom*** interactions to fulfill your ***Kingdom*** destiny.

You must learn and apply apostolic protocol with every loving molecule of your breath, and only then you will be able to flow, know, and grow in ***Kingdom*** success and ***Kingdom*** life as you set these basic needs for ***Kingdom*** matriculation in order. *Yes, we must set our lives in order. Yes, to "set it in order,"* we first—especially the *fivefold*—must receive and embrace order; then ***Kingdom*** citizens, then new believers, then general household, adults, youth, children, and everything around us and with us *must be set in order!*

Can untrained warriors fight in this battle!

Let's face it; the ***Kingdom*** *of God lacks discipline, has untrained warriors and disrespectful citizens. We must address and correct these issues of our* ***Kingdom****.*

The Church Will Live, and the ***Kingdom*** Will Grow When We "Set It in Order"

Order must first be established again within the local assemblies, state, churches, in our national standards, and within interglobal ***Kingdom*** ministries. We cannot fail to uphold ***Kingdom*** *citizenship, the process* and the order it brings.

There are RULES THAT GOVERN OUR ***KINGDOM***

The ***Kingdom*** of God has *rules* (most of which are broken on our moral substandard), which we allow to affect our personal relationships with God—therefore, our churches, communities, state, nation, and world have no order. Jesus confronted this lack of order constantly and finally said, "We would love the world, and *not the order* or the things of God."

This is the time to learn "***Kingdom*** *order,*" which affects us *morally, financially, emotionally, physically, spiritually,* and yes, even mentally. All my "mature" Christian life, God has placed order in my spirit. I was severely rejected for many years in ministry for saying that "*God has an order, God has a standard, and God has rules in the* ***Kingdom***." For years I had doors closed on the word God put in my belly because the churchgoers wanted to feel good and didn't want to go into the ***Kingdom***.

Now doors are open across the world for my preaching. Praise our God, no doors are closed to our ministry now! We have invitations interglobally and universally, but I had to stand up for the Word, the ***Kingdom***, righteousness, integrity, and holiness. I kept shouting "ORDER! ORDER! ORDER IN THE CHURCH!" I kept shouting for thirty-five-plus years *"This is out of order" until somebody heard me. Now people, true* ***Kingdom*** *citizens, they want help; they seek order and want truth! And I say hallelujah! It's about time!*

I could see as a young minister, and I still can see as a seasoned minister, as I go to churches and I *see the lack of order.* I could and can still see after thirty-plus years people out of order in the church building and in the service of the Lord as a faith builder in the ***Kingdom*** of God; WE must establish ***Kingdom*** order. A country without order will fail! We must have order.

I had the pleasure as I was in the Bahamas several times, to have visited (Pastor) Miles Monroe Ministry. Dr. Monroe, who is an apostle to the body of Christ and a bishop of many, has a table that those who seek membership must apply. As I told this to many pastors in the States, they did not understand the disciple or the accountability. But I did! I embraced the fact that someone is saying "You choose to be here, and it is my choice to have you here as well. We are both making a covenant to comply with order!

What do I see? As a twenty-first-century prophet, I see (truthfully) the lack of commitment of the people who call themselves Christians, and I see the *lack of people growing*. But Dr. Monroe is saying you must make yourself accountable to the ***Kingdom*** through stepping up to the plate of accountability. You must tithe, be faithful, and we need to know who you are and where you are. This is God's plan for us in the ***Kingdom*** as good citizens. You must begin to understand and receive deep in your spirit that the ***Kingdom*** has an order and that God wants so much more for us! So why do we not choose to embrace ***Kingdom*** *order and grow up in our faith*?

WE can take control of our spiritual growth, we can choose to grow up and become better citizens, we can choose to increase our faith, and we can choose to better our walk with Christ. So let's grab hold and set it in order; it all starts with one person, YOU! It starts with one mental commitment to see the ***Kingdom*** expand and grow with us, and we can do this. We can make up our minds to do this because as we do this, God will bless us. I know you are as I am; you want the blessings of God. So we must SET IT IN ORDER!

What do I need to set in ORDER?

For over thirty years, I stayed faithful to my assignment screaming "ORDER!" Yes, I knew God our King had an order. But it seemed like the church wanted to dismiss this order; they wanted to let everything and anything be done and thought our King would accept this behavior. Just because we think we have a "good church" does not mean that the King is pleased. Did his witness truly show up, or were we operating in the flesh of emotions and thinking that we have just been touched by heaven? *What are we doing in our walk with God that we do not even know the "wind of the flesh from the move" of God? Have you or have you not experienced a fresh wind and real move of God in years?*

Nothing but a joyful Noise, but not the wind of GOD!

I have several friends (pastors) who swear that their churches "*move*" in the Spirit. I visit their ministries from time to time, to find the same people shouting and dancing on the same cue. *No growth* inwardly is happening in the people and no real growth in their church, but the *music is good and they dance, dance, dance all night! But where is the FRESH WIND! The blowing of the wind of God that changes things?*

This excitement that we are sometimes experiencing *is not* the move of God, the presence of God, or the truth of God. It is just a lot of shaking in the wind.

Funny enough, as to who is doing the most dancing (guess who)? "Those with ever-present evil spirits." The spirits of *lesbianism, homosexuality, lying, and hatred flood their churches.* So I know this is not the Spirit of God.

We must begin to examine ourselves and our ministries: who's over the music ministry, the altar, the children's church? And what kind of spirits do they truly have? God would not call certain behavior a violation of his ***Kingdom***, or even an abomination, and then show up and bless it; let's get real!

Does *God,* our *King,* flood this type of ministry with His Spirit? Or is this another spirit? Yes, God loves all his children, but are we all his children? Yes, God wants to help us all; but are we all willing to change, or are we submitting our churches to immoral values all for the sake of music and "good church"?

Are you bold enough to preach deliverance, or are you just an "exhorter" and not a "real pastor"? Is this why our churches have not changed? Exhorters just encourage you, but a true pastor, shepherd, will shear your will if necessary for your sake as well as his.

We have some wonderful "*exhorters" who have assumed the role of pastors* and want to make the sheep feel good. A real pastor knows when to *shear the sheep* and is not *afraid* of "if they feel good"!

Real pastors do what is necessary *to keep the herd healthy,* even if they have to slay a "diseased sheep" or kill wolves, witches, or warlocks who flood our camps and take over. Because we have no shepherds or, shall I say, we have "scared shepherds" who are hiding from the truth.

This is not popular preaching and teaching today, but I pray your spirit will receive it with gladness and embrace this truth. NO, not popular, but it is biblical, and those of us who want to have *true* ***Kingdom*** *living will embrace this,* teach this, and receive God's true "*move*" within our service times and our person times of ministry within our homes, cars, jobs, and social experiences!

It's time for the "fresh wind" of God, "*a wind*" that will blow and shake things up and change things, *a real move of God*! This wind will also make ourselves accountable to truth and to preaching it and receiving it; "the wind of God" will blow if we let it until change fills our church services, our hearts, and our homes.

Why do you go to CHURCH?

Or should I say, the reason you should or *DO NOT GO TO CHURCH. You* do not or should not come to church to *feel good*!

Your ***Kingdom*** life that you are living should make you feel good! *Church is for training,* deliverance, salvation, and ***Kingdom*** school—to empower you, to refuel you, to have something to give someone else for their journey. To train you and teach you the ways of the ***Kingdom*** and of Christ and to get you to understand and know our God better, deeper, and wider through true revelation.

You go to the training center of God, "THE CHURCH," to Learn!

IF you are living a ***Kingdom*** lifestyle that embraces the love of God, and that is what will make you *feel* good. *You go to church, which is God's school (house), to embrace* ***Kingdom*** *truth* so you can line up your life to be pleasing to the King.

If another organization (not of our Christian faith) had not taken the term ***KINGDOM*** *HALL,* I would say "Let's make a change and every Christian pastor rename our worship and training centers to '***kingdom*** hall training and worship centers.' As you can see, we must embrace teaching and not feelings and emotions. When we go to fellowship, we must stop the churchdom. Let's go to the "***Kingdom*** and set it in order."

Chapter 4

The ***Kingdom*** Has an "Order"

*The **Kingdom** has an order. Even if you are not living in full protocol,* you still know everything has an order. We want to try and to establish some type of order for the ***Kingdom*** officers of the body of Christ. We can no longer say that we just let and allow anything to go on and happen. We need to establish some sort of method to our government. Will everyone embrace this order? No, however, many will because they, as I was for years, sought to establish some type of plan that we would agree on that would make us take our heads out of the sand and see the same thing for once in the ***Kingdom***.

There are qualifications for officers and leaders in every order and part of life.

Let's Look at the Qualifications of Those to Whom We Entrust Our Spirits

Qualification of an Apostle, Bishop, General Overseer, Elder

Not a novice—unless they be "pulled up in pride." Not a beginner, not a young person, not a youngster, not an inexperienced person. But a fully mature Christian who understands and has been proven in the faith by experience and has godly victories to be substantive in their testimony.

These are the people who should "lead us" in the major offices of the church of God, through his son, Jesus Christ. We do not want people practicing on us; *we want seasoned, matured gifts working with us, GROWING US UP AS THEY HAVE GROWN UP!* WE want matured believers, faithful and tried, loyal to the body of Christ to teach us and train us in his work, warfare, and principles.

I, as you are, am tired of these Johnny-come-latelies who have not even learned that there is still milk behind their ears. They have not even graduated from high school yet and are trying to pastor people who have been in the faith before they were born. Yes, you can rule as a "king" at any age, but not as a priest. The responsibility is too great for our souls to entrust them to "Mr. Johnny's baby boy because he is cute" or "Mr. Preacher's second son because his daddy says he is ready." No, not my soul, I want you to know the god you talk about. Otherwise, my daughter may be caught in your trap as you are trying to grow up. And you get her pregnant because you're still young but you marry somebody else because she's the right type of first lady." (And yes, this has happened too many times.) But why? Why did this happen? Because you were not ready yet, not mature, you, you did "not wait on your calling, to be able to walk worthy of your calling" so the church does not suffer while you practice being anointed.

Is there an age to be ready for Ministry, especially the office of Bishop or Apostle?

Everything in the ***Kingdom*** draws parallels from nature, so let's see. I believe that if our government gives us an age where they can lead us as a people, certainly God would expect no less.

To be the president of the United States (or any other country), you must be at least ____ years old! (You fill in the blanks, look it up, or ask somebody.)

To be a king, one must at least be ____ unless their predecessor dies early. To be over a standing ***Kingdom***, one must take the ***Kingdom*** at age.

To be a CEO, the average age is with years of experience in running the type.

To be the pope or cardinal, one must at least be the age of ____.

So how old do you need to be to be an apostle? (It may differ with some people.)

Having balanced this Holy Spirit with the works and the need to fulfill true apostolic works and requirements (I feel truly), one must at least be *thirty-seven* years old to be the head of the church.

The office of An Apostle is like the pope to the Christian church

How old would you want the pope to be? To consider him ready to lead the Catholic church, you want them to be mature, fully seasoned, and ready to stand tall. To be able to reign in power and authority, making their calling at election. Sure, let's say give or take *thirty-seven to fifty* years is the age considered for full maturity.

Under twenty-five, you are probably not ready

Who *cannot be an apostle (agewise)?* Anyone under twenty-five years old. *Why?*

The first reason is because it takes time to mature, even spiritually. Don't rush to the palace; complete your work like King David did, as a shepherd in the fields, before you go to the palace." Yes, know that you are anointed and appointed, but wait until you mature before you allow your appointment. NO one can take your gift or talents from you, but once you put on the robe, your life will change. Get fully prepared; kill your lion, your tiger, and your bear; and defeat your Goliaths because you cannot go back to the fields once you have entered the palace!

The second reason is that it would be impossible to have *completed the apostolic works* in full and with perfection. God wants you to know how to run the ***Kingdom*** fully, respectfully, and completely. You cannot just jump into pastorship and ride it like the boat of fellowship; and it is a long way from the boat of friendship. It takes time and work to LEARN HOW TO WALK IN YOUR OFFICE. You must have apostolic works to complement you as a pastor, bishop and finally an apostle.

Let's support this with the lives of other apostles and ministerial persons. (You must take time to study and review their lives.)

What Are Apostolic Works?

An apostle is the highest office in the "Christian church," the body of Christ. They are the called-out ones, the ecclesia; do recognize and embrace the office of the apostle as one that will never die and is still in operation as a gift to edify the body of Christ and has not been silenced or given by our Lord and Savior Jesus Christ to have done away with. As the other fivefold gifts will never die or be silenced, if you are in a church or ministry that only teaches in the gifts of the pastor as the only speaking voice to the edifying of the body today, RUN! This is wrong; these gifts are here to help us until the return of Christ.

As to the works you should have, each apostle and bishop should *have at least* (minimum) but not limited to *twelve levels of ministerial duties and service levels that they have operated in and spent time perfecting and maturing in each area.*

One should have served at least two to three years in each area to reach a perfect and mature state in the ability to teach on each area or train others in each area in the apostolic works. Some areas should have led to other areas and may have been done concurrently, which have led to their individual spiritual promotion and spiritual growth. *This has been creating a track level in their lives and a walk of faith for them while seasoning themselves in the faith,* ***Kingdom*** *beliefs, and personal experiences* with Christ, the Holy Spirit, and the Father God. This will establish you as one who can truly say they have come to be able "to *know* Him and then to *make him known*"!

These areas can include staff worker, missionary youth minister, choir, praise and worship, deacon, elder, greeter teacher, Bible class leader, women (dept) ministry, usher evangelist, prophet, pastor, senior pastor, newsletter staff, financial minister, bishop, cardinal, minister, security, armor bearer, administrative pastor, executive pastor, church planter, international missionary, department head and counselor, or other ministry work—*any person* seeking to be a true apostle must have at least twelve areas of works.

Not everyone will want to work for the title; some will want to steal it illegally and point fingers as to why they do not feel it is necessary to fulfill any requirements. *"GOD called me,"* they will say. Yes! God did, but he also said to "**perfect [mature] in your calling.**"

Now let me pause to say that "anyone who wants to follow someone not qualified to do spiritual surgery on you," go right ahead. I will probably see you in the "spiritual morgue" after you "bleed to death." It is your choice whom you follow in the ***<u>Kingdom</u>****, but you owe it to yourself to have the best! Especially when it comes to your soul!*

We find that those who disagree with this normally *are self-appointed apostles with no works, no stability, and an arrogant spirit.* They often prey on the members and have no financial integrity. The churches they pastor are a breeding ground for sin and are often filled with these kinds of homosexual persons' tendencies and flamboyant tendencies. Many women follow, seeking those men for "husband" (normally the self-appointed apostle), and persons of unstable mind-sets often follow these persons, who by the way usually "steal" other's *sheep* (breaking them away from their former church) to establish the *new* church.

These are not apostles; these are "hurt, immature people" who need to repent, resubmit to leadership, and be restored to the family of love.

As you can see, to gain this experience and become an apostle takes *years* and *years*. An apostle must have a "*vision* of ***<u>Kingdom</u>***, not churchdom and not dumb-dumb," *maturity*, and *grace, not cockiness and not kookiness*. Or even varied forms of *strangeness does not make you a prophet.* The way you roll your eyes, flap around, snap your fingers, look at your palm, call out phone numbers, the sound of your voice, or just because you do "antics or strange things" will not qualify you. You need to be seasoned, mature, and move with God; say what God tells you to say; and do what he tells you to do, correct, rebuke, love, and set in order. Otherwise, if you don't, one day the people will wake up and see that you are certainly not an apostle or a prophet but a fake, and then you will have to run to another town to do your tricks again.

Chapter 5

Problems in the Prophetic and Apostolic

The Eight Problems
In the Apostolic Order

Eight Problems We find in the Prophetic and Apostolic

We must address these issues honestly and openly to have a chance to fix these eight areas of problems in the prophetic and apostolic order. Until these areas can be addressed, the ***Kingdom*** *will not take the next level from the enemy because we are living on a lie and standing on a platform of deception. We must form a holy platform and embrace the truth of change. Let us expose truth in these areas, embrace the truth, and run with the vision of GOD so that the* ***Kingdom*** *can stand and withstand the enemy; but it must start from within.*

Problem #1
* Those with An "*Unstable Mind*" create problems in the prophetic

As said before, "*strangeness*" does not create a ministry appointment for you. Because you cry a lot, whine a lot, scream or holler, or even have flashes or have seen the light does not create *you* as a minister, fivefold or *apostle*. Make sure you are mentally stable before counseling, praying for, or laying hands on others. (This must be set in order.)

Ask the person you are following—who sent them out, when, where, how! You will be surprised at the instability you will hear.

Problem #2
** Those with "Homosexual Spirits create problems in the prophetic:*

Let's define spiritual homosexual spirits: (1) the "I can do it with myself and with myself only" spirit. This same kind of spirit of rebellion will reproduce after its own kind and produce isolation and independence, pulling away from normal fellowship and spiritual accountability; (2) an unnatural way of reproducing. Cloning activity—"everyone must dress like me and me alone. Otherwise, you will be ousted"; (3) a spirit *refusing to believe* "I am wrong. I am made to cohabit like this. God made me this way and I will not change. I will ignore scriptures that apply to me and I will be like I want to be in spirit of God's Word"; (4) a disloyal spirit, a backbiting and double-tongued spirit, a spirit of gossip and discord, and spirit of nonvalue of the truth.

Those with these types of spirits create problems for the prophetic move of God. They cause people to withdraw from the truth of God by their personal display and physical witness. Not believing the Gospel because of your outward show of discontentment toward the Gospel, believing that if you are not the first partaker of the Gospel, how can you tell others to partake of its truths and deliverance power?

Problem #3
**** Those with a "Joab Spirit" create problems in the prophetic:***

The independent spirit that goes against the leadership while in the camp, *"undermining the authority," vision, and direction of the house leader that is* in position. One must kill the spirit of Joab, the absolute spirit, the independent spirit, the spirit of adultery, and the homosexual spirit. In this reference, please adhere to a nonsexual definition of homosexual spirit.

Problem #4
**** Those with No integrity create problems in the prophetic:***

Many of the people you are following are nothing more than "Internet prophets and *apostles"; this will create and has created a lot of problems in the prophetic:* I once asked a person that was in my office, "Who 'consecrated' you? Who established you as an apostle?" I asked him this because he had only been saved about three months. I know I was there when he accepted Jesus. In fact, it was in one of my services that I called him out of the audience (he had gone to hear me because of the girl he was dating. In fact, he went to pick her up from church, thinking church was out; but because she didn't go outside, he went in and sat in the rear of the church. I spoke into his life and led him to Christ on his confession that he was not saved, nor had he ever been.

So he went back to my church on this day in South Carolina to thank me for leading him to Christ and to say "*You know, Apostle Rice, I am an apostle now, just like you!*

Puzzled and startled and confused, I began to ask him a lot of questions; and he answered me boldly. This thirty-plus-year-old man said that *he brought his papers off the Internet.* And to top it off, he told me that another local preacher, who was a pastor, had told him to do it *because he could skip the red tape and people trying to hold him down, telling him also that that is how he got into the ministry because no one would license him, so he just said he would get his own papers. He paid $350 plus shipping and handling, and now nobody can tell him what to do.*

I was shocked, mad, and appalled and said, "*How dare you buy your way into the **Kingdom** authority ranks?*" This person had only served three months and was the "pope" of the Christian community. "No way!" I began to say to him "*This is out of order*"—only to be in front of an angry person whose excuse was "everybody wants to hold people down." I said, "No, baby." I assured him no one wanted to see him grow more than I did and fast is OK, but this is not sane. I also let him know to grow in grace and peace and in order, not skipping (that's not right) and that the ***Kingdom*** has rules.

Problem #5
Those who can't repent create problems in the prophetic

This young man, Bobby P., he never repented. A few months later, he broke up the church he had started (in a young lady's house because he got put out of his apartment). He got the few members he had by stealing a family from a church he visited for three months. He then moved in about eight months; he was in the store front with about fifteen members and only kept the church open for two years, and then he scattered the flock and left town. Because he got caught by the young girl he opened the church in her living room, whom he was now living with, this the young boy he had doing the music ministry in her bed, having sex (yes, he was living in fornication in an active gay relationship, which she claimed she did not know). You cannot be in apostolic protocol if you live a "*bisexual lifestyle* or have a *whoremonger spirit*"; both of which he had, and this is what caused a lot of additional problems.

After he left town, many of the people he "*pastored*" went to me to "share their pain." You see, he also *left another young girl (eighteen) pregnant by him* and sent her away with a young boy (nineteen)—to be his wife (to cover it up quickly)—that he told to marry her, prophesied, and said, "This is your wife. Marry her now." This was messed up for years, and many people got hurt because he was not ready to be a sold-out witness for Christ!

You see, he was not prepared. Afterward, I also heard he went on the road "to preach" and had a "successful" following (he and his lover), but no one thought to follow up on where he came from.

Problem #6
Those who do not practice what they preach create problems in the prophetic

Let's continue with my story from above.

But my question to the person who told me of his *success* is, *What is spiritual success?* Who is really "succeeding in the ***Kingdom***"?

I must tell you; it may not be who you think it may not be! It may not be the megachurches or the big-named pastors who let anything and everything go on in God's house; I don't need to go on and on about how many pastors, bishops, apostles and other ministers are "undercover homosexuals, having adulteries, and many affairs within the church. They are also thieves, and many are downright liars, not living holy or with the mind-set of real ministry." They are truly more concerned about the offering than the truth of the Gospel that brings change and deliverance, nor do they want to be delivered themselves. They do not want the god of the Bible or the Gospel of the Bible. They just want to have a form of godliness with no power; *is this what you are calling successful?*

Well, I speak to your spirit that you would *WAKE* up! *Stand up, speak up, and tell the devil to shut up!* Take your Bible and read it, believe it, do it, and see it come to life in your life. *Rebuke the devil from speaking in your life, and take account of who is speaking in your spirit.* They can't speak "life to you if they are not living and alive with the Word themselves." ***Kingdom*** people, *don't follow a walking corpse.*

You will both end up in a large ditch. *Do not act like you do not know what sin is or how sin looks;* do not act like you do not understand when something is not lining up with the Word of God. Open your eyes, people, and see; *stop living in spiritual denial.*

I saw a movie, *Brokeback Mountain,* which cleared this up even more in my mind—that *the church* has its own spiritual *Brokeback Mountain* and *shepherds who are being buckaroos* who *camouflage their lifestyles of homosexuality by marriage,* children, and telling lies while praising God and thinking all is well; if you are a *true prophet/apostle,* God *will* "first speak" to you and *condemn these behaviors in your life before you can speak "in the true* ***Kingdom*** *authority."*

A Word to the Wise

You need to know that as a prophet of God, many of God's people truly *see* your flaws and sins, yes, even the ones who come to you, many are not bewitched and your deeds, which will be tried in judgment; Because you can "choose" *to repent,* and truly allow God to use you to affect ***Kingdom*** change. Integrity and holiness are still required for ***Kingdom*** glory and success.

Whoremongering is no better than homosexuality and scares many people away from spiritual commitment to ministry for many years; do not "lie or lay" with or to the sheep in the ***Kingdom*** (and lambs especially) for your own personal gain or pleasure. God will judge you heavily. I have known preachers who have five or six "girlfriends" in one church, a wife, and a boyfriend. This is no better than club hopping or the pimp on the street. We must not allow this in our leadership in the ***Kingdom***. WE must want and accept better for our lives.

Ask yourself, Why does the church house permit this abomination? (As my spiritual mother, Mother Ruff, would say, "This is utterly stupid, foolishness.") This must stop today!

If you are in such a church or are permitting this foolishness to happen to you (dreaming that you are the next Mrs. First Lady) or are doing this closing your eyes for the sake of the marriage, even pimping in the church house, stop now, get out, repent, and seek "apostolic protocol"; for the ***Kingdom*** of God is at hand, and God will judge you first.

Problem #7
Those Who Operate in unforgiveness and unrepentance create problems in the prophetic

Those who operate in unforgiveness will taint their ministry with practices that come from a "mad" spirit. That spirit is the one who *manipulates (by adding or subtracting from what God says) and divides the church (MAD).* This spirit will tell others a lie to defend its principles rather than change or repent. It will constantly talk about what happened five, ten, fifteen, or even twenty years ago. *It will always have a reason for its rebellion and will never see God's grace on hand in what they endured for knowledge or growth.*

I do not care how gifted they seem if they are *not living* ***Kingdom*** *lifestyles.* God is not speaking through them. A spirit is speaking, but it is *not* the Spirit of God.

Problem #8
Those Who Operate in Unrest create problems in the prophetic

A restless spirit will damage the church, ***Kingdom***, and the people they serve. One who holds on to this spirit will move all over the place as a nomad; with no accountability and no foundation, they will create bitter people because of broken promises and lying words of prophecy that do not come true. They must be truly delivered before allowing him to serve.

So let's discover why we need apostolic protocol in the ***Kingdom***.

Let's Look Up These Words

Webster's Dictionary is fine.

Apostolic:

Apostle:

Protocol:

While you have your dictionary out, let's look up

Patrol:

After looking up these words, why do you think we need apostolic patrol and protocol in the **Kingdom** *of God and in our personal lives?*

It's All About the **Kingdom**

Chapter 6

Eleven Steps to ***Kingdom*** "Maturity"

Maturity Is a Must!

"Let's Go!" and Grow Up in the ***Kingdom***

We Are on the Move!

Moving from the
Dumb-Dumb, through
Church-Dumb, to *the*
Kingdom*!*

Growing up in the *Kingdom*

The *Kingdom*: It's a process . . . .

One Step at a Time

To An "Expected" End

Eleven Steps to ***Kingdom*** *Maturity*

One Step at a Time

It's not too late to "captivate" the divine destiny in your life.

When God spoke to Abraham and said "*Get thee out,*" the process started with one step.

Abraham made the "*step*" to go into the "*new direction.*"

Leaving the familiar: We must take the time to get out of our familiar circumstances and lives and welcome the change. You must ask yourself, "Is this working for me? Are what I am doing and how I am doing it working for me?" *If the answer is* "*No,* this is not working for me," then *it's time to go* to another place. This place is in your mind, emotions, spirit; and of course, maybe a physical change is needed as well.

Christendom versus ***Kingdom***

In Christian understanding, we get into "one church" and stay there until we die. In the ***Kingdom****, we must be taught that we go to a church to develop in a specific area in our spiritual lives, and when this area is matured, we then must seek God and our current leaders for our next level of "schooling." We do not just stay in a church because it was "my grandmother's church." We go to "****Kingdom*** *school"—let's think of it as a "church* ***Kingdom*** *training center" to learn, be empowered, and be fit for the Master's use. We go there until we grow up in whatever this ministry has to offer. We do not go to be entertained; we go to become matured and learn. When we have learned what we have been sent to that training center to learn, then we are promoted! We graduate to another class. Now it's time to move to another schoolhouse, another training class. Our teachers are happy for our growth, and finally we receive a degree.*

This takes "one great step at a time."

Step One
Maturing to know you will walk alone . . .
It's time to be kicked out of the nest!

Leaving one's family church can be difficult, but it just may be time to grow. If I had stayed in my family church, I would not have been filled with the Holy Spirit as early as this in my life. I would not have been in ministry as I have been for over thirty-one years. (Because my family church did not believe that God could use a woman to preach, they are still not far from it now!) I would not have had the experiences of ministry to be able to share with you now. *Wow*! I am glad I followed God and left my family and went to a new land. I had to learn to walk alone with God and what he was speaking to me in my divine calling.

It was not easy; my parents were not happy and for the first eight years did not support my ministry. But I kept going, and today, they have fully accepted that God uses me mightily, and have seen many signs and wonders in my churches. I have ministered as a guest in my home church, and they have received me well. I was the first of (now) many women who went out of this church to become minister. I praise God. I did what he told me to do!

Step Two
It's time to know your calling . . .
Maturing to starting Your Personal life of Ministry

All of us are called to a "type of ministry." Maybe yours is not in the pulpit; maybe it is in the mission kitchen. Wherever it is and whatever it is, find it and *do it*!

Do not just sit in the pews of the building for thirty years and do nothing; this is not ministry or serving God! We all are called to do a work for the Lord and a work in the ministry we serve in as members. *This is your personal ministry*. Know it, develop it, and do it well and with faithfulness and grace, and watch God perfect you in it. Then he will make you ruler over much.

Step 3
Maturing to embrace the teachings of your leader and other great Christian leaders

I have never met this wonderful gift to the ***Kingdom*** of God; however, I have read many of his books. Bishop-Pastor Dag Heward-Mills of Lighthouse Chapel International ministries writes wonderful books on *Loyalty & Disloyalty*. If you have never been taught how to become loyal, you need to read these books before going into any type of membership or ministry. Especially for following another leader, pastor, bishop, or apostle, you need to have the spirit of loyalty in your life.

That's another "great step," but it must be done with the greatest of *class*. If you are to begin a ministry, it cannot be done at the expense of other people's ministries. Give people credit for what you learn from them. Do not proselyte, but be glad for mentors afar, and teach as you have been taught. You do not have to undermine other people; we have all learned from someone else. That God's design and plan. Embrace it with grace.

Step 4
Maturing in your Mind
Changing Your Mind-set

Take one step at a time

You will only change your mind-set with much prayer and rehearsing over and over what you wish to become. This will take one step at a time to get rid of the negative and embrace the positive in your life. But you must start with one step—one positive confession, one positive thought, one positive book, and one positive prayer. It all starts with one day and one *step* at a time.

Your mind must change to go into the ***Kingdom***. Your perception must change to a positive one and your lifestyle will become brighter and better. Take the step. Find out what is negative in your life and begin to change. You have the power to change *yourself*! You are empowered to change *yourself*! You have my permission to change *yourself*! *You* must embrace that change is good; and to be accepted into the beloved of the ***Kingdom***, God expects you to change. *No*, you are not all right like you are. If we were, Jesus would not have died for us. We all have to change! This is not about being *bad;* it's about becoming better, good, great, and then excellent.

This spirit of excellence will then begin to reflect in everything you do. It will change your environment, your life, your love walk, and your ***Kingdom*** lifestyle. The changing of your mind-set to be the absolute best, to walk an A+ life, is the best living ever.

You must ask yourself how to create an ***A*** *type of lifestyle.* Ask yourself, how does an A type of person dress, act, or think? Is an A life wearing hooker clothes; being uneducated, broke, drunk; taking your money to spend impressing women or men who mean you no good; cursing your children; getting put out of your home every other month; living off the system; and not improving? Is it waiting on food stamps every month to sell for "stuff," keeping people around you who are negative and full of problems and dramas? It is being with someone who has "always something bad going on"?

Ask yourself, *Is your family a drama type of family? Are your friends drama queens? Do you surround yourself with people going nowhere fast?*

This type of existence is *not glorifying God! No,* it is not!

If you have truly answered yes to these questions, you need a *fast and furious change.* (Stop, read here now, and go to the "thirty-one days to turn around" chapter RIGHT NOW! And start on your change today.) *This is not an A+ life; this is an F-style lifestyle,* a failing type of lifestyle, a zero, a substandard type of living. You can make the change today for your better tomorrow! I will be with you every step of the way!

If you are not so bad as to have a yes on every question but you have a lot of yesses presented in the scenario, still you need to know, however, that there great hope. Yes, there is good news; *you can change your life* today! Life changes are great! How do we begin to make the changes we need in our lives that will bring us again to hope in the greatness that is within ourselves?

It starts by finding somebody living an A lifestyle and telling them you want to change. Find somebody outside your drama. How about telling your caseworker you want to go to school and become something different? Find your pastor and tell him that you want to be different and ask him to help you to change. Find your employer and tell him you want to get better on your job and be promoted.

In other words, ask somebody that is doing good to help you to do better; ask them how they started and got on the path to success. A change in your mind will change everything about you. Once these changes come, your finances will change and increase. Then you will see yourself moving over from *nothing to something GREAT!*

Step 5
Maturing to become a faithful follower

As a sidebar, I was in a service one day at an associate's church, and he was preaching. He had a good-size church, membership of about four hundred people, and a staff of about twenty. One of his ministers kept looking funny (on the pulpit) during the sermon and afterward called me to the side, telling me, *"I really could not get into the service today because the pastor preached this same sermon last year on the same Sunday and used the same topic. The same points were emphasized. Other people may not have noticed, but he has done this several times this year."* She went on to say, *"He is supposed to be full-time. It seems like he could give us a fresh word instead of hanging out. It is like he pulled this sermon out again and preached exactly the same thing."*

She went on to say that she would be "*getting out of that church very soon*" because the pastor was "*not feeding her.*" Without me saying anything, she turned and left and just walked off. And went on to *tell at least three other ministers the same thing.*

I said this to say that if you are going to be in full-time ministry, *work for the Lord every day as you would for any other job. Because people like her are watching us.* Bishop and I personally work almost fifty hours for ministry and then do our personal study time just like we would for any other job. We do not go fishing on the Lord's time just because we can. This would not be fair. WE do not just lay around and get canned sermons; we actually study to hear what God wants to say weekly and daily and minute by minute before we minister to God's people.

We do not take off to pray "for weeks at a time" as an excuse to not really work, especially during our workdays, other than our thirty minutes for prayer line, which we try to make every day, just like we ask others to do! In other words, *we do not fake our work time* by goofing off or making personal calls during our "work hours." We work for the ministry full-time in administration and serving. And God blesses us for our labors.

We also have an evangelism schedule and a marriage to work on, as well as our local church schedule. So we manage our time very well and depend on the Holy Spirit to lead us in our time management every day.

So if you want to go into full-time ministry, expect to work, create extra income for yourself, and expect to be available to serve. This is why we need full-time people in the ministry.

Step 6
Changing Your Finances—
Maturing in Your Mind-set about M*oney* Must Change

Take one step at a time

Money does matter; however, no one is just going to *give you money*, nor will it *drop from the sky. Money will not just appear for you; you must create it for yourself.*

Money *must be thought of as your friend. "Keep it around you and embrace it." In the* **Kingdom**, *money is our resource to get the means to an expected end. If you do not have it, you will not get the results you want. You will not maintain the happiness you really want to see in your life. Money is your friend; let it hang around you sometimes.*

To change your thought on money, you must embrace how you treat money. Do you respect money? Do you treat your money well? And do you allow your money to treat you well? To have a change in the process of your mind about money, *you must know that money wants to be "attracted" to you. Don't always look for ways to spend your money; look for some ways to "keep" some of your money. Then create ways for your money to make money for you. Don't live broke, and don't live poor! For the **Kingdom**'s sake, glorify God in your **Kingdom** living.*

In many families, one person of the family has a grip on this fact, and other family members "sponge" off or soak up their resources, trying to get them into the same predicament as they are—broke!

Every month, they need to borrow "twenty dollars," they need help on the light bill, they need gas in the car, they need . . . they need! However, the next week, you see them spending money on "junk" and not saving for the day, the week, and the next week. If you are going to stop this cycle, you must learn to *say no to them the next time they ask you for money*!

My parents are near eighty, and their family still tries to "bleed" them when I am not around. When I am around, I stop it. My mother's family has no problem, borrowing all the time.

However, they always have beer in their hands and are always shopping. They get money, all of them, but they are cursed not to keep it; most of them do not pay tithes and do not value money. They have not improved their lives; over fifty years, it's the same. "Can I borrow?" "What you got for me?" Many of you have a family and the so-called friends like this. You are afraid to tell them *no* because you do not want to lose their "friendship or make them mad at you." So what if they get mad? Maybe they will get better.

To create a new you, you must learn the word *no*! And you must mean it. Otherwise, others will always enjoy more of your finances than you do, and you will never develop an inheritance. I know, for a fact, that these family members will never leave an inheritance for their children. My parents have developed a nest egg of savings, but the devil in the non-money attractors of the family wants them not to have anything to leave either. This is a "cankerworm spirit" that comes to eat up what someone else has planted. One day my parents will be gone. I wonder if they will stop eating, drinking, or living. *No*, of course not; they will find someone else to "leech off."

Some people work hard with two or three jobs, while others lie around and do nothing but wait on the workers and their finances to come in so they can spend them. When you tell them no, they will get mad. But it's your right to say no and mean it. This is the first step in changing your mind about money; stopping other people from spending your money, just because you don't want to make them mad.

I am not talking about helping somebody sometimes, when you can. But if you notice a regular pattern, then *stop* them; you are not helping them. And by helping them you are not helping yourself. Money management is a must. Make money your friend, before others. If they stop speaking to you, it's OK; you just kept more of your money. These people are not in your corner; they just need you to be in their corner. After all, it's your money they are asking for.

If you find yourself in this loop with them, stop and get out; don't borrow from them. Manage your own money better, and you will see the steps to increase money in your life.

Step 7
Maturing as a full-time minister
Leaving Your Job for Full-time Ministry

This is a true step of ministry. Many ministers have made this step too soon, and some people have not made this step soon enough. Being called into full-time ministry should not be a struggle; it should be a blessing. Let me help you to be successful in this transition. Find out if the church can afford you, and then plan to establish at least four other ways of ministry income to assist in your income levels. You will find that you cannot expect to go into full-time ministry by just depending on the people you pastor and the funds they put into the church for the ministry. This fund will fluctuate greatly with the members, their attitudes, and their faith. It will go up and down, depending on their jobs, family makeup, and decisions of other expenses. It will even change by the content of your message. Happy sermons, more money. Rebuking sermons—oh well, (we know) this may drop the pan. Maybe this is why preachers preach happy sermons instead of relevant sermons. If God has called you to begin a new ministry, get out of there and get your members from all the unsaved souls that need to be saved.

Don't steal sheep or lambs; there are enough people who need Jesus to fill your church, there are enough backsliders to fill your church, and there are enough people who must be delivered to fill your church. Find these people and truly start fresh. Don't break up another person's hard work to fulfill your destiny. That's not how the King or the ***Kingdom*** works.

If you do this, *you will have to endure this coming back* to you and your ministry at least once, maybe twice, or three times. (You will reap what you have sown.)

A fact for you not to start your ministry this way is that with church hoppers, *they* (church hoppers) never stay! They will leave you faster than they left the people you took them from. As soon as you get going, they will leave you, hanging out to dry every time because they are not loyal—not to the person they left (the ministry), and they will not be loyal to you. And by the way, if you stole them from their last ministry, you have taught them "to be disloyal, to have no respect for the leader, and go off whenever they want to follow another shepherd." You must be careful what you teach the people you lead by the deeds you do and the words you say to and about other ministries.

Step 8
You must mature to an honest assessment of yourself!

Let's Get Real—Some of Us Have "Failed" Every Assignment God Has Given Us—

We Are Not Highly Favored, yet . . . . . .

To be highly favored, *we must have completed to assignment and the task; completing the task, let us come to know our god like to other. It builds our faith.* Mary's task was not completed with her assignment when Jesus died; at this point, she was just a mother with a son who, in those days, was considered *crazy*; it was not until He (Jesus) rose that she received the glory—"the unprecedented glory."

For thirty-three years, she was mocked at, picked on, and known as the woman who was pregnant before she was married. Unlike today, this was embarrassing, not highly favored. *To be pregnant without a husband*, it was not a badge of grace, but of shame.

After years of shame, to top it off, her son was making everyone mad in the city they lived in; he was saying he was the "son of God." This was not really a comfortable place.

After all these years of being a "nomad for a son," he had finally made the entire town made enough to beat him and hang him. This was not a feeling like being highly favored. Her son was beaten and put to death like a criminal before everyone. *Not highly favored.* Then he died, and people laughed at her again. She was still "not" feeling so highly favored; for three days and three nights, she had to believe God and her promise like never before. That's why she was at the tomb *early*; she was waiting to be glorified and was paid off for all her pain. Her Son "rising" would make her blessed and highly favored; she needed to know that he had risen. She needed to complete her assignment, and when it was over, she had the victory!

"Hail Mary, mother of the Savior, you are blessed and highly favored."

Why? Because she kept the faith. I know she told Jesus the story of the angel and the Visitation over and over and over and over. He knew who he was because his mother would not let him forget. She never moved away; she never ran; and she never quit in the midst of her pain or embarrassment, in the mist of being rejected, picked on, and looked over. **She earned the *title*.** Can you keep the faith like Mary did? Can you stand to be stressed, persecuted, or embarrassed, and still hold on?

What a shame that such a lifestyle has become such a cliché now; we want to wear it on a T-shirt while smoking a cigarette. Do not lie to yourself about where you are; always tell the truth about you to yourself, and strive to improve and mature to another level.

Step 9
Maturing to become Blessed and Highly Favored In the ***Kingdom***

Take one step at a time

There are seven steps to become "blessed and highly favored."

What does it really take to be "blessed and highly favored?" Everyone is always talking about "they are blessed and highly favored." It has become a cliché in the church, but it should be a lifestyle of living—***Kingdom*** living. This step will develop in you a divine presence in your daily walk and your ***Kingdom*** purpose.

You must embrace every step (one at a time) to be blessed and highly favored. This is not something you can name or claim; you must walk this out with every fiber of your being.

You must have a *"divine visitation."* God through the Holy Spirit will visit you in your spirit.

You must be given *"divine instructions."* In this visitation of the Holy Spirit, you will be given specific ***Kingdom*** instructions.

You will be assigned a *"divine assignment"*—something that only you have been assigned to do in your life.
You will be given a choice to have a *"divine acceptance"* of assignment; you will have a choice to say yes or no. Once you answer, you will be held accountable for your answer.
You will be blessed with *"divine grace and faith"* to complete the task assigned to you.
You will be graced with *"divine boldness"* to fight the tiger, lion, the bear, or your Goliath; in the face of the enemy, you will not waver.
You will be emerged in *"divine determination."* Nothing or nobody will be able to stop you until you complete your task.

When you can line up with these ***Kingdom*** *principles for being "blessed and highly favored,"* then you can wear the T-shirt. Only then will you be able to say "I am blessed and highly favored."

> Like Mary, the Mother of Jesus, I had a visitation. I was given instructions, an assignment. I accepted the assignment. I was filled with the grace and faith to continue in my assignment. I embraced the boldness and diving determination to fulfill my assignment, and God got the glory out of my life though this assignment.

Step 10
Maturing to understand that You Must Lose Something to Be Highly Favored

I understand the pain of this assignment and the fact that I had to lose something or someone that I loved. But it was worth it all. You must also lose your *pride,* and you *will* be blessed and highly favored. You must be able to *go* through to get to that. Why am I "blessed and highly" favored? *I paid a price.* I do not say this common saying, nor should we because it sounds quite spiritual. Only say this *after you have paid the price* and have seen it through to the fullness of understanding, standing upon the ground of *faith,* and speaking the ***Kingdom*** language as you embrace your assignment.

Because I know what it means. It means something to me. In the ***Kingdom*** of God, I have the victory of the fight, and I am blessed and highly favored.

I must ask you like Bishop T. D. Jakes did; however, can you stand to be blessed? Can you stand to be picked on for thirty-three years to wear the T-shirt, or do you need to think about it again the next time someone asks you "How are *you*?" and just reply "I am fine, thanks be unto God and his son, Christ Jesus!"

Step 11
Maturing to be transportable, and relocatable for the *Kingdom*s sake!

Many times you need to go to another land and country to succeed in ministry. This can be a great way to see the hand of God move on your behalf. Don't be afraid to go. If you are sent by God, you will be provided for.

When we first left South Carolina, we moved, and God moved with us like never before. And we are still seeing God move with us. God will give you the best when you follow him into your promise. Moving can be a *great* thing. Moving can be a mind-fulfilling blessing. Moving can take pressure off you from being "overly dependent" toward family and friends. By leaving, you can teach them how to be interdependent—on God and not on you.

I was talking to a *family member* who told me that she had moved to another city, Georgia, to be exact. The problem with this is that *her daughter worked very hard, struggled with two children, and finally was doing great in life. She* went to school when no one else in her family did, and she now had graduated from college and moved to Georgia. This overneedy and very dependent *mom* had moved to Georgia following this daughter and, worse, had taken another daughter and her children with her. I thought this was so sad that they would crowd her new space and her newfound freedom in life, her God-given and earned place. I felt that this was an "Abraham and Lot" dependent type of connection, where, of course, Lot and his "connections" brought *drama* with them. God never told Lot to move; he told Abraham to move. Be careful when you *go* to not let others who are not called to follow you; they will only cause you problems.

Kingdom maturity is a great, and we should all seek to grow greatly in the ***Kingdom*** of God. Do not be stale, frail, or pale in growing; do not become lame or seek fame. Just grow up godly in righteousness, peace, and joy in the Holy Ghost—that is the maturity in the ***Kingdom*** of God. Each step is a level of perfection and grace, with challenges and victories; we must embrace and know that each level is step and each step in another level of maturity in the ***Kingdom*** of God. At each step, there will be a new fight and new conquests, and at each level, there will be a new frontier and a new land to conquer; remember you are a giant killer and are not a grasshopper! It will not be easy, but growing up is worth it!

Let's face it to grow up—there will be some bumps, bruises, and bloodshed.

There will be "bloodshed" in the ***Kingdom***

—*as you are birthed*
—*as you grow/* mature in the ***Kingdom***
—as you learn what makes you mature
—as you learn the "order of the Spirit"
—as you learn to cultivate souls
—*as you give birth,* there is pain!

Do *not run* from the pain or *blood*!

Blood will be shed—as you are defined—in your gift

—*as you are purified*—tried by fire
—*as you are identified*—as being loyal or disloyal
—*as you die to self-rebellion*
—*as you fight the "good fight"* in the ***Kingdom***
—as you fight and go against ***Kingdom*** wolves
—as you define the principalities of the "sin" in your life and as you face disobedience
—as you conquer and come "against the spirit of *error in your life.*"

There is bloodshed in the ***Kingdom***

You will *bleed,* and your blood will shed; you will also see others bleed, and your leader will even bleed at some points or times. They defiantly will have bloody hands! Face it; you also will bleed!

Just like our Savior shed His blood to conquer and become victorious, so shall we. *Bleed*—this is the principle of the ***Kingdom***.

If it does not *cost* you something, you will not respect it. It must cost your *blood, sweat,* and your *tears.* The first area we must work on in this area is ourselves. Take the next twenty-one days to work on yourself, your family, and then your ministry. Do chapters 20 and chapter 15 to help your mind be renewed to the ***Kingdom*** principles and pathways.

Chapter 7

Kingdom "Rules" for ***Kingdom*** Destiny

Learn the *Kingdom* Rules
for *Kingdom* Destiny

Let's Learn the ***Kingdom*** *Rules*

Coming out of just receiving Christ to becoming a ***Kingdom*** is just like a child being born in a country (receiving Christ). But until you mature, you really do not understand or operate as a full citizen. So it is with spiritual ***Kingdom***ship. Many believers are born in the ***Kingdom***; however, they do not understand their ***Kingdom*** rights, benefits, or obligations to the ***Kingdom*** of God. To understand this, we must mature (grow up), stand up, speak up, think up, and challenge our immature nature of playfulness, games, and inappropriate behavior. We must follow the ***Kingdom*** rules of speech, dialect, and language. The language of God's ***Kingdom*** is *faith.* I often know the immaturity of one by their true faith. What do you really believe God for *truly?*

Many have started their ministries without this basic ***Kingdom*** principle. They do not have the experience of faith or know the ***Kingdom*** language; most of them do not know the language because they do not know the King. They have entered into the Christian ***Kingdom***, and they do not want to adhere to ***Kingdom*** rules, the order of the ***Kingdom***, or the order of our heavenly Father. They believe they are exempted from the spiritual police and spiritual patrols. This has offended and hurt many sheep who have a sense of the ***Kingdom*** to go astray and develop their own ***Kingdom*** language.

"Blessed and Highly Favored"? Are you really?

I said I wanted to review this cliché again in depth because I know we Christian abuse this saying more than we do many others. I really want you to understand what I talk to become, blessed and highly favored and to be able to live in it. You can obtain this level of maturity, but it takes power and authority and a matured mental choice to retain it.

We say a lot of clichés that we do not understand the meaning of like "Say hello to a believer. How are you?" "I'm blessed and highly favored." Is the cliché any of the following?

First: This praise was given to Mary to encourage her on her journey that would almost kill her, "Mary . . . thou art blessed and highly favored."

Second: You've been chosen to carry an assignment of the Gospel that was given to you to bear before you were born. You will be talked about, lied on, and possibly put to death. But remember, you're blessed and are chosen to carry the assignment out!

So when someone tells me this cliché, I say, "What's your assignment, and are you willing to die for it?"

Third: She would have a refined relationship with the Father that no other person would experience; she would be hated by men and women. Envy and jealousy would be on her shoulders always. She would have to suffer her child being beaten, scorned, and put to death; and there would be nothing she could do about it but believe she was blessed and highly favored.

Fourth: Her reward would come, but she had to faithfully endure and keep the faith in the promise. She had to PAY A GREAT PRICE! Do you still want the title of "blessed and highly favored"? After all, it was only said in the scriptures to one person in all the writings of the Word, so it is a tall order. I ask you, can you stand up to it?

I say this because a lot of us try *to start our ministries on another person's anointing, promises, or visions. What you need to start your ministry with apostolic protocol is a personal encounter with God for yourself.*

You cannot start a church to make friends, money, fame, or recognition. "This is churchdom" and not ***Kingdom***.

Let's Talk about the Church in its Current Stage

I have found that most of the ministries, hundreds, have *no protocol.* Everyone basically does what they want to do; there is no anointing and no true move of God. Yes, people move, jump, and have motions but no deliverance, healing, or true ***Kingdom*** strength that is in the vein of God's army.

This hurling of the Gospel cause the people to faint. *Sixty-five percent of the membership is on some type of medication.* There are *seven to ten funerals per month,* adultery, fornication, and all manners of evil. Communion is taken as a ritual. No repentance is prevalent. *Holiness is out of the question.* Hell or accountability is not mentioned. And the "church" is a free-for-all. *People wear the highest symbol* of the Christian church (*the cross*) and curse with the worse profanity and then say "God bless you."

Because this is the lifestyle of the some Christian let's say about 85 percent. Those who preach Christian accountability are *silenced by the "big boys" of the Gospel* who "fail" Sunday after Sunday to bring ***Kingdom*** accountability and cause many to look their true ***Kingdom*** destiny.

Just imagine with me for a moment: If on "one given Sunday, *every preacher in the world takes a risk and preaches real repentance, calls our sin and sinful naturism, encourages accountability, and suggests that we all live by* ***Kingdom*** *rules,"* people would get saved "for real," renounce sin, and embrace godliness. People who are "shacking" would get married, families would be restored, and lives would change.

If we all could dedicate one month to Acts 2 and create a temple where God could dwell in, "what a time this would be for the ***Kingdom***!"

No one could leave your church *because pastors would network, require membership and accountability, and send people back to their leaders for reconciliation*; and if they went to your church one Sunday, they would have the same message. The enemy of ***Kingdom*** division would be destroyed as we preached the Gospel. *"Wow! What a church!"* This is *"****Kingdom*** *unity"* at its best with change and spiritual growth that must appear because of the unity.

I once mentioned this to one of my AME friends; he laughed and said, "Pastor [I was pastor then], you want these people to put me out of *my* church?" I said, "Are you more interested in having a 'church' than a ministry where God's tabernacle can dwell? Can we count on you to be true? Or just another preacher?" was my question to him.

Needless to say, this "upcoming minister" quit going around us; he never invited me to preach again at his church and soon disappeared into the crowd of "let the people do what they want to do. As long as they come and pay, I get my check, and we have 'good church.'" And the souls of the people, oh well, they must like it; they go. This is not ***Kingdom***.

In starting your ministry and your spiritual destiny, you must not personally and/or collectively be a "sellout" to the world of commonality and ungodly principles that do not adhere to the ***Kingdom*** rules. Do not chance your soul for popularity.

If you do not root in this principle, you will just be gathering people in a devil's dew. I am not the "prophet of doom"; however, *I am a true prophet.* And a true prophet must sound the alarm; for those who hear it, great. There is a powerful world of ***Kingdom*** glory; for those dead to truth, your ministry will not truly glorify the King and His ***Kingdom***.

Leaving Your Job for Full-time Ministry: Just a quick apostolic point: This is a great big leap of faith and a gigantic step of love for God and his people! *Hear God,* have a plan, obey God, and in following him, you will learn to trust him. Do not lie to people for gain of money; tell the truth and trust God. And you will succeed in full-time ministry.

This is another mind-set, however, that you must face when time and finances challenge you to stick it out for the sake of the calling.

Leaving Home for ministry growth!

Sometimes your ministry will blossom better if there is a transition to a completely different location. It is just a simple fact: God is good everywhere; however, certain plants just grow better in certain soil and regions. Know what type of tree you are, what type of plant you are, and what type of soil you need. Then collide with your destiny.

I will speak more on these two areas in apostolic protocol session 3.

Can we grow to understand and embrace the rules of the ***Kingdom*** of God? Yes! Yes! Yes! How? It is simple, three simple rules to help you to embrace ***Kingdom*** rules.

Rule #1 *Change Your Mind-set*
Leave what you thought you knew behind; become new wine in new skin.

To create newness in your life, you must change your thought process. Archbishop James Rice, my mentor, teaches that you must get a vision of success to change your mind-set.

I agree you must change what you see, say, dream, taste, eat, and belong.

Every day, you must believe for something new and great. Normally this is a twenty-one—to thirty-day process.

So get one thing you want to change, find out how to change it, and begin to put it in practice—see chapter 11 for the twenty-one-day turnaround.

Rule # 2 *Change Your Finances*
Create a currency magnet to yourself **. . .** *begin to respect money as a purpose in the* ***Kingdom****, draw money to you, and have an assignment for it.*

Changing this mind-set will change your finances. You will spend better, make better choices, and fund the ***Kingdom*** fully.

The *Kingdom* is depending on you to fund its purpose!

If you are not tithing and supporting the ***Kingdom*** with offering, take the "cross off your neck"; look at your checkbook. Does your wallet match your verbal commitment? Are you "giving as much to the church," at least, to match your light bill, credit card payment, or Walmart bill spending?

Have you ever given enough in one offering to have a church party? (You know, the same amount you spend on a cookout party for your friends?) Where does your checkbook really say your treasures are? This is also a test of your maturity in the ***Kingdom***.

Rule # 3 Trust God, Really Trust God!

The promise of God and ***Kingdom*** rule of finance is to support the ***Kingdom*** and give God an opportunity to restore money to you while building your faith. This will change your finances and destiny, but we must follow this basic ***Kingdom*** rule (Deuteronomy 28).

Once you change your mind-set, your finances, your way of viewing church-down versus ***Kingdom***, and stopping the dumb-dumb, you will be on your way to the favor of God, erupting in your lie. Favor will hunt you down and overtake you, blessing will sandwich you on all sides, and wealth and riches will live in your house.

Then and only then can you move into the *seven stages* of "being blessed and highly favored."

You must qualify to get the "Crown of Life"

What Does It Really Take to Be Blessed and Highly Favored?

Seven Stages of Being Blessed and Highly Favored

1) ***Divine Visitation:*** Where you sat down, stood up, walked, drove, went to the park, or whatever, but you know that another being of the holy trinity spoke to you about a ***Kingdom*** assignment.
2) ***Divine Instruction:*** From this divine visitation comes a divine instruction where you hear what your instructions are; it is an "I want you to do . . . .")
3) ***Divine Assignment***: This divine instruction is your ***Kingdom*** assignment. Sometimes, *after perfecting* one assignment, God will add to your assignment to edify the body and you even more.
4) ***Divine Acceptance***: God gives us a choice; that's why we must make sure when we say yes to God. God will not hold us guiltless. We must be ready to give up the *world* and *sin* when we take up the yoke of ministry. Sometimes this yoke is heavy. Because we keep our eyes on another prize while we say "we are following our calling," we stumble and fail unnecessarily and trip others as we fall.

Some people say that God called me so I went; I didn't want to. Our Father will never make us take any yoke of the ***Kingdom*** that we don't want. So if you're *not ready,* don't accept it. Ask God for time and grace; and our Father, who loves us, will love you until you are ready to fully submit. In the meantime, study to show you're self-approved.

5) ***Divine Grace* and *Faith***: For those with a "heart" after God and ***Kingdom*** principles, *our Father* gives us divine grace and faith. We make mistakes, we grow, we learn, and we must know that divine grace and faith will take us through every storm.
6) ***Divine Boldness***: Can you do what God *has told* you to do in the divine visitation? Can you do it? Can you stick to it? Will you hide your true instructions? Do you remember your divine assignment? Can you boldly tell the enemy's camp no? I will stay to my *divine visitation, instruction,* and ***Kingdom*** *assignment.*
7) ***Divine Determination***: In the *final stage* to "becoming blessed and highly favored," we must stick it out; God called me to the

ministry thirty-eight years ago. It was not popular to be a female minister; now it's so popular. Thank God for the "trailblazers in our lives," who made this path easier to reach; they had divine determination. I remember those who preached before me, mentored me closely and afar, and the determination they had, and have today. Just a few pastors: Dorothy L. Pearson, Pastor Hattie Mickens, (Pastor) Dr. H. J. Jerry Clark, Bishop Doris C. Rice, Pastor (mother) Julia Lakin, Elder Elva Davis (deceased), and others of true faith.

These women are truly "blessed and highly favored" and have lived to bless many through their ministry, holding on to holiness and faith and birthing many men and women of faith; some say "thank you" and others don't. I say thank you.

Today, when I meet other young women in ministry (below twenty years) and new, they have so much to say; *they have all the answers until the pressures of ministry come,* and then I hear *"they closed, quit, and are no longer even going to church.* They left the ***Kingdom*** and the faith." Then I am so grateful and I remember the words of the song:

> So many falling—by the way side,
> Lord, help me to stand. Take me by my hand and lead me on.

The Last Step: "**Step 7": *Divine Determination***
This will take you to successfully meet your ***Kingdom*** assignment, and that will lead us to ***Kingdom*** growth.

Now let's go and be "blessed and highly favored!"

Chapter 8

Developing ***Kingdom*** Character

Empowered with Grace and Glory

Two Powerful Characters of the *Kingdom* That Will Lead You to Your *Kingdom* Destiny

Receiving The Character of the ***Kingdom*** Grace and Glory.

Kingdom Character(s) Grace and Glory

I remember when God changed my name; I was sitting on a pulpit in Bethel AME Church in Columbia, South Carolina. I was really listening to Pastor's (Brailford's) message. I heard the Lord say "Enter in, I want to say something to you." *I took three breaths, and I was in a cloud, looking down at everything else. I said, "What is it, Lord?" and he said to me, "I am giving you a gift. I give you grace."*

Smugly I said, *"Grace?"* See, truly I was thinking that I already had "grace," and I thought grace was something every Christian had. So what was this big thing? So he and I (the Holy Spirit of the Lord) went back and forth.

I said, "*Grace?*" and he said, "Yes, grace." I said, "Grace, Lord?" and he said, "Yes, grace. In fact, *I'm changing your name.* I am not only giving you grace. You are *grace.*"

Well, because I knew God, I knew when God gives me a gift, it's good. I began to give thanks. I found myself floating back from the divine presence of God into the church service.

I realized God had truly spoken to me. He had said something to me that caused me to want to leave the service and seek God some more for His Word—just one word will change, *will change* your life.

I endured service remaining in a state of gratefulness because I *began to realize* God does *not* tell you He is going to give you something you already have. So I obviously did not have grace, but needed it. So I asked the Lord, "If I didn't have 'grace' before you just gave it to me, what did I have?" *"Class," the Lord said, "you had class. Now you have class and grace, and I am also going to give you 'glory.'"*

"Lord," I said, "I don't want *your glory."* He said, "*Stop it, not my glory, but glory for you and your ministry. I give my glory to your life and ministry, and I place the spirit of grace over you from this day forward. I anoint you with grace and glory."*

I was overwhelmed with the flow of the anointing that fell on me like never before. It was another measure of his love and anointing for me, but more so, I felt it was another part of his *character and* ***Kingdom*** *identity* that he wanted me to know "assured" that I would share it with the body of Christ.

On arriving home, my first stop was to find a dictionary and look up for *grace* and every word identified with it, followed by *glory,* followed by *class*, followed by ***Kingdom***, followed by *holy*, followed by *righteousness*, followed by *gratefulness*, followed by *loyalty*, followed by *adoration*. I just had a worship service in the dictionary, a praise party in God.

Grace

Kingdom Grace

When *God changed* my name, I thought that just happened in the Bible. I did not understand what he was saying to me until I researched his "Word."

When God gives you a word, message, thought, or vision, it will never hurt to *look it up*! I know you are "deep and wonderful," but please look it up. Especially before you try and teach it to others. I listen to people (ministers) read and then misinterpret what they have read; take these words, for example:

bitter versus *better* — *man* versus *mane*
slip versus *slap* — *letter* versus *litter*
set versus *sat* — *missing* versus *messing*

See, just a change of a letter can change what God is saying; so look closely, read assuredly, speak clearly, and look it up to find a clearer meaning of what the *word* means.

So I found out *"grace" was a dynamic gift,* and I was so pleased to have had a grateful spirit.

Let Us Define Grace

Grace: (1) a beauty or charm of form, movement, or expression; (2) goodwill favor; (3) a prayer of thanks; (4) a delay granted for a payment or obligation; (5) the love and favor of God; (6) a title of archbishop, duke, or duchess; (7) a showing of kindness, courtesy, or charm (8) marked by luxury, ease and elegance.

Wow! There I was, "Lady Grace" by the spirit of God.

Glory

To experience *glory,* I had to understand grace; it took years to reestablish and retain "my ideal" of ministry by adding these *two gifts.* God opened up my mind to ***Kingdom*** ministry. It really wasn't until these gifts declared dominate eminence did my ***Kingdom*** lifestyle began.

Let us define glory: (1) great honor or fame, adoration, splendor, prosperity, heavenly bliss; (2) delightful or enjoyable, better than that, excellent, grand; (3) rich, beautiful, celebrated, remarkable; (4) praiseworthy, admiration. Again, I had to tell the Lord "thank you." I went back to the day he revealed these words to my life, and even today, I am moved with deep graciousness to him for these two simply powerful and well-used ***Kingdom*** gifts. Remember, before I had grace and glory I had "*class.*"

Let's Look at Class

> 1) A number of *people* or *thing* grouped together because of certain likeness, (2) kinds or sorts, (3) social or economic rank, (4) grade or quality, (5) a group taught together that operate under the same teaching or respect, (6) formal, regular, or simple, (7) famous as traditional or typical.

When I read this, I said, "How stoic! Boring and typical of churchdom, but not at all reflecting ***Kingdom***."

Kingdom Grace

Kingdom *grace* is what every fivefold ministry person needs—I can say *must have* because I obviously participated in the ministry for over twenty-one years without the spirit of grace being manifested in my life. I was "taught" to be a "hard woman in ministry." Don't smile; walk talent; be bodacious; and prophesy hard, loud, and fearful. Let people know the "wrath of God." This was my training in ministry through observation and participation with the men and women of God who preceded me.

Now, God said, "[Rice] you are grace, my daughter, *you* are grace." I cried like I never had before; all the time I labored in prayer, intercession, warfare, and worship. Now I was in the midst of "grace." My life changed, my character changed, my ministry changed, and I learned a different side of ***Kingdom*** *identity.* I had sung the song "Amazing Grace." Now I know what "grace" really meant.

I want you to experience *grace of the **Kingdom***: "the form and movement, experience the goodwill and favor, the showing of kindness, the courtesy, the suppleness, the harmony, balance, smoothness, and true charity." This is ***Kingdom*** grace.

To have grace in my ministry allows me to enter into the prophetic realm with truth and reason and be able to truly minister in grace. Before grace, I thought prophecy was only about "land exposure." If you were in a sin and God told me to tell you, out it would go (anybody there/here/now)! Well, the ministry of grace allows me to say the same things but with the character of God: smooth, sweet going down, then (bitter) working it out on the inside. This took many years of reform to tone it down and *allow the second half of* the gift to begin to blossom in my life and ministry. Remembering grace and glory!

The ***Kingdom*** identity of grace and glory gives us fluid movement in His spirit, His Word, and His life reflecting success, honor, riches, fame, and remarkable people who celebrate heavenly bliss, having a delightfully enjoyable lifestyle that is admired and brings God ***Kingdom*** praise and ***Kingdom*** growth. Why? Because people want to be a part of something that is *working well*!

Before grace and glory, my ministry and life were "dreaded," as I now view it. I didn't even know I needed grace—thank God for the Holy Spirit. He will give you what you need; you are open to his love, teaching, breaking, training, and influence.

Without Grace

I was a minister, a pastor, but I didn't like "church, church people, or church stuff!" And it showed. And yes, again I was a minister, *a "miserable minister."*

I was tired, burned out, and disappointed in "church folks" who can really beat a church leader down, those who you have minister to for years that just can't catch the vision and don't grow to understand their ***Kingdom*** purpose.

Some of my disappointments came from church people who were revolving doors and had problems everywhere. It seemed as the more we tried to pour into them, the more uncommitted they became. That's because they were "church people" and not "***Kingdom***-minded citizens," and I was a "***Kingdom***-minded pastor." So we were not fitting.

This was making me bitter. There was no "***Kingdom*** joy" in my life because I had people "in churchdom." As I was called to "***Kingdom***," I was trying to pull these people into what I saw. But when I received grace and glory, I just walked out of churchdom and people began to follow me into the ***Kingdom***! Am I helping anybody? (Is anybody right here been there? Are you there now?)

You must understand, as I had to learn that "leading people are *not* pushing people." If you spend all your years pushing sheep, they will never be led. Many of us, like I did, spent too many years pushing sheep: *this makes you tired, weary, disappointed, mad, angry, frustrated, worn-out, rejected, feeling forgotten, and brokenhearted.*

But if you get in front of them and *lead* (just flow and go) in ***Kingdom*** grace and glory, you will come from behind sheep dung and lead up front. Trust God to have the right sheep to finally join you or be born to you, following you as you live out your ***Kingdom*** destiny and teach them how to live out their place in the ***Kingdom*** as well. Now I love ministry, and the sheep of God who are sent to our pastorate. I love living and teaching ***Kingdom***.

Not My Sheep—I'm Not Their Pastor

I had to realize that not everyone is my lamb. As pastors, we must learn that not everyone is assigned to our spiritual district. Not everyone is on our ***Kingdom*** role sheet under our leadership. We are not their shepherd, and they are not our sheep; we just passed by each other as we were both looking—I, on my way to find my sheep (who'd hear my voice), and they, on their way to find their pastor (whom they can hear).

I remember sitting in Florida one day as Apostle M went by for a counseling session—she was to discuss the "*woes*" of ministry and her church. It began to be obvious that she seemed to have great problems. As she discussed the "trials of ministry" and lack of obedience of the people, I began to reveal to her *the ministry of grace,* to let go of things, people, places, and dreams (for people) that really do not belong to her.

I told her how we (Christian leaders) waste precious years *trying to "pastor people" who do not belong to us. We meet them for a season* and they were just supposed to pass us by on their way to their shepherd, and *"we are to let them go* on our way to our sheep" as well.

What Does This Mean?

Kingdom *grace* gives us enough love to let go of people whom we cannot help.

"Sheep *hear* the voice of the shepherd." *Another* they will not follow. So sheep *who do not listen to you* are *not your sheep.* That does not mean you are not a great shepherd, just not to this particular sheep.

So why hold on to people and waste their time and yours for five, ten, or fifteen years? When one person can speak into their lives, an instant change will come!

How to Get Rid of the "Stress" of Pastoring!

Sheep, find your shepherds. Shepherds, find your sheep, and then you will grow and be blessed! And your sheep will grow and become obedient to the shepherd and to God.

This will make the stress leave your ministry. You will pastor stress free!

It took me over twenty-five years to learn this. I wasted a lot of time and energy.

When someone is not supposed to be in your fold, let them go! If you don't, they will continue to cause problems for you and the rest of your flock.

I speak now to members of the fold: "Sheep and lambs, when you can't *hear* (grow by the Word of God) where you are and *obey with joy,* causing no sorrow to the leadership, then you are in the wrong place."

This shepherd is and maybe a good person and pastor; however (unless you are a wolf that will not listen to anyone), he/or she is not your shepherd! That is why you have not grown in nine years. Let's face it. You are not called to this fold; this is why you are barren and not producing fruit. It's just that simple.

I did not say when you "*can't agree,* that this is not your shepherd." *God does not send you to a place to agree, but he sends you to hear.* Most of the time when we don't agree, it is because *we don't* understand; our position is to swallow and follow as a sheep and reproduce "lambs." This is our true place *in the* ***Kingdom***, not to instruct the shepherd. We do not even understand our role. How can we instruct our leaders? But two can't "walk together" unless they agree. Right! If you are "walking together," that means you are equal. God has not called you to be equal with your spiritual leader. They are leading you, not walking with you; even when you are walking beside them, they are still directing you. They are guiding you, not waiting for you to tell them what to do.

Your girlfriends or guy friends are your equals, never your spiritual leaders. That's the problem in our minds sometimes and why we do not respond well to instructions. We want to be equal in everything. And we are not. There are some spiritual parents in the ***Kingdom*** and some sisters and brothers. We are not all on the same level with our calling and gifting or leadership anointing. Just face the fact.

I remember one time my parents were talking to me about going to my church for membership. And my father jumped up and said with a stern face, "No, that's all right because if I come over there with you, you are going to want to tell me what to do, and I can't have that 'cause I'm the daddy". You see, he was not willing to relinquish his natural authority for spiritual authority. I said, "That's true, Daddy, so I understand." And we went in peace.

See everyone cannot receive you as a spiritual authority in their lives, and this must be OK!

One must know that they have to carry the responsibility of leadership, and cannot allow this to get mixed up in friendship, partyship, or partialityship.

The president, king, priest, bosses, spiritual leaders, *the owners* make, create, and carry out decisions that will be *what's best* for the company, church, nation, and world at large. Some of you can't even balance your houses, at least look out for every household in the ministry, and have faith for all the people to succeed. I encourage you to strive to learn what a good sheep does instead of trying to figure out what the job of the shepherd is.

Many of us *disagree.* However, we do not leave the country, job, or nation. But when we *disagree* with a local assembly (or church at large), we *leave.* We no longer want to be a *Christian* **Kingdom** *citizen;* we renounce our faith. Our basic banner and flag, "Christian," no longer flies over our houses or hearts. I tell people over and over that *"people hurt us on our jobs. We get fired or quit. But we go get another job."* We do this because it's vital to our social need, physical well-being, and level of want. Most of us would never remain out of work for one to five years. But we do and know people who remain out of a church for one to five years thinking they are all right.

Being led by our own imagination and falling prey to our own thoughts and "spiritual patrols," we are on the verge of spiritual shipwreck and spiritual rebellion.

Sheep that are gone astray must return to the fold; you must allow yourself to be brought back into the heart of worship and fellowship. Do not be a *spiritual renegade*—find a spiritual parent today—submit, come under authority, and regain your ***Kingdom*** assignment.

Fly Your Flag Proudly, No Matter What You Are Still Christians in the *Kingdom* of God

I remember being invited to a home of someone I considered somewhat solid in the church. I knew she had a long way to go into ***Kingdom***. However, we began the conversation, and she was excited to tell me how someone had gone to her door, "Jehovah's Witnesses." And she told them this and that and that she was *not a Christian*!

I was appalled as I listened to her excuses. I tried to tell her, "No matter what, we are still Christians, **Kingdom** believers, and citizens of heaven." She just did not get it.

I told her I am confused as to why she thinks because someone else has *disgraced* the faith that she should reject who we are because they are not acting as she believes they should. *Because someone else does not act like a Christian does not change my testimony* and should *never* change who you are.

Yes, people are wearing crosses and cussing. Yes, people are running around and doing all manners of evil, but that only allows me to minister more ***Kingdom*** grace and glory! Yes, I am a Christian, and I won't take it back.

We Need to Know What a Christian Really Is

Christian: "A believer in Jesus Christ as the prophesied Messiah, with 'the basic foundation, principles, and life directions coming from the teaching of Jesus Christ, the Son of the living God; a verbal profession of Jesus as Christ, as the Lord of your life, which is based on his life, as presented in the Holy Bible; His preaching, teaching, and reaching of the lost; His death, burial, and resurrection; one who is presenting or professing the qualities as taught by Jesus. One that has or is in the state of having love, kindness, humility, and dominion—the state of being Christ-like is a Christian."

As you see again, one should understand any *word* before we receive it or reject it. *Being a Christian or not is not based on what someone else does not do; it is based on what I do. This is the only thing that makes my confession valid.* Not someone else's like, dislikes, or disrespect for what they should be. This should never affect my testimony or yours.

Needless to say, this conversation ended abruptly with the person getting up and walking off. However, I remained in grace and glory because I realized *she* was *not* my *sheep.* I was not called to pastor her, and she would probably need to hear this from someone else to receive it. Or to receive it in herself that she is a Christian. I was only there to eat a meal, not to convince a person (a minister) who they were. This was not a babe or a lamb; this was just someone who just wanted to be stuck on a nonimportant point.

I was OK with this. Years ago, I would have said she was Satan, gotten offended by her action, and walked out. However, because of knowing my ***Kingdom*** assignment, I felt *this revelation was her loss,* and I continued to *hold my "pearls" tight.* Wow! What power to know that you can just let "them who do not hear your voice go!"

Do You Know the Role, of One Sent "Higher" than you, in Your Life?

Weeks later, my friend Missionary Humes and I had a conversation. I shared with her my conversation and how I was finally "delivered from trying to help people who wanted no help or could not hear my voice."

To my surprise, she said, "Apostle, some *people don't know the role of the pastor.* They think they know just as much as people who are really greater than they are. Their pride makes them want to seem greater than they really are, and they try to talk when they should be listening." They do not know the role of one sent higher than they are that are sent to really speak to them and help them in their lives."

Just like John the Baptist, even though Jesus was his cousin, John knew Jesus was higher than he was.

I remember another time with Dr. Pastor Miles Monroe, of the Bahamas, who was here in the USA, in Fort Lauderdale, Florida, in a conference, saying, *sometimes people go to him talking when they should be listening, telling him "how great they are and how wonderful their ministries are"* while they have small ministries or works compared to his; really, instead of making him listen to them, they could be learning from him how to be even greater.

I began to watch this with the people *who talk with Bishop and myself,* and I noticed the same thing. People (ministers) unseasoned with only ten years or less under their belts entreat and engage us in conversation to tell us about themselves. Pastor Monroe said, "To be great, you must listen to those greater than yourselves. *Ask questions, and do not try to impress them with your glory. Enjoy their glory while they are in your presence,* and you will be a better person after the conversation."

Kingdom *grace and glory will teach you that it's not important to win every disagreement or to be the center of every conversation.* It's all right to let people stay in "dumb-dumb or churchdom until they are ready for ***Kingdom***." ***Kingdom*** *sheep* will find you—love your grain, exalt you, help you, be happy for you. They will support you and give the word about you to others for ***Kingdom*** enhancement. They will know their purpose to help you and give to you (their shepherd) health, rest, and the greatest gift of all, the gift of "growth."

These sheep will yield to your words, and be happy you are their shepherd. A ***Kingdom*** sheep-citizen will eat out of your hand and never bite you; a ***Kingdom*** lamb-citizen will understand the language and receive it and grow.

Kingdom Sheep Reproduce

Kingdom citizen reproduce ***Kingdom*** citizens without hesitation. ***Kingdom*** citizens love the king and the queen, and they love the ***Kingdom***. They take care of the land and their ***Kingdom*** assignment.

So when I received ***Kingdom*** grace and glory, I stopped worrying and I "pressed" toward my ***Kingdom*** assignment, taking new paths, and going in ***Kingdom*** directions. The glory be to God!

Back to Apostle M

In the final days of counseling this "self-appointed" apostle (Apostle M), I found her to *be the problem.* This lady truly *lacked* "***Kingdom*** identity, character, guidance, and spiritual truth." she would go by and just tell untruths and had no reasonable excuses when these stories were defeated as *not* truth. At this point, I asked the Lord, "Why are so many sheep eating poison grain, from her, when they are not confined to do so?" This woman was the epitome of "lies." She would just *make up lies (they all knew she had a problem with the truth).* I soon broke contact with her *after calling her to "apostle protocol."*

Being a chief apostle whom she (by her statement) had self-appointed as her "spiritual mother," I asked her to go to my home, *where I confronted her untruths* (a type of spiritual intervention). Of course, after this meeting, *she ran from our covering.* I then saw why the sheep were in disarray—*she was still in "dumb-dumb faking churchdom and nowhere near **Kingdom**."*

This type of person has not entered into any type of real accountability but seeks to drain true ***Kingdom*** warriors and spiritual parents of the grace and glory that God has provided them. They want to continue in denial so they can prostitute the gift. Please be aware and don't cast your pearls to them.

I called this person several times afterward to meet, very simply, to see if she would repent and be salvageable. She did not want help. She was under shadowy rude; finally *I asked her to discontinue me from her schedule. Wow! What a relief!* A burden removed, a yoke destroyed. And all I had to do was make a decision to stop the dumb-dumb.

*See, there are some people you cannot pastor, mentor, coach, teach, lead, or train in **Kingdom**. They pause in "dumb-dumb," build a house, and stay;* so if you are not going to live there, leave them—because they are not *even* moving into ***Kingdom***.

This is good for laypersons; it is good for leadership and fivefold members. *This is good for everyone.* If a person is "stuck," *determine how long you plan to be a ditch puller.* Are you equipped to pull this load? And what if it does not want to come out of the ditch?

When do you move on? When?

OK, ***Kingdom*** citizens know when to let go; a ***Kingdom*** leader knows when to say "*This is not working.*" Make a full assessment and move on. If you don't, you will force the hand of God to move on your behalf.

I always say there are three types of moves!

Even God moves in threes.
When God Moves—He Moves

God will Move:
He will move (the situation) *up*. You will go higher in him and get better!

God will Move:
He will move the situation out, repositioning you in another location mentally, physically, financially, or out.

God will Move:
He will move the situation *out*! He will cause *the situation* to "die."

So when we experience movement—*the movement of God—truly expect change.*

When you ask for help, *expect God to move.* And most of the time this movement *will* start with you. When God *speaks to your spirit to let go, let go!* Why is this so hard, so long, so challenging, and repetitious? Why so we have to be exhausted to move?

The kings and the constitution say "we do not have to put up with, go through, or embrace some things we *choose* to go through." The King even speaks through the Holy Spirit to us and says "Stop!" on a lot of things we continue to do. Even after *we hear clearly that this is enough,* some people really feel bad when they cannot be the savior; they do not know that WE all already have a Savior! Jesus the Christ! He has already won the battle for us, been beaten, suffered, and died! He did all that for us so *that we will live well and guilt free without "OPP" and "OPD."*

Live free of "OPP" other people's problems* (or) *other people's drama.

This is a "*bad mind space.*" If you are stuck, you need to find the strength within yourself, and you personally need to unstick yourself, so do not wait to be rescued. Unstick yourself. Use the Holy Ghost power you have received from the King, the authority of the cross, the wisdom of the Word, and get out of the mess you are in! Once you are out, STAY OUT! Learn how to enjoy life, and for the ***Kingdom***'s sake, enjoy. For ***Kingdom*** living, breathe, relax, and trust the King!

Chapter 9

How to

Bring "Glory" to the ***Kingdom***

My Life Is Wrapped in
Kingdom **Glorification**

Does Your Life Glorify God?

Kingdom *Glorification:*

When you learn to trust the King and become obedient to his ***Kingdom*** leadership, the ***Kingdom*** spiritual patrol, and your spiritual parents (your set apostle, your pastor, and your assigned spiritual coach), you will find the *grace* and *glory* in your life.

When *your life allows God* to get *have-occupy and maintain full access at any time, any place, for any reason,* this "glorifies God and creates him a place to be shown off to be used and to be glorified." This lifestyle of being wrapped in his glory will be illuminated in you and bring ***Kingdom*** *glorification, or glory to the* ***Kingdom*** *of God.*

God is able to let the *dominion of his principles abide in you and his glory shine through you, as you are committed to be an ambassador of his truths and principles.* Others will see your *practiced consistency* and *faithfulness* to the ***Kingdom*** constitution and will want to live *a better* (moral, holy, righteous, joyous, and beautiful) lifestyle, like you do. This is what brings ***Kingdom*** *glorification.* ***Kingdom*** *glorification* is what we do that causes the ***Kingdom*** to look good enough for somebody, anybody, and everybody to want to be a part of.

Having a Piece of the "*Kingdom*" Pie

I *personally* know many people who have risked their lives, live in fear, limited access, and everyday hiding. All for what, "*a piece of the American pie.*" You see, we have made *America look good.*

The ***Kingdom*** of *America looks so good* until people are smuggled here every day. They leave their country—"***Kingdom***"—to come to America to live their dream of success. Why! Because they feel "this ***Kingdom***" has something better, so they "*quit*" (*leave)* or "transfer" to another lifestyle and living area because America has been glorified!

People come here every day because of this *mental glorification* as well. It must become so in the "***Kingdom***" of God; *we must make the* ***Kingdom*** *look so good* that others would throw down their "*old lives*" and *come to* the new ***Kingdom***, the ***Kingdom*** of God.

This ***Kingdom*** must be made to *look* good, sound appealing, and be gratifying. It is our job as ***Kingdom*** citizens to produce a hunger for others to take a bite of the "heavenly pie."

We must glorify the ***Kingdom*** of God by our walk, talk, and lifestyle. I have spoken to many pastors, leaders, and ***Kingdom*** gatekeepers who have not glorified the ***Kingdom***.

They teach (by example, word, and deed) that the ***Kingdom*** has misery, brokenness, weariness, sickness, and despair. "*Poor* us—we just saved filthy rags, hallelujah," God (our weary and worn King) just wants us to make it to heaven, forget down here—just make it to heaven, and it's a hard journey, but we can make it."

This sign of the ***Kingdom*** is a sign of despair. Who (in their right mind) would want to go to this ***Kingdom***? I would not want to be a part of poverty, sickness, and despair.

I want something better than what I have now! If I trade my car for a worse car, I am crazy. *I should want to trade* for a better vehicle. Not a worse life, a better life is what I need; I need to give away the bad to get better, not worse. When we do not teach ***Kingdom*** lifestyle as a plus, we give a wrong interpretation of the ***Kingdom***.

Stop the Wrong Interpretation of *Kingdom* Living

Stop this wrong interpretation of the ***Kingdom***. Who would want to risk their lives to go to this ***Kingdom***? Ask yourself how *can I live* (such a lifestyle, have such *a conversation*, do such *a service*) *a life* that will glorify my King in such a way others would want to go to this ***Kingdom*** because of *my life*?

What have you said today that will want to make somebody give their lives for the King and become a servant of our ***Kingdom***. (*This is true salvation.*)

It's not the "rolling on the floor, falling out, shaking, and baking." When you are finish with all that, *what's better in your life* or anyone around you because you are in the ***Kingdom***. You should be better. After each experience with God!

I have a funny but real story to tell you; sometimes when I am praying for people, they often fall down under the power of God, many times for long periods of time (ten minutes or more). When these people get up, I ask them, "What did God say to you?" They look bewildered and say, "Nothing, I did not hear anything" or "I don't know." I ask them "Then were you just taking a nap?" This is funny to me; how can you be taken into the presence of God and go back with nothing, NO change, no power?. How can this be? Or after they shout, dance, and speak in tongues for long periods, I ask them, "*What did God say*?" or "*What has he spoken to you?*" I get the same response, *"I don't know" or "Nothing, really."*

People of God, if you enter into the presence of God, get the best his presence has to offer; do not go back empty-handed. *Why go into the King's presence and get nothing*? Learn to reach into; you pull out something, or why go in? Going in before the King, you take something in, and you receive something in return; it's just that simple.

However, we must train our mind that our King wants to speak to us and give us good and gracious gifts before we leave his presence. He wants us to tell everyone he is a good King.

Many people, after they reach America, call back and tell their families "Come to this land!" and their families come.

They don't know the language, style, ways, or anything; but they come! Having everything unfamiliar, they change their allegiance for the unfamiliar. Why? Because this other ***Kingdom*** has been glorified, talked about, and built up by a "new" citizen who has experienced greater things than he had before.

In the church, we don't feel a need to discuss the good of the land—***Kingdom*** of God. But we need to change this. We need to change our ways, change our talk, and let our life glorify the ***Kingdom*** of God; and our ***Kingdom*** citizenships will grow in leaps and bounds. If we allow the ***Kingdom*** to be glorified in our lives and come out of our spirit and our mouths, others will come, and our ***Kingdom*** be glorified.

***Kingdom* Grace and *Kingdom* Glory**

What does It Take to bring Glory to the ***Kingdom*** of God?

*To Have **Kingdom** Grace and Glory*

This will automatically bring or cause an increase to the ***Kingdom*** of God. Anything that look good and is attractive will cause someone to want to have it! Does your *life produce* additional ***Kingdom*** citizens? Is your church growing because of your citizenship? Do you tell others how great it is to be in this country? Do you really value being a ***Kingdom*** citizen? Remember, just because you are in a country does not make you a citizen.

A *citizen* is the one who *owes allegiance* to a state, nation, or group by birth, naturalization, and is legally entitled to *full* rights. *Allegiance* is the "duty of being loyal to one's ruler, country, or nation." *A citizen should be devoted, have honor, and respect for the land they have taken on as their country.* The person who has *naturalization* is the "one whose citizenship has been granted legally after applying for it and received acceptance from the country/nation that one seeks to enter." They as well should have this same loyalty, respect, and honor.

What Will It Take To Create Glory in the ***Kingdom***?

I like the thought of "owed allegiance." It is our duty to be loyal to our *Christian* ***Kingdom*** because we owe *God our allegiance,* having been accepted into the ***Kingdom*** of God through His son, Christ Jesus. Now is the time for true ***Kingdom*** loyalty. Some of us do not feel this loyalty because we have *not become legal.*

We do not value the naturalization process. We want the benefits but without the obedience to ***Kingdom*** rules; so we *invade* a country, wanting our own ways for all the benefits, glory, advantages, and benefits. But we don't want to seek, accept, or adhere to ***Kingdom*** rules. This is not the spirit of ***Kingdom***, grace, and glory, but ***Kingdom*** rape and discord.

I was at an event one time with persons of mixed natural origins—Jamaicans, Bahamians, Americans, Europeans, Canadians, Austrians, and such. At one point, I heard a person (non-American) who lived in America, had an American husband, and American child blurt out (because someone made a comment on a TV show about parentage, that a star was not the father of a child—nothing major). At that comment, she blurted out, "All of America is going to hell." I said, "What?" She repeated, "All of America is going to hell." I said, "Well, *if all of America is going to hell, where does that leave you?*"

I really wanted to say, *"Dare you, you are in our country, take our benefits, live in American glory, and condemn America? You are not a loyal citizen."* I wanted to say "If America is that bad, why are you here? And you can go home. This is my home. I must make it better. I have nowhere to run. *You have a choice,* you came here, and now you're despising this great land. If you can't *be loyal,* leave."

But I said enough to make my point that this was disrespectful, stupid, rude, and unacceptable to our ***Kingdom***; this was an ungrateful comment. She was actually condemning herself, her family, and everyone "in America." How can you condemn something you say you love? She was in a sense acting like a terrorist (one who comes in as one who loves something, only to destroy it or do it harm). She claimed to love America, like we say we love the church.

However, we act as *spiritual terrorists,* to the ***Kingdom*** of God. We act like we are in the ***Kingdom*** of God; however, we speak against our

King and ***Kingdom***. We speak foolishness and death to our fellow citizens. This is as disrespectful, as this lady from another country loves her past life, her past husband, and her ex-family members more than she does her present life, her present husband, and new family. It is so with us. We in the ***Kingdom*** act like we love sin more than we love salvation, our past life more than our present life.

Do not be a spiritual terrorist!

When I studied this more, I realized this is how the so-called Christian-***Kingdom*** citizens really live and act. Let's give additional examples.

We go to a church every week and condemn the pastor, choir members, staff members, and everyone we see; we don't like the church, and we even say, "Ain't anybody right in this church?" *But we don't leave*; we do the same thing with jobs. We are not grateful or loyal. It is amazing that because of *unloyal people* who go to the church and say "God sent me here" only to leave weeks later, we now look at people and say *"I wonder how long they are really going to be here?" Because we leaders have heard it all before.* The ***Kingdom*** citizens are so unloyal and so ungrateful that I know the King is displeased. We are never happy about our blessing, no matter how great. This is wrong.

I once had a member. When I met her, the first thing she asked me was to pray for her, saying, "*Apostle, pray for me, I need a new job. I hate my job.*" Then I found out later she had been there for *ten* years. Nothing was holding there; she just needed to have *something to complain about* because she was *not* loyal, not a true citizen of her job. Of course, *three months* later, I discovered that she was a big part of the problem—*often negative, never happy, a poor mother.*

Why did I say a "poor mother"? Because her children were undisciplined. In fact, I think she strongly disliked being a (single) parent, and this was reflective on her as a parent. We worked with her children, got them trained in church discipline, and had her daughter, a beautifully spirited young child, singing on the choir, She was a great vocalist. I think her mother was jealous of her gifts and talents, Finally, when the children were great, she stopped going to church because of—you guess it—she received rebuke for being out of order!

To tell her story however, *one year later,* she was still "singing" the same song. "*Woe is me!* I hate my job." She could **not bear *Kingdom* fruit;** *there were no new members because of her membership* (no one followed her to church, and if they did, they left quickly). She was spiritually impotent. And this type of citizen is *not* a good representative of the ***Kingdom*** of God.

This behavior must stop if we must go forth in building the ***Kingdom*** of God. His grace and glory must consume our lives; his grace and glory must be large badges worn proudly, graciously, and with joy.

People must see something in your life that will cause them to be drawn to the spirit and ***Kingdom*** *of God.* We must talk about how *good* it is to be a Christian; we must talk and show others the love of our King. Jehovah-jireh, El Shaddai, God the Father, Abba, the Great "I Am"—*whatever you call him is not the issue; knowing him and making him known is what the* ***Kingdom*** *of God is all about.*

Do something for the ***Kingdom****! To make it grow and increase, do the work of the evangelist! You stop and do the work of the King and the assignment of the* ***Kingdom****.*

Stop complaining about those who door knock and witness for Jesus and ***Kingdom*** impact until you do something; do anything and everything to enhance, glorify, and show the grace of God to someone to go into the ***Kingdom*** of God.

A Prophetic *Kingdom*, that brings glory to God

In the *Kingdom*, "Prophetic Services" Are Needed for *Kingdom* Hearers!

I have gone to many services (several different services, several different places, and several different times). These services were *supposed to be "prophetic."* However, nobody *prophesied;* the people shook, *screamed* (really screamed a lot), ran around, and hollered. They prayed for people doing a lot of *shaking*, spitting on *people*, pouring oil, and such stuff. Nobody really got a real, complete, understandable word.

But the people jumped up and down, moved by beating drums and music; excitement of music, songs, and praise made the people move, but there was *no true* Word from the King.

I soon found out people love "titles in the ***Kingdom***," but they fail to flow *in the gift of the title,* in the true appointment *of that title.*

Or what about the person who is *supposed to be the prophet* that *asks you questions* to seek answers and *then says "God told me"*? *This is not prophecy. This makes us all look bad and does not bring grace or glory to the* ***Kingdom*** *of God!*

Let me help you. "We all ***may drive*** *or* ***ride in*** *a car every day. This does not make us a car.* We use the vehicle to get to the place we need to go from commencement to the designated point." However, we get out of the car to fulfill our destiny (assignment or purpose). We get back into it and go to our next destination. My *point* is that you use the vehicle several times a day/week/month. But you get out and fulfill your assignment. This does not make you the *car.*

God will allow you to be used in a gift for his glory, but that does not mean that you maintain that gift as a primary gift of operation.

I ask you again, Are you a Car?

In the ***Kingdom*** gifts, God allows us to use many gifts to arrive at our ***Kingdom*** *assignment.* This *does not* mean this is *who we are;* we just are allowed to operate a vehicle to get to whom we need to minister to. That may be prophecy, healing, administration, teaching, gift of wisdom, or whatever vehicle we need to "drive" to get to our assignment.

You may have had a dream, told it to, or gave the meaning of it to someone; and it came to pass maybe often, maybe a lot. And God used you in interpretation several times; however, this does not necessarily make you a dream master. You may prophesy and it came to pass or you use the other gifts often, but this does not *make you* a prophet.

Like the car (that you expect to crank) when you turn it every time accurately and dependably, so must a gift operate in your life before *you can assign* yourself as "that."

Wise leaders know that; God does what he wants to do with us as he wants to We are his ambassadors on assignment for his *Kingdom*!

Pastor Benny Hinn just says, "I am a teacher with a healing ministry of the Word of God," though gifted in the area of healing. Bishop T. D. Jakes just says, "I am a preacher, pastor, and worshiper," though gifted in the area of deliverance, prophecy, and book writing. I, Chief Apostle Rice, say, "I am a worshiper, psalmist, deliverance minister, and preacher/pastor," even though I flow in prophetic utterances as a master prophet and am seasoned in many areas.

Jesus asked the disciples, "Who do men say I am? And who do *you* say I am?" But as for himself, he said, "I am Son of God." I do what my Father says for me to do. I fulfill His will. He never said He was ______ (any list of names). He just operated and glorified the ***Kingdom*** of God. Can we be more like Jesus and glorify God, Jesus, and the Holy Spirit? Not with noise, but with *"**Kingdom** power."* Let this mind be in you, which was also in Christ Jesus that "our Father" may be glorified.

Kingdom *authority will not let people call you something that you know you are not. This causes a rift in the authority that is supposed to be over you.*

In one of our services, one of the mothers in the church got up to **"***say a few words.***"** *When she got up, she then called one of the newly elected deacon a pastor* and went on to say that this is what the Lord told her! And this is what she sees.

True or not true, this lady was so out of order that I doubt the Lord spoke anything to her at all. However, this type of prophecy can get many people off track, and when the leaders of the church do not agree with this, give instruction to them and tell them to wait or make them be trained before going forth, causing them to wait on their callings. The ones who have gotten this out-of-town prophetic word are angry; you see, they were the "spoken-over ones—I have been spoken over"; they get mad and leave the ministry because the enemy makes them think they are being held down.

I was at a crusade recently, and the floating prophet, just in town for thirty days, told the people he was going to lay hands on them on a certain night and ordain, send them forth, and anoint them to the Gospel. He also said for them to not let any jealous leaders stop them from their ministries." I thought, *Oh boy, we are going to have a mess on our hand.* You see, this type of person will not be able to be trained easily because they have the "anointing already." They will operate in zeal but not according to knowledge. And because this preacher is leaving town, he just gave a kid a loaded gun and a sharp scalpel and told them to cut everybody they see, shoot the gun, and declare war on the devil.

This type of sending forth is wrong. And if you were sent forth like this, humble yourself and get under a local pastor who can judge your gifts and develop you in the ministry and teach you how to walk worthy of your calling. Do it quick before you kill somebody with your anointed self.

Get sent forth right as an ambassador, to bring the ***Kingdom*** Glory!

The body of Christ will thank you for perfecting your gift and truly being birthed and not "pastored" into the ***Kingdom***. Your spiritual parent does not need to be a *fly-by-night one-night stand who does not even know your mother's name.* But your father will know you and your mother, and together they legally will bring you into the ***Kingdom***. Don't settle for the halfway, get the best the King has to offer you, even though it tarry. WAIT on the Lord and your leaders to strengthen your hand and your way.

This is right before God. Remember you cannot skip ***Kingdom*** rules and you cannot make up your own rules; you must do it correct in the ***Kingdom***.

Taking ***Kingdom*** authority (with grace and glory) will be able to tell you what really glorifies your father and what glorifies your spiritual parents; you will learn with authority how to be under authority first, then how to be in authority, learning what glorifies God and what does not bring ***Kingdom*** glorification.

Kingdom *grace and glory is not being a "wimp."* It just is another tool of knowing when and how to *pull your* ***Kingdom*** *authority badge,* not using excessive force to handle a situation but knowing when we should pull the *oil, sword, word, or heart* and *minister to the need at hand.*

God spoke to me about ten years ago and said, "*Take authority over your life.*" Again, I thought I was in *authority,* so back to the dictionary. *Let us look at* **authority***:* the "power or *right to command, power or influence resulting from knowledge,* prestige; an expert, a scholar, professional; o*ne who knows; A specialist.*" One with the ability to command, and other obey." Again, I said *wow!* Another power word. I cannot stress to you how important it is to fully *know* and *understand* a word before you can fully minister (to help and serve others). If you want to talk to others, keep a *dictionary* around you (two or three, they may add to or take away information).

Chapter 10

Developing as a

"***Kingdom*** Specialist"

The *Kingdom* Is in Need of *Kingdom* Specialist

In school, we know that a kindergarten *teacher* is important, vital, and a necessity to good *foundation growth*, impartation, and basic skill development.

However, we do not expect to stay in kindergarten for five years. In fact, it is ridiculous to stay in one grade for five years. No offense, but we would consider someone who has stayed in kindergarten for five years as *special, slow, or retarded.*

Yes, we label people who do not promote, as we expect, by a tried time line. And we call this normal growth.

I do have to say, after thirty-eight years of ministry, there are too many "*special*" people in the ***Kingdom*** schools, "the church." These "special members" have not graduated to the next level of ***Kingdom*** learning and would never graduate to ***Kingdom*** maturity and become ***Kingdom*** *citizens.*

I must finish with what I started earlier by saying that "just because a person lives in a nation (especially if he is not born there), he does not become a citizen."

Until he finishes the "courses," he is not a citizen. The same is true with the ***Kingdom*** of God. *Until you complete the* ***Kingdom*** *courses and pass and become* "*legally* and spiritually matured," you are *not* yet a ***Kingdom*** *citizen.* You, like any other *nation,* are there; but are you a citizen?

We must promote ***Kingdom*** advancement to our students. OK. (Pastors, put the pressure on!)

How Do I Get to Be a *Kingdom* Specialist?

We must all pass through these phases to become a matured "specialist" in the ***Kingdom***.

In every other field, there are those who matriculate higher and deeper in their field of study, and they love it so much that all they do is talk about that. They are specialists! It takes time, extra time and work to be titled as specialist or a master in a field. God did not say not to become a "master" or specialist in a spiritual field. He said that "there will not be many masters or specialists!" Why? Because he knew people would not take the time to do so!

Let's Take the Time to Grow Up

When we are in the ***Kingdom*** *kindergarten,* we get saved; delivered; set free; learned ***Kingdom*** language, how to put the other ***Kingdom*** citizens, and play "good" together. We learn what habits we should have. We learn our ABCs and 1-2-3s, our basic constitutions, and then we should move on to the next level in our faith. However, in this class, the teacher must watch you always and babysit you. *The teacher cannot leave you alone for any amount of time* or do anything different because you may do something you have no business doing. However, we must make up our mind to go farther in life than kindergartener life. This lifestyle is for a short time. We grow and go to the next level. *No* one should have to call you for church or to be on time or to be faithful in your membership unless you are still in kindergarten class. Otherwise, move on and grow up!

Stop Being a *Mad* Kindergarten Teacher

At this point, it is no need to be a "*mad* kindergarten" teacher; you specialize in Christian practices—outreach, deliverance, pampering, bottle-feeding. Don't despise your area of specialty and authority. A true teacher pushes their students to the next level. We need you specially in the ***Kingdom***!

If you have done your job well, "*someone will* want to be a kindergarten *teacher*" like you.

Let them go through the necessary growth process and train them well to help their next teacher out. However, all others encourage them to "*grow on.*" You have taught them the value of salvation, deliverance, Christian forth; now let them go—seven—to twelve-year-olds.

Do not get caught up in offense when your children *grow up*. Remember, they will have at least *fifteen other teachers* before they graduate.

Next level specialist—*Kingdom* "Middle School" Student and Teachers

This teacher will teach the next level of growing in the ***Kingdom***—faith, obedience, love, faithfulness, gifts of the Spirit, basic ***Kingdom*** principles, and rules of the constitution; established need of ministry and calling may be identified at this level. "What do you want to be when you grow up?" is often identified at this stage. At this stage, backsliding is not a thought; we develop skills and practices for the ***Kingdom***—*no nap time, no whining, no complete babysitting.* There will be some freedom but still under the watchful eyes of the teachers. You may have two to three teachers at this level and should give yourselves a maximum of five years to get out of middle school.

Next level specialist—***Kingdom*** "High School" *Students and Teachers*

We know that high school is the time to put away with the toys and get to work; career paths are chosen, colleges decided, drivers' licenses are received, love blossoms, and everything else you have learned for the *last twelve years are* honed in toward a lifetime of personal (***Kingdom***) development.

At this point, it may be OK to decide this is your *lifetime spiritual goal*—to understand the Word and operate in the high school ***Kingdom*** level. Just as with all high school students, this *should not be the final point of your spiritual enrichment, but another goal.*

It is good to stay in a *high school church* until you *fully graduate and mature,* deciding this area should be written, discussed, and agreed upon as to your graduation date; as depending upon your mind-set, this stage can take from five to ten years (limit yourself) to graduate and seek the constant inspiration from your leadership.

College—Everybody does not go to college, but all should want to go!

College: natural and spiritual, *can be very hard.* It is a time of focus (you would not think so by American ways sometimes).

However, college is for *focused people* with an *expected goal.* It is for people who have a *dream* for a specific career path. In today's colleges, there are still many levels of maturity. Some very immature and some ready to "buckle down."

However, college tuition is still the same amount for everyone. *Everyone pays a price to be developed, matured, seasoned, and receive practical application.* They are *tested* over and over again and *tried,* molded, and instructed. There are "basic" courses that everyone had to take, and then we move into the courses directly related to "what we want to do."

You have to want to spend more time to become a specialist!

Some courses require more math; some require more science. Whatever it takes to complete your course of study you take, *you map out and plan to grow and succeed.* The same is in *"**Kingdom** school";* we discover what area of ministry we would like to operate in.

We learn, become seasoned, and are tested; real ***Kingdom*** school begins to define who we are in the ***Kingdom*** citizenship. An accountant does not study music as a major. There must be "*personal time,*" developing your personal skill. In college, you must become responsible and must practice to perfect your skills.

My daughter was in school to become a music teacher. High school was her preference at college; there were many days of extra practice. And each semester, she had to learn a new instrument at the decision of the teacher. There were *choirs,* rehearsals, practices, and more practices.

At the end of the year, there was a final performance, and the instrument learned that semester had to be performed on. The teacher wanted to know what Ara knows. Only when what was *known* to her was *proved* could she pass, and this goes on and on, again and again for four to six years. Then and only then does the *college* say you are ready to graduate. Some quit, some change colleges and majors, some stay longer, and some graduate with the greatest sense of accomplishment and power—and so it is in the ***Kingdom***.

Kingdom College—"Students and Teachers"

Kingdom *school* is the development of ***Kingdom*** standards being taught by *college graduates* who have the required experience, skill, patience, and knowledge to formulate required information, participation, and motivate ***Kingdom*** citizens to matriculate to higher heights in ***Kingdom*** work.

With this said, *"**Kingdom** college" is not for everyone.* However, it is for anyone who seriously wants to understand where the King, our god, has dominion, his sovereign way, and his divine principles for our lives, directions, and future. ***Kingdom*** *college* produces ***Kingdom*** living—like *college* should produce a *more fruitful* lifestyle providing resources, hope, and a better redeemed life of abundance.

Kingdom College allows you to focus on what called you to do!

Kingdom college gives you an obtainable goal to work for the citizen of heaven and earth. ***Kingdom*** *college also* produces *kings* and *priests* and defines the roles clearly and with authority to fulfill every expectation of growth and development.

Kingdom **College is not playtime**

Like in natural college, some go to get drunk and are not really here to learn; they are here to play, "seeking fun stuff." In the church, some do the same things! Prophetically speaking, some go to play and have a good time and be moved by the music and fame.

Others go to party and dance (never grow up and always watch other people slide by). But some go to learn, put foolishness aside, and grow in the grace of God.

I take pride in myself and thank God for me being a "*college* ***professor*** *for the* ***Kingdom***." We operate a ***Kingdom*** "college-style" ministry; all the Greater Harvest Christian Center Churches Worldwide Inc. operate in a "***Kingdom*** campus" and with a training-school mentality.

We specialize in *training leaders for the* ***Kingdom*** *of God* because we know who we are. We don't expect everyone to embrace our ministry or "college" because it's not for them. Some people go to only have a nap; others, they go to play, chew gum, and have recess. They are in kindergarten.

I love babies, and I enjoy three-year-olds; however, I am not a kindergarten teacher. I am not. I know it!

Why? How do I know? Well, personally, *I don't like sitting on the floor*. I don't like *repeating, repeating, repeating, repeating*. I don't like singing songs about alphabets and colors ("songs with no substance to the word"). Do I know how to teach in kindergarten? Sure, and I can operate as a middle school and high school teacher and as a principal as well. I have been there doing that! But that is not my specialty.

This *does not make me a bad person; it makes me a* ***Kingdom*** *college graduate and teacher of college-level-minded* ***Kingdom*** *students. I am one that knows her place, and I know what I am most fluent in.*

So when kindergarteners come to "color and play with glitter" (a type of church mind-set) and they need "their diapers changed," bottles made, and "want to *crawl around*," we often don't *fit* with them; and they leave because you can go in kindergarten, but you must want to grow up, and do it fast.

Have You Been in Kindergarten Too Long?

They are in kindergarten with a fifteen-year track record and enjoy naps and teacher playtime. Our *ministry* is, however, *no* playtime experience. We have skilled professors who believe students are here to *learn, grow, know,* and *show* the love and ***Kingdom*** purpose of God.

Are You Ready for *Kingdom* College?

*A **Kingdom**-college ministry* will mostly operate alike. (They may vary in some small things.)

However, you can expect the following:

- True (Word-based) praise and worship
- Forty-five minutes to one hour of solid teaching
- Training for leadership and leadership growth

A direct plan of expansion
A demand for spiritual reproduction and *fruit*
A request and solid of tithes, offering, sacrificial giving.
A "pastoral" sheep and shepherd's type style of overseeing
Your leaders to know your name, address, phone number, and call you into accountability
To have "homework" assignments, personal training, and overseeing
To be corrected when you are wrong, and a solid teaching is given

You will find out *what you are called to do (in the ministry)*. The pastor will really "be in authority" and not the deacon or advisory board. Everything from the music to the working of the church is "Word" based; if the Word does not say it, it probably will not happen.

This is a big change for some people. (You will think at some point that these people are crazy because you will begin to feel that everything you ever learned about "church" is wrong because it was not based on the Word.) And many of you run away at this point when you ought to be opening up a new attitude and embracing change for the better.

You will be stretched for excellence—over and over again. They will have a heartbeat for your children to grow in the Word and faith as well. They will be concerned about your evangelism and Christian ***Kingdom*** works. They will have a strong prophetic presence and flow. They will limit church gossip and deter wolves from among the sheep.

When you find one of these churches, *do not run away from them to return to the familiarity of the past. God is trying to grow you up. Stick around, and you will see that you have just encountered a college ministry!* This will do you good.

The *college* ***Kingdom*** *ministry* will force you to grow, see yourself repair broken pieces in your life, make financial assessment, build family business, and your personal Christian destiny. ***Kingdom*** college will require you to *self-study,* take notes, review, worship, and build your faith.

Everyone Should Want to Go to High School and on to College

Everyone should want to go to a "high school, college church." During your years of college, you will finally grow up.

If you take it seriously and *establish your purpose early,* your ***Kingdom*** college ministry may be your final rest in ministry.

Internship and Residencies

Before practical application, you have nothing—it's just paper. *Practical application* will allow you to experience *ministry life firsthand.* You will be able to get behind the scenes—up close and personal.

However, this level is a level that should be appreciated the most. This is the "*ultimate perfecting level.*" It will also allow you to experience your leader, teacher, and coach up close and personal as well.

The person who used to babysit you, smile, and wave at you is now in your face and making you accountable for everything you do and say, looking over your shoulder and finding all your mistakes. You will work long and hard and rarely get any credit.

This is the proving stage to see if you are really what you say; many people run from this internship phase and want to go straight to their jobs. With no experience, these people go into the jobs without this oversight and the on-the-job training necessary to do well. They often kill and hurt innocent people trying to learn their jobs.

You must use what you have learned; you must use it or lose it. In a ***Kingdom*** college ministry, after approval, you should be ready to step into ***Kingdom*** leadership with ease and grace, obtaining the spirit of the section of ministry you are assigned to, specialize in, *flourish in,* and *bring fruit forth* from where you are planted.

This is why "***Kingdom*** *authority*" must be in the church. *Without* ***Kingdom*** *authority, the church moves in jealousy, envy, spite, and every evil work.*

Remember the following:

1) ***Kingdom*** *authority* allows you the right to influence resulting from knowledge. *A specialist* is a powerful person. When you are a specialist, you don't have to push, direct, compete. People will seek you out for your specialty.

2) When you are a specialist, you are free enough as a specialist to refer to another specialist. Mental health and deliverance may not be your specialty. Your specialty must be praise or worship. Be comfortable in your area and allow others who may not belong in your classroom to be promoted *or* demoted to another teacher.

A good specialist does not take all patients; a good pastor cannot take all members. Take them if you must and refer them if you must. "*Lead* them to *greener* pastures."

A specialist will realize whom they are to help. Stop *fighting with sheep* that belong to another pasture; lead them with **Kingdom** authority to their (new teacher) planned growth point in the ***Kingdom***! It's all right to see your students graduate; even the best will someday "grow on." Learn to *release people* with grace and ***Kingdom*** authority.

Becoming a ***Kingdom*** *specialist* takes one final stop of ***Kingdom*** authority. It is for those, like me, implanted with *one vital message.* (You are a specialist.) This message will grow and mature until years of study and depth produce a product. *My specialty is Christian maturity:* "developing and training" the ***Kingdom*** citizens to *grow* up!

Postgraduate *Kingdom* Specialist—Master

As a *postgraduate,* you are required to research, write about document, and prepare a thesis. This thesis is your completed work of studies and prepares you to receive a master's degree in that area of study.

As a ***Kingdom*** *specialist,* it is so as well. I love it when people ask me what is a "master." Prophet, teacher, preacher, psalmist—simply put, a person *experienced* enough to teach others *successfully;* a person having control over something; a director, mentor, teacher of the gift one possesses; a champion, connoisseur, instructor, or leader of an area in which *time and experience* has proved his or her skills as above proficient.

If you are going to be declared as a "master" or specialist in the ***Kingdom***, you must put the time in and keep challenging yourself to grow up in the ***Kingdom*** business of God.

Kingdom authority will demand "attention" be paid to you personally and within your ministry. Make sure if you have progressed and perfected your ministry to become a *specialist* for the ***Kingdom*** *of God.* Know whom God has called you to be and rejoice, learn, and grow so that the ***Kingdom*** seeks you out for your gift and ***Kingdom*** specialty. God told me to take "*authority* over my *life*"; what's my life ***Kingdom***? In other words, he said *learn* the ***Kingdom***, develop in knowledge, and set yourself as a specialist for ***Kingdom*** "growth and development." And I did—it has been a college of prayer, intercession, prophecy, teaching, pastoring, and loving God.

God needs *specialists* in the ***Kingdom***. The **Kingdom** *spiritual guards* "are always changing." But additional specialists are *not* being developed fast enough. *There should be more than one* foot specialist, ear specialist, heart specialist, mental specialist, and emotional and physical specialist in the ***Kingdom***.

Yes, everyone has a pastor, but the pastor should have enough ***Kingdom*** wisdom to know when to refer his sheep/lamb to a specialist without feeling guilty. It's time to step up, grow up, and come up to ***Kingdom*** maturity.

Chapter II

Living the "***Kingdom*** Life"

Where Are You in the ***Kingdom***?

Are You Growing Up *in Christ's* Spiritual Maturity in the ***Kingdom***?

-God's Expected End (Maturity)

Living the Real "Mature" Life

Ask yourself these questions and answer them honestly, then ask yourself these questions three months from now and answer them again honestly. One year from now, do the same thing, three years from now, and five years from now. The question to ask yourself first is "Am *I living a* ***Kingdom*** *life, and am I fulfilling my expected end of maturity in line with the plan of God?"*

____

____

How do you know you are? or Why are you not living the ***Kingdom*** life?

____

____

____

Next, ask yourself the following series of questions:

What's your spiritual grade (now)? ______________________
Are you "promoting" classes properly? ______________________
Is it time to change grade? ______________________
Are you becoming spiritually matured? ______________________
Do you have ***Kingdom*** expectations of maturity? ______________

How to grow up and know it?
Signs and tests of maturity

An Expected End Reaching

Spiritual Maturity

What's the process (The spiritual guide of maturity)?
(A) Look at it *like life.*
Once you're born
Infant
Toddler
Adolescent
Preteen
Teen 13-17
Young adult 18-20

The sky is the limit, often wild and unsettled, making a lot of mistakes, and learning about life, consequences, and penalties of adulthood.

Rebirth 1: New Adults (*twenty-one to twenty-nine)*
First mind-set and changes to maturity, college grads or first permanent or long-term job, possible truly "born again" time in your life

Rebirth 2: Stable Adults (***thirty to thirty-nine)***
Second mind-set change—possible restructure of future, career, and settling in, often a new time of changing ministries and settling into knowing yourself in Christ.

Rebirth 3: Established Adults (***forty to fifty-five)***
Third paradigm shift—possible home ownership and looking for retirement job, career, or owning of own business, often will change church again, seeking church to raise a family in, and settle into your ministry in.

Rebirth 4: Senior Adult (1) (***sixty to eighty years)***

- Retirement
- Rebirth 4 retirement grandchildren, looking to be drama free, can volunteer, and become ministry specialist if dedicated to church. Will reevaluate again to see what is now not fitting lifestyle and patterns, will be quick to dispose of nonworking items in life and family. Very protective, values good friends, and wise council more than ever. Normally will not change ministries again unless death or moving occurs.

Senior Adult (80-99+)
2nd childhood phases or freedom phases depending on health

Active and healthy—will attend all functions, will work harder in the later years to ensure heaven, and have less temporary concerns, may travel a lot to see children or grandchildren if able. If not, they will be faithful members until death.

Inactive and unhealthy—will not attend church or functions much, will need a lot of spiritual at home care. Unhealthy—may require a lot of prayers and visits, family may become attached and some will become members, some will reject your presence as minister and will cause havoc.

What your "learning" scale and spiritual scale should reflect by *years saved.*

(B) Look at it like *education*

Grade (or years) Saved What you should know

1-2 years saved	Preschool	Salvation, books of the Bible Should have completely read the entire Bible at least once. Should be able to pray for at least fifteen minutes, a Word-filled prayer by the end of two years, and do five minutes of praise and worship.
3-5 years saved	Kindergarten	Faith, General overview of Bible General knowledge of Old and New Testament General characters of our faith General application of the Word Psalms and Proverbs overview Should have read the entire Bible at least twice Basis principles of our faith Should know basic evangelism scriptures and be active in evangelism weekly. Should be able to pray out loud, scripture prayer for at least thirty

minutes. Should be able to do at least three praise-and-worship songs.

6-9 years saved Elementary Medium of Christian principles
Grasping of scripture quotations
Good working knowledge of Bible and principles, where to find a scripture
Should know major and minor works of faith and be able to overview the chapter with its content.
Should be able to lead others to salvation and do basic home Bible studies with new believers.
Should be considering or working faithful in at least one department in ministry.
Understand and be able to operate in basic praise, prayer, and worship for at least forty-five minutes to one hour of prayer. Should be able to do five to seven praise-and-worship songs, should be able to pray for others while on the altar, phone, or in a crisis.

Should also know:
Basic praise
Basic worship
Basic healing
Basic deliverance
Basic study skills
Basic scriptures for evangelism

10-13 years saved—Middle School—Same as elementary, but much more advanced.

14-18 years saved—High School—More defined to gifts and callings
More impact in the local community on behalf of your church and vision
More understanding of the Word of God. Being able to rightly divide

the Word of God, teaching local in house classes and grooming others in the faith
More understanding of the vision of the house
More assistance to the in-house leadership
More godly in grace and glory

19+ years saved—College Level—***Specialty field of service***
Same as above and with a greater anointing and purpose of ***Kingdom*** direction. A full-time minister, a full-time assistant, and a full-time ***Kingdom*** keeper.

19+ years saved—Should definitely be the

- ✓ *In-house teachers to new students and members, teaching only as they have been taught, graced, and developed (but only if you carry the spirit of the house).*
- ✓ *Should be fruit bearing, with strong evangelism and an evangelist, have intercession and prayer warriors, know the operation of said ministry partaking in and other current ministries in-house. Should know the ministry of missions and service to the church as well as and ministry administration*
- ✓ *Be able to present themselves and their leader for other open door opportunities to do, network, and establish ministry outreach.*
- ✓ *Have and develop good loyal shepherding and lay pastor skills*
- ✓ *Be able to lift the service and carry on exhortation in the absence of the leader.*
- ✓ *Anyone saved over twenty years should be able to teach a message of hope and salvation, no matter where you sit in the ministry.*

Kingdom Assessment

As in the nature, one in a million students is a genius and skips grades or progresses overwhelmingly fast through high school; however, this is not the normal. Most of them learn on a regular pace. And so it is in the Spirit. The Bible says "to be not a novice [beginner], least you will be puffed up."

Be careful of persons who aggressively skip grades and want to promote themselves as teachers when they need to be taught.

Pastors and leaders, be careful of those who are saved many years but fail to develop spiritually. Both the overzealous and the underzealous growth can be a harm to ***Kingdom*** citizens and even to the person themselves, as the entire plan and destiny of God.

We must be balanced and have balanced growth in the ***Kingdom***. Stagnant members are dead members and should be skimmed away for new growth to happen.

Growth Chart—How Well Do You Follow?

How often do you attend service? ____________________

How well do you participate when you are there? ____________

How many church activities (extra) do you attend? __________

How many church activities (extra) do you participate in? ______

How many church activities (extra) do you lead? ____________

How long have you been in this church? ________________

List any leadership or strong activity roles.

____________ ____________ ____________
____________ ____________ ____________
____________ ____________ ____________
____________ ____________ ____________

What are your spiritual growth plans for the next two years?

____
____
____
____

Make a copy of this page and discuss it with them as soon as possible to help you increase your spiritual growth and ***Kingdom*** destiny.

Who is your current pastor/spiritual leader?

____

How well do you serve them and your ministry? (rate 1-10) _____

Who are your spiritual parent(s)?

________________ ________________

Where did you come from? _____ When were you birthed? _____

____________	____________	____________
Parent(Mother)	Parent (Father)	How were you birthed?

Other spiritual coaches in my life, spiritual mentors, and coverings

Spiritual Mentors

List five personal spiritual mentors who have directly imparted into your life by the laying on of hands and prophetic words.

____

____

____

____

____

____

Call them and thank them today or send them a thank-you card with a current picture.

When you mention spiritual mentors and do they know they are your mentors? ______________________________

Spiritual Coaches—and in what areas

List three to five spiritual coaches you have had in ministry areas!

__________________ __________________ __________________

What do you expect from your present spiritual leader(s)?

____

____

____

____

____

____

____

____

____

____

____

____

____

____

Do you have other ministerial experience, and where did you get your training?

____

____

____

____

What do you give in return to your leader for all your expectation?

____

____

____

Now that you have charted your past, you are well on your way to spiritual growth in the future. You can see your strong and weak area and can prepare to mature in the next six months as a spiritual champion. Let's get ready to go to the next level.

Chapter 12

Kingdom School

It's Time to Study to Show Ourselves Approved

Study Tools Needed for the *Kingdom*

You need more than your Bible to grow and do a great study; there are many study helps to help you understand God's Word better and clearer, so plan to invest in yourself if you plan to be a dynamic minister. Those of us who minister to you greatly study greatly; we read bibles and other books. We pray and enhance ourselves to have something fresh to share with you. Yes, the Holy Spirit is our Helper, but God told us to STUDY to show ourselves approved and be able to rightly divide the Gospel. Have you really been taught how to study? Then it is time to learn; especially if you have been graced to pastor.

When wanting to enhance your ministry growth, you need the following:

- Your Bible
- A dictionary—(regular) standard and a biblical dictionary

To reach any higher level of understanding, you must study higher.

Understanding is the ability to have "comprehension, the power to think and learn to have intelligence, to agree with, to stand under (or with), to take as a fact."

The ***Kingdom*** has "*suffered violence*" and has been taken by force in the area of "*ignorance.*" We refuse to go one step further to learn anything. We think we have it all. This is not the case; we need more of Him (God and His word).

We can't just get it all from our *limited understanding. We must "study to show ourselves approved."* Especially, those who are ministers must reach farther for ***Kingdom*** understanding. Our constitution (our Bible) *must* be understood, comprehended, researched, studied, learned, developed, and put into action.

The enemy will try to steal your zeal for studying and respectful research. I hear people who call themselves preachers who, if you really listen to them and take the time to write down what they have actually said, would have "not less than" *500* hallelujahs, *250* "Praise the Lords," and *350* "Thank you, Jesus" in *one sermon* and have a lack of solid materials or biblical teachings—all this in a twenty-five-minute service. This is bottled milk! When you study more, you will need less bottled milk. and require more solid food. When you know His Word, you will use less-repetitive speaking and dead filler words! Really, where did we get this type of speaking from? Not from Jesus, this is not ***Kingdom***. This is emotional stirring and bodily exercise, which profit very little. We must give our king a good name by "prais[ing] the Lord in spirit and in truth." This is truly only done by preparing a good, solid Word sermon! And like I like to say, "Before you *hoop*, walk it out." In other words, "*Before the gravy, please give me some meat and mashed potatoes.*"

Again, no offense, preachers, but *Jesus* (our example) did not preach or teach like this; so where did we get this? Not the even the Holy Spirit, who is a reflection of Jesus and speaks like the Father. When we have good, solid teachers who are not "hooping," we call them boring. We must learn to endure good "preaching" and not good hooping. Really, where did we get this foolishness? Why does it appeal to our flesh as "good church"? Nothing is "good church" that does not cause you to change and become better in your living and your giving. We must learn what is "good" and what is truly not good.

I am told that "crack" makes you feel good; however, we all know that this is not good and will make you do things that are not good. Do not fool yourself with what is truly good. Some of you are in "spiritual crack houses" and are taking "*spiritual crack.*" *It makes you feel good, but it is not good for you.*

We can't hide behind explosive "noise" to camouflage our lack of understanding, research, and sermon development. As ***Kingdom*** citizen, you receive these "junk food, microwave meals, and canned food" because you do not require more.

Somebody is gonna love this and get delivered today!

If you are still *receiving* kindergarten sermons (the same type and way) over five years, you are not growing. Then it is time to come out of the "spiritual crack house" so you can grow up in Jesus and your ***Kingdom*** assignment. Do not be fooled; I don't care how gifted the ministry is. *No ministry* is set to equip you in every area of your life.

That's why Jesus went from place to place; *his ministry did not change! He changed! He went from place to place!* He preached the same way; however, when the time came to leave, he left. Most pastors cannot *do this,* so sheep must change pastors at least every *seven years.*

There ought to be growth. *You should outgrow your chair, develop your ministry, serve in another* area of ministry, and *outgrow the same "old" teaching.*

How do you know when you have outgrown the ministry and are ready to be promoted?

My bishop says, "When you can preach what I preach better than I preach it [with understanding—not just parroting], you are probably ready for a promotion [in-house first and/or] to another vineyard. If you still have not conquered what I am preaching and living it out in victory, you are not ready to leave this classroom."

The ***Kingdom*** is always in need of new laborers

*The **Kingdom** is always in need of new laborers. No one is trying to hold you back.* You should seek to advance to ***Kingdom*** *leadership* and to pastor your own flock. *Have a dream* to grow out of your parents' house, and *parents have a dream* for them to *grow up*! It is not a reflection as negative ***Kingdom*** citizenship but true ***Kingdom*** growth.

How Do I Grow in the ***Kingdom***?

By studying to show yourself approved and you start by opening your Bible and asking God to help you to grow and understand the constitution. You cannot say you do not understand this wonderful and life changing book, You must take the time to learn to love its facts, principles, and love stories to us, the King's children. WE will learn to appreciate and embrace our inheritance, for the Glory of God is in us to receive him and his Word. In Jesus's name, go STUDY.

Learning how to study the Word
Five simple study principles that will enhance your life

I. *Be real in your commitment to study*—studying is not just reading, especially speed reading with no hope to retain information. Slow down, and hear yourself read, understanding what you have read, and be able to say it to someone else today!

II. Plan to invest*—books, tapes, and video*: *Books, tapes, video, any learning material that will increase you in your biblical studies. Look at Christian TV. Begin to take good notes at the church you attend. Go home and look up what was taught and try to resay it in your own words.*

III. Plan to expand your spirit and knowledge by attending special events, conferences, Bible school, Bible studies, and ***Kingdom*** classes. In other words, plan to invest additional time in additional ***Kingdom*** learning, even if you have to pay for it. It is worth the information you will receive and how you will begin to grow. Also attend Christian motivation *and* business education.

IV. Plan to get to know your God, our ABBA Father; His son, Jesus the Christ; and the Holy Spirit. Get to know them daily. "Seek them while they can be found, call upon them while they are near, and they will hearken to your request." Yes, they do want to hear from you, and then you will see yourself growing at a fast pace and even in a greater anointing. Expect God to begin to speak to you, as you read his word.

V. Get a notebook and write down what you study, what you pray for, and what you are expecting, In thirty days, look at it again and see what God has done for you. Find someone to tell about what studies you have, and expect them to grow with you, if they don't tell someone else.

Someone wants to know God with you as you learn more about him. Your light will shine, God will be glorified, and the blessings will come to you.

Kingdom Maturity Is a Must, *Kingdom* school is No choice . . . . . .

Because I am a specialist in "***Kingdom*** *maturity*," you can say to your *people, "I'ma going to send you to Chief Apostle for a month so you can learn this area and come back matured in the faith." Or "Chief Apostle is coming to impart to us this month the area of______ so we can grow in our faith."*

I am a teacher of ***Kingdom*** *school. I teach others how to bloom in the* ***Kingdom*** *of God. Going to* ***Kingdom*** *school is like "basic education for your child"; it should be NO CHOICE! You must want to learn and enhance your own self to grow in the* ***Kingdom***.

I heard the Lord as he told me to tell the ***Kingdom*** population that *"they must immediately take on the spirit of* ***Kingdom*** *maturity, which means to grow up in their responsibility to LEARN in* ***Kingdom*** *school." Yes, they must GO TO SCHOOL; they must put themselves on a healthy regiment of* ***Kingdom*** *knowledge, wisdom, and* ***Kingdom*** *understanding. Pastor Mike Murdock has wisdom school and other schools and camps for short-term learning of large principles. Pastor Leroy Thompson, in*

*Louisiana, has money schools and prosperity camps. Pastor Kenneth and Gloria Copeland have faith schools and camps, and I do **Kingdom** schools and school of the prophets and ministerial camps. Many other pastors and leaders have conferences and bring the gifts for the body together to help us grow up in the **Kingdom** and our faith. As I said in this book, DO NOT MISS YOUR SEAT! For if you do miss your seat, you miss your **Kingdom** connection. Go and be blessed as you mature in the **Kingdom** with education and faith.*

One day, in service, I was teaching on the army of the Lord. There was "a member" who thought she was God's gift to the ***Kingdom*** and that God had given her an assignment to go around and minister to the homeless. This was without my permission. She said God sent her to our ministry, but she was never submitted. She would put her ministry above everything we were doing—services, training, and direct assignments. She was a *renegade,* out of order most of the time, *never on time,* and always out of step with what we were doing. I assigned her as an usher. God told me to humble her. She thought she was above this position. *She did have a gift of exhortation,* but she wanted to be called a prophetess or evangelist. Let me say, she rarely brought anyone to church with her; and whenever she would bring one or two persons, they were always "needy" or out of order.

Kingdom Maturity means discipline

This day, as I said, I was teaching on the army of the Lord, and she was laughing, laughing silly, for no reason. I asked her to stand up and asked her what the problem was because she was disturbing my sermon and church. *She haphazardly stood, still smirking, looking around at the other members.* I asked her again what was funny; she continued to laugh. God spoke to me and said this was a "*rebellious demon, mixed with pride, and kill it*" and to have her to drop down and do ten push-ups. God told me to have her drop down and do ten push-ups. Even though I thought this was strange, I obeyed the Lord. I said, "*OK, solider, drop and give me ten push-ups!*" She immediately stopped laughing and rolled her eyes at me and said, "*I can't do push-ups. I have a bad back.*" I said, "You can do half knee or whatever." At this point, she refused to do any. She didn't even try! This was an exposed demon of disobedience seen in the natural army; we do not disobey our commanding officer!

I immediately felt the Lord lead me to teach on this spirit and how it comes to deflect from those of us who want to do better and see better. *I also told them that in a real army, when the commanding officer tells you to do something, you do it! So why do we think we can refuse in the army of the Lord to follow our leader's orders?*

I told them that she was not a solider of God, but of Satan. Yes! I exposed this demon, and I also told the ministry that if she could not follow and respect leadership, she was not welcome in our college, our ministry, or our church.

Are you a whisperer?

See God needs real soldiers in his army, not fake wannabes who mean our ministries no good!

I later found out *why God needed to expose her,* because she was secretly trying to take *ungodly authority in the church; she was calling other members and directing them like she was the voice of the church, all behind our backs.*

She had "webbed" a web through unauthorized and ungodly communication among several members who were intrigued with "her anointing," which was not in existence. *She made a lot of outward gestures like she was so spiritual (punching the air like she was fighting demons or devils or something,* walking around, quickly swinging at the air, and always spitting up stuff).

In all her antics, she never once acted like she had *a bad back or any other problem.* I knew this was a forest of emotions and not real; however, some people, to find out, were taken in by these spirits pretending to be so great.

I am glad God showed the church who she really was before more destruction could happen. About a month later, she called Bishop and said that "God told her" to take a month off from church; (of course) she never returned. Praise the Lord!

We did not know who she was influencing until she left. In her leaving about four weak-minded and feeble clan members of hers (the people she webbed with her emotional web), they left right afterward; these were the *people she was "ministering to "unauthorized," yes, even over the phone; and when she thought I was not looking, she was pulling them to the side to "whisper" to. You see, she had stolen the hearts of the weak and feeble who were not attached to the shepherd.* We must watch this and this type of people.

Are you a whisperer, or are you being whispered to? If you are, stop this and tell your leader the wolves are among us! Scream for your life. The wolf is here!

We need to know the spirits that infiltrate the church and try to stop you from growing in the ***Kingdom***. It takes a real eye of discernment to see these little demons that slide in like snakes to take you away from your true shepherd.

We Need true Spiritual Coaches willing to help the team!

Coaches Train us, Push us, Yell at us, and cause us to get better!

In the year of *2009,* God called me to be a *spiritual empowerment coach.* See, I have matured in the spirit, and gifting of coaching and empowerment is in my life. I live an empowered lifestyle, and the ***Kingdom*** has needs of my specialty.

After, I released myself to the body of Christ because I know who I am, and the body of Christ has received my gift. (I am so happy; now I coach pastors and fivefold leaders to know their gifts and talents for the ***Kingdom***.) *Why?* Because they need to be empowered in the *spiritual camps* of the ***Kingdom*** principles, ***Kingdom*** healing, and ***Kingdom*** success.

I feel very much fulfilled. I/We (Bishop Rice and myself) have committed to saturate the ***Kingdom*** with knowledge and the *Word of God*. We go to churches for three, nine, and twenty-one days ***Kingdom*** **c***amps*! Depending on the need and the faith of the people, *we* also teach the s*chool of the prophets, the school of ministry, and various* ***Kingdom*** *classes allowing others to gain certification, ordination, and associate* **degrees** through Harvest University; we do these classes on location, with host churches in their local areas, and rise up real prophets and ministers for the ***Kingdom*** of God.

You must be ready to be equipped for the battle. *You must be ready to be educated; you must be ready to be schooled.*

We empower the leadership with *three-day* leadership camp, *five-day* ***Kingdom*** (camp) revivals, and conventions, the move of God. While we are in the city, we help the leadership and host *two to three* days of pastoral empowerment: We *overview* the administration, *help them* set up books, *address* issues, *help* to develop *skill* assessments, *review fund*-raising techniques; we *preach, teach, prophesy,* and we *coach* others in their ***Kingdom*** "*college*" experience.

Other times, we "*coach*" from "in-house ***<u>Kingdom</u>*** camps." In other words, we have taken ***<u>Kingdom</u>*** authority and are *producing* our own kind of specialists in the ***<u>Kingdom</u>***—sons and daughters who embrace our wisdom, experience, and specialties in ***<u>Kingdom</u>*** authority! I encourage people to take an assessment of themselves and chart their progress for twenty-one days to see where they are truly at spiritually.

Let us assess ourselves.

Chapter 13

Kingdom Spiritual—Maturity Assessment

and

Growth Overview Charts

Your Personal Spiritual Assessment

Use These Same Principles to

Make an Assessment in your Ministry

Your Family
Yourself
Your Finances
Your Health

To make this journey better, find a partner to journey the assessment with you. If you can't find a journey partner, then start alone; after all, it's your own success we are working on.

Chart yourself

Day 1: *This is where I am right now in my life.*

Days 1-7	Present	Goal	Mission	Levels to measure
Rate yourselves 1-10 *each area	Where am I? 1-10	Where do I want to be?	What is going to take to get to my goal?	Three things to do to make the change
Spiritually				
Mentally				
Healthwise				
Financially				
Socially				
Family				
Church				

Days 1-7

Midway **review and rechart your changes**

	Present	Goal	Mission	Levels to measurement
Days 8-14	Where am I now?	Where do I want to be?	What is going to take to get to my goal?	Three things to do to make the change
Spiritually				
Mentally				
Healthwise				
Financially				
Socially				
Family				
Church				

Days 8-14

Assess your changes and rechart your success!
Now live it out! And grow in other areas

	Present	Goal	Mission	Levels to measurement
Days 8-14	Where am I now?	Where do I want to be?	What is going to take to get to my goal?	Three things to do to make the change
Spiritually				
Mentally				
Healthwise				
Financially				
Socially				
Family				
Church				

Days 15-21

	Present	Goal	Mission	Levels to measurement
Days 15-21	Where am I now?	Where do I want to be?	What is going to take to get to my goal?	Three things to do to make the change
Spiritually				
Mentally				
Healthwise				
Financially				
Socially				
Family				
Church				

Personal Maturity Assessment and Review

Day twenty-one: What have you changed, and how are you going to keep this change?

What did I change?	My new level	How will I maintain this change?
		(1) (2) (3)
		(1) (2) (3)
		(1) (2) (3)
		(1) (2) (3)

Chapter 14

Learning about Our *Kingdom* Constitution

Two Hundred ***Kingdom*** Constitution Facts for Every ***Kingdom*** Citizen

Two Hundred Things Every ***Kingdom*** Citizen Should Know

It's finally time to test your ***Kingdom*** and spiritual knowledge. How much do you really know about the ***Kingdom***, Christ, and the god we serve?

This is the first-year test I use to certify all ministers. *However, every* **Kingdom** *citizen should know these basic* **Kingdom** *questions to lead others to Christ.*

Enjoy, learn, and grow in ***Kingdom*** teaching and these ***Kingdom*** facts.

Do You Know Your Bible?

*Do you know your **Kingdom** Constitution?*

Two Hundred Vital Questions and Answers Every Christian Should Know

A Special Section of Compiled selected questions and answers for your ***Kingdom*** Growth

These resources were compiled from various study sources and resource materials, handouts, and staff assignments in Harvest University by Chief Apostle Dr. J. G. Rice during the years of 2002-2007. They are also sanctioned for use by Harvest University Bible College 2008 for the course of Ministry 101 and are used as training materials for Greater Harvest Christian Center Churches Worldwide since 2007. Our chancellor (Apostle Dr. J. G. Rice) and our dean of finances (Bishop James R. Rice) believe in the education of every ***Kingdom*** citizen and push all ***Kingdom*** citizens to continue to learn on a daily basis; because of this, we grow in maturity and faith as we continue to study to show ourselves approved.

How to Use This Section

This section was originally designed as a college course in a little booklet. It is designed to broaden the Bible knowledge of new Bible students, current believers, and all ministers from junior age through adult.

The questions in this section may be used in a variety of ways:

1. Supplemental lessons for a Sunday-school class. They are arranged topically and may be used separately, in groups of three, or as a whole group.

2. Elective lessons as a substitute for a regular lesson of a given quarter. You may use a lesson a week for twelve weeks and have one week for review.

3. Preparatory class for those contemplating church membership.

4. Bible drill work in connection with an evangelistic meeting or otherwise.

5. Bible training course for new Christians.

6. Home instructions.

7. Weekday or Sunday evening classes.

8. Trivia games and fun time at home.

The Kingdom Constitution

We must seek to understand our constitution; though this is a slight overview of information, learning it and using this information will help you to understand our constitution better;

Our constitution, which is our bible, must be studied and embraced a lot better.

We must continue to seek knowledge as it will help us to be better Kingdom citizens.

The Bible

How much do you really know about your ***Kingdom*** *Constitution?* We have carried our bibles around weekly and under our arms religiously; however, do we seek to know our Bible? This section will push you to get to know your Bible, beginning with learning the books of the Bible, Old and New Testament.

A basic question would be first, can you list the books of the Bible? Can you do it by alphabets, or by Old and New Testament, or can you do it by sections, major and minor prophets, history, poetic, or books of poetry, and so forth? Do you know five books right off the top of your head? Go on and say them right now, out loud. How about ten books? Say them if you can! Challenge yourself to grow in this area and to become a student of the Word. It may be a strong leap for you, but please take it.

Alphabetical Listing of Bible Books

Do you know your books of the Bible?

First Test

This is your first test to see if you are serious about learning. Get a paper and pen and write down the books of the Bible. Yes, list them and see how many books you know from memory; then check them against the following pages, see what you missed, and retake the test tomorrow.

You get three times to get them all right. The third day, retest yourself often to see if your scores and knowledge increase.

Grades for the test:

Sixty-six books	*A+*	*Forty books*	*C*
Fifty-five books	*A*	*Thirty books or less*	*D*
Fifty books	*B*	*Twenty books or less*	*F*

Don't cheat yourself! Give yourself a chance to grow, strive for an A+ within three days.

Second Test

Our second test is to divide the books by sections. You can then test yourself with dividing the books by Old and New Testament. Grades are the same as above by correct placement. Go for it and do it for yourself.

You are now on your way to becoming a good *Kingdom* citizen.

Welcome to the ***Kingdom***

Books of Our Constitution

Acts
Amos
1 Chronicles
2 Chronicles
Colossians
1 Corinthians
2 Corinthians

Daniel
Deuteronomy

Ecclesiastes
Ephesians
Esther
Exodus
Ezekiel
Ezra

Galatians
Genesis

Habakkuk
Haggai
Hebrews
Hosea

Isaiah
James
Jeremiah
Job
Joel
John
1 John
2 John
3 John
Jonah
Joshua
Jude
Judges

1 Kings
2 Kings

Lamentations
Leviticus
Luke

Malachi
Mark
Matthew
Micah

Nahum
Nehemiah
Numbers

Obadiah

1 Peter
2 Peter
Philemon
Philippians
Proverbs
Psalms

Revelation
Romans
Ruth

1 Samuel
2 Samuel
Song of Songs

1 Thessalonians
2 Thessalonians
1 Timothy
2 Timothy
Titus

Zechariah
Zephaniah

The *Kingdom* Constitution:

How Much Do You Know about Your Constitution?

The ***Kingdom*** *Constitution is filled with treasures; let's go treasure hunting.*

1. What is the greatest book in the world?
   Answer: the Bible

2. Who wrote the Bible?
   Answer: holy men under God's direction.

3. How many men did it take to write the Bible?
   Answer: forty

4. About how many years did it take to write the entire Bible?
   Answer: fifteen hundred years

5. How many books are there in the Bible?
   Answer: sixty-six.

6. What are the two great divisions of the books of the Bible?
   Answer: Old Testament and New Testament.

7. What does the word *testament* mean?
   Answer: "will" or "covenant"

8. How many books are there in the Old Testament?
   Answer: thirty-nine

9. How many books are there in the New Testament?
   Answer: twenty-seven

10. In what four parts is the Old Testament divided?
    Answer: law, history, poetry, and prophecy

11. How many books of law are there?
    Answer: five

12. Name the books of law.
    Answer: Genesis, Exodus, Leviticus, Numbers, and Deuteronomy

13. How many books of history are there?
    Answer: twelve

14. Name the books of history?
    Answer: Joshua, Judges, Ruth, 1 and 2 Samuel, 1 and 2 Kings, 1 and 2 Chronicles, Ezra, Nehemiah, and Esther

15. How many books of poetry are there?
    Answer: five

16. Name of the books of poetry.
    Answer: Job, Psalms, Proverbs, Ecclesiastes, and Song of Solomon

17. How many books of prophecy are there?
    Answer: seventeen

18. Name of books of prophecy.
    Answer: Isaiah, Jeremiah, Lamentations, Ezekiel, Daniel, Hosea, Joel, Amos, Obadiah, Jonah, Micah, Nahum, Habakkuk, Zephaniah, Haggai, Zechariah, and Malachi

19. Into what four parts are the books of the New Testament divided?
    Answer: biography, history, letters, prophecy

20. How many books are there in biography?
    Answer: four

21. Name the books of biography.
    Answer: Matthew, Mark, Luke and John

22. How many books of history are there in the New Testament?
    Answer: one

23. Name the book of history in the New Testament.
    Answer: Acts

24. How many books of letters (epistles) are there in the New Testament?
    Answer: twenty-one

25. Name the books of letters.
    Answer: Romans, 1 and 2 Corinthians, Galatians, Ephesians, Philippians, Colossians, 1 and 2 Thessalonians, 1 and 2 Timothy, Titus, Philemon, Hebrews, James, 1 and 2 Peter, 2 and 3 John, and Jude

26. How many books of prophecy are there in the New Testament?
    Answer: one

27. Name the book of prophecy in the New Testament.
    Answer: Revelation

28. Name, in order, the books of the Old Testament.
    Answer: Genesis, Exodus, Leviticus, Numbers, Deuteronomy, Joshua, Judges, Ruth, 1 and 2 Samuel, 1 and 2 Kings, 1 and 2 Chronicles, Ezra, Nehemiah, Esther, Job, Psalms, Proverbs, Ecclesiastes, Songs of Solomon, Isaiah, Jeremiah, Lamentations, Ezekiel, Daniel, Hosea, Joel, Amos, Obadiah, Jonah, Micah, Nahum, Habakkuk, Zephaniah, Haggai, Zechariah, Malachi

29. Name, in order, the books of the New Testament.
    Answer: Matthew, Mark, Luke, John, Acts, Romans, 1 and 2 Corinthians, Galatians, Ephesians, Philippians, Colossians, 1 and 2 Thessalonians, 1 and 2 Timothy, Titus, Philemon, Hebrews, James, 1 and 2 Peter, 1, 2, and 3 John, Jude, and Revelation

Old Testament History I

Creation—Period of the Judges

1. What does the name *Genesis* mean?
   Answer: “beginnings”

2. Quote the first verse of the Bible.
   Answer: “In the beginning God created the heaven and the earth.”

3. What event marks the beginning of Bible history?
   Answer: the creation of the world

4. Who were the first people God created?
   Answer: Adam and Eve

5. What command of God did Adam and Eve disobey?
   Answer: Do not eat the fruit of the tree of the knowledge of good and evil.

6. Who was the first child born into this world?
   Answer: Cain

7. Why did God send a flood to destroy the earth?
   Answer: because men were very wicked

8. Who were safe in the ark during the flood?
   Answer: Noah and his wife, their sons—Ham, Shem, and Japheth—and their sons’ wives.

9. What was the first thing Noah did when he left the ark?
   Answer: built an altar and worshipped God

10. What great structure did people try to build after the flood?
    Answer: the Tower of Babel

11. Who is called the father of the Jewish nation?
    Answer: Abraham.

12. How did God test Abraham?

Answer: He asked Abraham to sacrifice Isaac, his son of promise.

13. Who was the father of the twelve tribes of Israel?
    Answer: Jacob

14. Who was Jacob's favorite son?
    Answer: Joseph

15. To what high position was Joseph called?
    Answer: second in command to the pharaoh of Egypt

16. Who, in the Bible, is best known for his patience?
    Answer: Job

17. Whom did God call to lead the Israelites out of slavery in Egypt?
    Answer: Moses

18. What did God give Moses on Mount Sinai?
    Answer: the Law

19. In your own words, give the Ten Commandments.
    Answer: You shall have no other gods before me; make no graven images; don't take the name of the Lord in vain; remember the Sabbath day and keep it holy; honor your father and mother; don't kill, don't commit adultery; don't steal; don't bear false witness; don't covet.

20. Who was chosen to lead the Israelites after Moses's death?
    Answer: Joshua

21. What was the first city the Israelites conquered in the Promised Land?
    Answer: Jericho

22. Who were the only people saved in Jericho?
    Answer: Rahab and her family

23. What did Joshua want the Israelites to decide?
    Answer: whether they would serve God or the heathen gods of their neighbors

24. Who with God's help, used an army of three hundred men to defeat the enemy?
    Answer: Gideon.

25. Who was the only woman to judge Israel?
    Answer: Deborah

26. Which judge was taken captive because he got a haircut?
    Answer: Samson

27. Which young woman left her home and family to go with her mother-in-law?
    Answer: Ruth

28. Who was a great prophet and the last judge of Israel?
    Answer: Samuel

Old Testament History II

The ***Kingdom***—United and Divided

1. Who was the first king of Israel?
   Answer: Saul

2. Who was the greatest king of Israel?
   Answer: David

3. What part of the Bible did David write?
   Answer: most of Psalms

4. Which king of Israel was known for his great wisdom?
   Answer: Solomon

5. What part or parts of the Bible did Solomon write?
   Answer: Proverbs, Ecclesiastes, and Song of Solomon

6. After Saul, David, and Solomon ruled, what happened to the ***Kingdom*** of Israel?
   Answer: It was divided into two.

7. What was the name of the northern ***Kingdom***?
   Answer: Israel

8. What was the southern ***Kingdom*** called?
   Answer: Judah

9. What happened to the northern ***Kingdom*** of Israel?
   Answer: It was destroyed by an enemy nation.

10. Why was the ***Kingdom*** of Israel destroyed?
    Answer: because the people refused to obey God

11. What happened to the ***Kingdom*** of Judah?
    Answer: The Babylonians destroyed the cities and took most of the people captive.

12. Which four young men were taken to Babylon to be trained for important positions?
    Answer: Daniel, Shadrach, Meshach, and Abednego

13. Where was Daniel put when he refused to worship the king?
    Answer: in the lion's den

14. What great prophet told of the coming of Jesus hundreds of years before He was born?
    Answer: Isaiah

15. What prophet was thrown overboard into the sea because he disobeyed God?
    Answer: Jonah

16. Which prophet told the city where Jesus would be born, and what was the city?
    Answer: Micah, Bethlehem.

17. Who was the last prophet of the Old Testament?
    Answer: Malachi

18. When the Jews returned from Babylon, who helped them rebuild the walls of Jerusalem?
    Answer: Nehemiah

19. Which brave young woman risked her life for the sake of her people?
    Answer: Esther

The Christ

The Early Life of Jesus

1. Who is Jesus of Nazareth?
   Answer: the Christ, the Son of the living God

2. Has Jesus always lived?
   Answer: yes

3. Quote a scripture that tells of this.
   Answer: "In the beginning was the Word, and the Word was with God, and the Word was God" (John 1:1).

4. How did Jesus come to earth?
   Answer: He was born of the Virgin Mary.

5. Where was Jesus born?
   Answer: in Bethlehem of Judea

6. Who is Jesus's father?
   Answer: God. "I am that I am," Jehovah, our God!

7. Who went to see and worship the baby Jesus?
   Answer: shepherds and wise men

8. Who was taken to Egypt?
   Answer: Herod

9. How did Herod try to get rid of Jesus?
   Answer: by having all the boy babies killed

10. How was Jesus saved?
    Answer: He was taken to Egypt.

11. In which city did Jesus grow up?
    Answer: Nazareth

12. How old was Jesus when He went to Jerusalem with Mary and Joseph?
    Answer: twelve years old

13. What was the special mission of John the Baptist?
    Answer: to prepare the way of the Lord

14. Who baptized Jesus and in which river?
    Answer: John the Baptist, Jordan River

15. What did God say after Jesus's baptism?
    Answer: "This is my beloved Son, in whom I am well pleased" (Matt. 3:17).

16. Where did Jesus go after His baptism, and what happened?
    Answer: Into the wilderness, He was tempted by the devil.

The Ministry of Jesus

1. Where did Jesus do His first public teaching?
   Answer: in the synagogue at Nazareth

2. What one message contains most of Jesus's teachings?
   Answer: the Sermon on the Mount

3. What well-known group of sayings comes from the Sermon on the Mount?
   Answer: the beatitudes

4. Quote the beatitudes.
   Answer: "Blessed are the poor in spirit; for theirs is the ***Kingdom*** of heaven. Blessed are they that mourn: for they shall be comforted. Blessed are the meek: for they shall inherit the earth. Blessed are they which do hunger and thirst after righteousness: for they shall be filled. Blessed are the merciful: for they shall obtain mercy. Blessed are the pure in heart: for they shall God. Blessed are the peacemakers: for they shall be called the children of God. Blessed are they which are persecuted for righteousness' sake: for theirs is the ***Kingdom*** of heaven" (Matt. 5:3-10).

5. How many men did Jesus choose for His special helpers, and what were they called?
   Answer: twelve, called apostles

6. Name the twelve apostles.
   Answer: Peter, Andrew, James, John, Philip, Bartholomew, Thomas, Matthew, James the brother of Jesus, Thaddeus, Simon the Zealot, and Judas Iscariot

7. To whom did Jesus direct His teaching?
   Answer: the lost sheep of the house of Israel (the Jews)

8. What are some of the names Jesus called himself?
   Answer: the door, the vine, the light of the world, the good shepherd, the bread of life, the way, the truth, the life

9. What special teaching method did Jesus often use?
   Answer: the parable

10. Name some of the great parables of Jesus.
    Answer: the good shepherd, good Samaritan, prodigal son, lost sheep, lost coin, wise and foolish virgins, the talents, unjust judge, wedding garment, Pharisee and publican, rich man and Lazarus, rich fool, parables about the ***Kingdom***

11. What incident marked the end of the popularity of Jesus?
    Answer: the triumphal entry to Jerusalem on what is now called Palm Sunday

The Later Life of Jesus

1. What special things did Jesus begin the night before He died?
   Answer: the Lord's Supper

2. After they ate the Passover meal, where did Jesus and His apostles go?
   Answer: Garden of Gethsemane

3. Who brought the enemies of Jesus to the garden?
   Answer: Judas Iscariot, one of the apostles

4. Which Roman governor allowed Jesus to be sentenced to death?
   Answer: Pilate

5. How and where was Jesus put to death?
   Answer: crucified, outside the city of Jerusalem

6. Where was Jesus buried?
   Answer: tomb of Joseph and Arimathea

7. What great event took place on the third day after Jesus died?
   Answer: He came back from death.

8. Who was the first person to see Jesus after His resurrection?
   Answer: Mary Magdalene

9. Give at least three appearances of Jesus after the resurrection?
   Answer: to Mary Magdalene, to the women, to the two on the road to Emmaus, to the ten apostles in the upper room, to the eleven in the upper room, to the seven apostles by the Sea of Galilee, to over five hundred persons at one time.

10. What important order did Jesus give before He ascended to Heaven?
    Answer: the Great Commission

11. In your own words, give the Great Commission.
    Answer:

All authority has been given to me in Heaven and in earth. Go into all the world, teach all nations, baptizing them in the name of the Father, Son, and Holy Ghost, teaching them to do all that I have told you to do. I'll be with you to the end of the world.

12. Just before He ascended, where did Jesus tell the apostles to wait, and why?
    Answer: in Jerusalem, for the coming of the Holy Spirit

The Church

The Beginning of the Church

1. What is the church?
   Answer: the society of people who believe in Jesus and are striving to do His will

2. How can we know the will of Jesus?
   Answer: by reading the Bible, by prayer, by the Holy Spirit speaking to us, by our spiritual leaders, and by spending personal time with him in meditation.

3. Where do we read of the beginning of the church?
   Answer: Acts chapter 2

4. When and where was the Christian church established?
   Answer: day of Pentecost, AD 30, in Jerusalem

5. Who is the founder and head of the church?
   Answer: God, through his son, Jesus Christ

6. Quote a scripture about this.
   Answer:

   > Simon Peter answered and said, "Thou art the Christ, the Son of the living God." And Jesus answered and said unto him, "Blessed art thou, Simon Bar Jonah for the flesh and blood hath not revealed it unto thee, but my Father which is in heaven.
   >
   > "And I say also unto thee, that thou art Peter, and upon this rock I will build my church; and the gates of hell shall not prevail against it." (Matt. 16:16-18)

7. Who adds to the church?
   Answer: Jesus Christ and those who spread his Gospel

8. Who made the laws of the church?
   Answer: Jesus Christ

9. Who can become members of the church?
   Answer: all who obey Christ and have received him as personal Lord and Savior

10. Where can we find the right name of the church?
    Answer: in the New Testament

11. What are some of the names given to the church in the New Testament?
    Answer: church of Christ, church of God, household of God, body of Christ, house of prayer, pillar of fire, pillar of truth

12. What name best shows that Jesus Christ is the founder and head of the church?
    Answer: church of God in Christ

13. What scripture records this name?
    Answer: Romans 16:16

14. What are some New Testament names for the members of Christ's church?
    Answer: saints, brethren, Christians, disciples, friends, children of God, labors of the Gospel

15. When were Christ's followers first called Christians?
    Answer: "The disciples were called Christians first in Antioch" (9 Acts 11:26).

16. What scripture teaches us the importance of the name of Christ?
    Answer: "There is none other name under heaven given among men, whereby we must be saved" (Acts 4:12).

New Testament History

1. Who preached the first Gospel sermon?
   Answer: Peter

2. What was the result of Peter's sermon?
   Answer: Three thousand men were baptized for the remission of their sins.

3. What did the followers of Jesus do after the day of Pentecost?
   Answer: "They continued steadfastly in the apostles' doctrine and fellowship, and in breaking of bread, and in prayers" (Acts 2:42).

4. What did the enemies of Jesus do to Peter and John when they healed and reached in the temple?
   Answer: put them in prison

5. What was the attitude of the early church?
   Answer: "The multitude of them that believed were of one heart and one soul" (9 Acts 4:32).

6. When Peter and the other apostles were told not to preach Jesus, what was their answer?
   Answer: "We ought to obey God rather than men" (9 Acts 5:29).

7. Why were Ananias and his wife, Sapphira, struck dead after they brought their offering?
   Answer: They lied to God.

8. Who was the first to die for this faith in Jesus, and how did he die?
   Answer: Stephen, stoned to death.

9. Who was sent to preach to the Ethiopians' eunuch?
   Answer: Philip

10. What was the result of Philip's preaching?
    Answer: The eunuch was baptized and went on his way rejoicing.

11. Who was a persecutor of Christians?
    Answer: Saul of Tarsus

12. What happened to Saul as he was going to Damascus to imprison some Christians?
    Answer: He was blinded by a great light.

13. Who spoke to Saul and what did He tell Saul to do?
    Answer: Jesus. He told Saul to go into Damascus and wait.

14. After three days what happened to Saul?
    Answer: He received his sight back and was baptized by a preacher named Ananias.

15. What good works was Dorcas noted for?
    Answer: She made clothing for the needy.

16. What did Peter do for Dorcas? What was the result?
    Answer: He raised her from the dead; many believed in the Lord.

17. Who was the first Gentile convert?
    Answer: Cornelius

18. Who was the first of the apostles to die for his faith?
    Answer: James, the brother of John

19. What effect did persecutions have on the church?
    Answer: "The word of God grew and multiple" (Acts 12:24).

20. Where was Saul's name changed to Paul?
    Answer: while he was on the first missionary journey (Acts 13)

21. Who were the first people to be converted in the continent of Europe? What city?
    Answer: Lydia and her household, Philippi

22. What did Paul and Silas do after they were beaten and thrown in prison?
    Answer: They prayed and sang hymns.

23. What happened to the jailor at Philippi?
    Answer: He was baptized.

24. In Athens, what did Paul say when he saw an altar inscribed, "To the Unknown God"?
    Answer: "Whom therefore ye ignorantly worship, him declare I unto you" (Acts 17:23).

25. With which husband and wife did Paul live and make tents within Corinth?
    Answer: Aquila and Priscilla

26. When Paul preached to a great crowd of Jews in Jerusalem, what happened to him?
    Answer: He was arrested and put in jail.

27. How many missionary journeys did Paul make?
    Answer: three

28. Name some of the men who worked with Paul.
    Answer: Barnabas, Silas, Luke, Timothy, John, Mark

29. Tell some of the hardships Paul had to endure as a missionary for Jesus.
    Answer: beatings, stoning, shipwrecks, hunger, thirst, cold, nakedness, robbery, imprisonments (see 2 Corinthians 11:23-27)

30. Why did Paul finally go to Rome?
    Answer: as a Roman prisoner to appear before Caesar

31. What is Paul noted for besides his preaching and missionary work?
    Answer: He wrote the New Testament's letters from Romans to Philemon and probably Hebrews.

32. Which other church leaders wrote letters that are a part of the New Testament?
    Answer: Peter, James, and Jude (both half brothers of Jesus), and the Apostle John

33. Who wrote the book of Revelations and where was he living?
    Answer: the Apostle John, on the Isle of Patmos as a prisoner

The Mission of the Church

1. What is the primary mission of the church?
   Answer: to seek and save the lost

2. Quote the Great commission.
   Answer: "Go ye therefore, and teach all nations, baptizing them in the name of the Father, and of the Son, and of the Holy Ghost: teaching them to observe all things whatsoever I have commanded you: and, lo, I am with you always, even unto the end of the world" (Matt. 28:19, 20).

3. What does the word *missionary* mean?
   Answer: "one who is sent with a mission or task"

4. Who is called the great missionary and apostle?
   Answer: Paul

5. What scripture shows the importance of sending missionaries?
   Answer:
   "Whosoever shall call upon the name of the Lord shall be saved. How then shall they call on him in whom they have not believed? And how shall they believe in him of whom they have not heard? And how shall they hear without a preacher? And how shall they preach, except they be sent? As it is written, how beautiful are the feet of them that preach the gospel of peace, and bring glad tidings of good things!" (Rom. 10:13-15)

6. How can we help in the missionary task of the church?
   Answer: We can learn about missions, pray for the needs of the missionaries, give money to help with expenses, send new missionaries to the lost, and go as missionaries.
7. When will missionary work be completed?
   Answer: when every knee bows and every tongue confesses that Jesus Christ is Lord (see Philippians 2:10, 11)

The Christian

How to Become a Christian

1. What is the first step in becoming a Christian?
   Answer: faith in Jesus Christ

2. How do we get this faith?
   Answer: by hearing the Word of God

3. Quote a scripture that shows the importance of faith.
   Answer: "Without faith it is impossible to please Him: for he that cometh to God must believe that he is, and that he is a rewarder of them that diligently seek him" (Heb. 11:6).

4. What is the second step in becoming a Christian?
   Answer: repentance

5. What is repentance?
   Answer: sorrow for sin and complete surrender to Jesus

6. Quote a scripture that shows the necessity of repentance.
   Answer: "Repent ye therefore, and be converted, that your sins may be blotted out" (Acts 3:19).

7. What is the third step in becoming a Christian?
   Answer: confession

8. What is the confession we are to make?
   Answer: Jesus is the Christ, the Son of the living God.

9. Who was the first to make this confession?
   Answer: Peter (Matthew 16:16)

10. Quote a scripture showing the necessity of making this confession.
    Answer:
    "With the mouth confession is made unto salvation" (Rom. 10:10).

11. What is the fourth step in becoming a Christian?
    Answer: baptism

12. What does baptism represent?
    Answer: the death, burial, and resurrection of Jesus Christ

13. Quote a scripture that tells us that.
    Answer: "We are buried with him by baptism into death: that like as Christ was raised up from the dead by the glory of the Father, even so we also should walk in newness of life" (Rom. 6:4).

14. What happens when we obey Christ in baptism?
    Answer: We are born again receiving the gift of the Holy Spirit. (See Acts 2:38.)

15. Quote a scripture showing the necessity of the new birth.
    Answer: "Except a man be born of the water and of the Spirit, he cannot enter into the ***Kingdom*** of God" (John 3:5).

Christian Growth

1. Name at least four physical acts essential to Christian growth.
   Answer:
   Bible study, prayer, Lord's Day assembly (church attendance), partaking of the Lord's Supper, fellowship of giving through tithes and offerings, evangelism, and increasing the ***Kingdom*** through soul winning.

2. Quote a scripture that shows the importance of Bible study.
   Answer: "Study to show thyself approved unto God, a workman that needeth not to be ashamed, rightly dividing the word of truth" (2 Tim. 2:15).

3. Quote a scripture on the importance of prayer.
   Answer: "Pray without ceasing" (1 Thess. 5:17). "The effectual prayer of a righteous man (person) availeth much" (James 5:16).

4. What scripture speaks of the importance of regular Lord's Day attendance in worship?
   Answer: "Not forsaking the assembling of ourselves together, as the manner of some is" (Heb. 10:25).

5. Quote a scripture about the Lord's Supper observance.
   Answer: "This do ye, as ye drink it, in remembrance of me. For as often as ye eat this bread, and drink this cup, ye do show the Lord's death till he come" (1 Cor. 11:25, 26).

6. Quote the scripture that shows the importance of regular, systematic giving.
   Answer: "Upon the first day of the week let everyone of you lay by him in store, as God hath prospered him" (1 Cor. 16:2).

7. Quote one or more scriptures that tell of the need for soul winning.
   Answer: "Lift up your eyes, and look on the fields, for they are white already to harvest" (John 4:35; see also Matthew 28:18-20).

Continuing the Christian Life

1. Who has Christ appointed to abide with us and comfort us in the Christian life?
   Answer: the Holy Spirit

2. Quote a scripture that contains this precious promise.
   Answer:
   I will pray the Father, and He shall give you another comforter, that he may abide with you forever; even the Spirit of truth; whom the world cannot receive, because it seeth him not, neither knoweth him: but ye know him; for he dwelleth with you, and shall be in you. (John 14:16, 17)

3. What fruits of the Spirit should be found in the Christian's life?
   Answer: love, joy, peace, longsuffering, gentleness, goodness, faith, meekness, and temperance (Gal. 5:22, 23).

4. What is the greatest of the Christian virtues?
   Answer: love

5. Quote a scripture that tells us this.
   Answer: "Now abideth faith, hope, charity (love), these three; but the greatest of these is charity (love)" (1 Cor. 13:13).

6. How can we possess the love of God and be victorious Christians?
   Answer: "God is love; and he that dwelleth in love dwelleth in God, and God in him. Herein is our love made perfect, that we many have boldness in the Day of Judgment" (1 John 4:16, 17).

7. Quote a scripture that tells how long a Christian should remain faithful.
   Answer: "Be thou faithful unto death, and I will give thee a crown of life" (Rev. 2:10).

Chapter 15

Learning to Become a More Attractive <u>***Kingdom***</u> Citizen

How Can I Become a More Attractive *Kingdom* Citizen?

Three Laws of *Kingdom* Attraction

The laws of attraction will work for you when you develop these *three biblical* ***Kingdom*** *principles.* Then your blessing will run you down and take you over.

Learning these principles will bring overtaking blessings your way.

Three Points That Will Make You More Attractable!

1. *With Other* **Kingdom** *Citizens*
   1) *Speak* the truth one to another.
   2) *Pray* one for another.
   3) *Do* good one to another.
   4) Be dependable and fair.

2. *With Your Spouse*
   - A wise woman builds her house.
   - Love your wife like Christ loves the church.
   - Submit one to another.

3. *With Other Persons*
   - A friend show themselves friendly.
   - Let your conversations be holy.
   - Drop the negative (blessings and curses are in your mouth).
   - Don't let unbelievers influence you (set your affections above). You did run well, but what did hinder you?
   - Remain honest.

Chapter 16

Taking
"Twelve Steps" to My Miracle

Kingdom Miracles!

With My Name on It

Miracles, with my name on it!

There is a miracle for you in the ***Kingdom***. Don't let anyone talk you out of your "***Kingdom*** miracle." *Take the twelve steps to your miracle with the 2 Chronicle 7:14 challenge.*

It is the challenge of "miracles" that I am asking you to take. You are not challenging me; you are finally daring to believe God!

Is a ***Kingdom*** *challenge, you must start on your way to your miracle!*

I invite you to take *a fifteen—to—twenty-one-day miracle challenge*; God wants to give you a miracle with 12 easy steps, you too can experience a miracle!

Second Chronicles 7:14 assures us that miracles will come to you, *but you must meet your miracle halfway! Stop thinking that you do not have to do anything but put your hand* out to receive your miracle. No, this is not so; we must work our faith and our prayer life to get a miracle.

You must be serious about this like never before. You can start by making a date with God, yes, establishing a time of fasting and prayer to receive your miracle. Fasting and praying for twenty-one days will be a joy and a happy time, a short time, to see the hand of God move on your behalf. This time will go by so fast. Don't blink; a miracle will be at your doorstep! As you begin to see, God move on your behalf; you will do this over and over and share it with others as well. You will not look the same, feel the same, or act the same in twenty-one days. Get ready for your miracle.

Get your bible and let's go into his word, 2 Chronicles 7:14

I believe that this is the formula for your miracle. If you need a miracle and follow this pattern, you will see your miracles. Let us fast for fifteen to twenty-one days.

These days are full fast. First turn off the TV. The TV can be very bad for your faith, depending on what you are watching, of course; however, I suggest *no* TV (or only watching religious TV) definitely, *NO secular music or shows.* Cleanse and purify your spirit by reading your Bible and praying as you are going into a time of *war*! And victory!

Remember you must meet God half way to get your miracle.

Your miracle is *waiting for you* at a certain point; what are you willing to do to get it? If you keep doing what you have always done, *why do you expect something different?* You will only get something different if your change and press into what you wishing to and reach for. *Reach for your miracle with your faith.* Use the extra time you create when turning off the TV to build up your faith in reading and confessing good, positive things over your life. Get the negative influences out of your atmosphere. And create a atmosphere for the Spirit of God to come into, and bring your miracle.

Some things come only by fasting and praying; we must *stretch* ourselves again into ways of different types of fasting and a mode of special prayers, *focused prayers,* and prayers of expectations. "Whatsoever you believe when you pray, have faith to receive it, and it shall come to pass." Here below is a simple type of fasting that you can successful embrace and apply to your life as you transition into your space of received miracles.

A General Fasting Schedule

In addition to fasting to create a clean atmosphere, you may abstain from food and other things that have consumed your "spare" time as well, give your body a break, and clear up your mental and emotional atmosphere. WE have addressed already the need for clean environmental space, so stop the foul and negatives from entering into your space through TV, friends, Internet, phone, or any other gateway. Then you are ready to clean the inside once you have created a balance atmosphere of spiritual calmness.

First week: Eat no meat.
Second week: Eat only pure vegetables (cooked or raw).
Third Week: Drink only water for two to three days (preferred with lots of prayer).

Next three days, eat only soup—fresh soup, home prepared preferred. With meat or no meat, the choice is yours.

Last days Come back to light, small meals until you see your miracle.

Let's begin our walk to our miracle in twenty-one days or less!

We begin by studying and embracing a plan that will help us to create the miracle we are wishing and expecting to receive.

Study this scripture *(2 Chronicles 7:14) every day* and "confess." Say out loud and with boldness: "I ______________________ am God's [son or daughter]."

I confess that I am wealthy, healthy, and wise; I set my mouth today to agree with God about me; and I am an "earthen vessel full of good treasures." I am sent by God to manifest his joy and his glory in this earth. I pray and set my mind to meet God with his Word over my life to cause a great cosmic clap in my life, and I prepare my mind to receive the good things God has in store for me. I only agree with goodness and faith, joy, and expectance of miracles today in Jesus's name. Doubt and unbelief, I cancel your assignment; you do not have a partner to agree with, so leave, and do not come back. I pray with full power and faith over my life, and my house hold today I believe that

"I am blessed and on a divine assignment and mission for the ***Kingdom*** *today! Jehovah, acknowledging you as my Father God, and Jesus, your Son, as my Lord and Savior, the giver of every good and perfect gift toward me. I am humbling myself and praying, believing, and receiving today the good gift in my life. Father God, through your son Christ Jesus, I am calling and called by your name. I am purposely seeking your face for instructions and for favor, for grace, mercy, and the hand of your glory to move in my life. Father God, I am turning from my wicked way., I renounce any sins that I have committed before you openly. I do know that you will grace me in all my doings as I live sin free. Therefore, I can expect great things to happen to me today, this hour, this week, this month, and forever. Your desire for me to have the good and best of this land I occupy, so I speak to the giants in my land and curse them to move, die, or become my blessing. I live in favor. I have the favor of the* ***Kingdom****. I wave my 'favor flag,' and you see me, know me, and bless me. I expect healing in my land and a miracle in twenty-one days or less. In fact, I expect to see signs of it today coming my way. I look to the hills from which cometh my help, knowing that my help is on the way! I expect you to help me, Father, in every area of my life. I am expecting the healing hand of God toward me and my needs today!*

"Because I know my Father will show up on my behalf, I thank God for his miracles and breakthrough in my life today, in Jesus's name. I now walk into my miracle, direct my path today Father for my spiritual connections of

grace, glory, and favor! My miracle is now! AS I open my heart today, I see and thank you in advance for every type of miracle you have planned for me today! I live in a miracle zone! I create miracles through your wisdom that rests on me NOW!

"I wrap the love of God around me, and it shields me from wicked thoughts, imaginations, or darts that may come my way. They will miss me in Jesus's name, and only the darts of miracles will hit the target in my life that God has intended them to affect. I am empowered to prosper. Everything my hands touch is a success. I soar in power and authority, and people want to give to me good treasures every day. I receive the ***Kingdom*** *treasures with joy!*

"I have a plan of success and I am prepared to used the treasures I receive to grow the ***Kingdom*** *of God. Money finds me for the sake of the* ***Kingdom*** *and the sake of the Gospel so that I may dwell in peace in the land and eat the fruit thereon.*

"My miracle is on the way. I will know it when I see it. I will embrace it and make it work for my good! My miracle is here now! I can feel it! I can see the glory of God in my life more today than yesterday. I am changing and I am expecting God to work it out for and with me, so I rest in God! I am in his perfect will. I am a 'miracle magnet.' What others do not get, I receive for I am a prosperous steward over the little, and he makes me a ruler over much. God takes from the wicked and give their inheritance and current possessions to me daily. He takes from the unprofitable servants and gives to me. He causes me to produce and grow with the fertile soil and crops of plenty. Jehovah loves me and I love him. Jesus loves me, and I love him. We are all in agreement that I should have his best miracle and be promoted and blessed today. Yes, I praise you in advance for my miracles in Jesus's name. I thank you for it today, Jesus!"

The Twelve-Day "Miracle" Plan

Twelve Principles to your Miracle

Let's look at what 2 Chronicles 7:14 is really teaching us and meditate on these principle for the next twenty-one days.

The twelve principles to your miracle are revealed within this chapter.

Principle # 1 *If my people*

Establish yourself as a ***Kingdom*** citizen (2 Chronicles 7:14).

Principle # 2 *Who are called by my name*

Allow yourself to be called by his name.
Establish *whom* you belong to; it's not about our name. It is about *His name.*
Would humble themselves

Principle # 3 *Humble yourself:*

Tell the truth to God, repent, and be real in truth. Ask God and Holy Spirit to help create a new you.

And

Principle # 4 *Pray*:

Really pray—get, you, a small book of scriptural prayer and pray the Word of God. Forfeit your worldly mind-set of praying and teach yourself how to pray the effective Word of God.

And

Principle # 5 *Seek my face*:

Seeking God is equal to being able to meditation (Psalm 1:1). Sit and think on God's Word; get one passage of scripture a day and think on it (just a short passage). We must purpose to say to the Lord, "Thy will in my life be done, now and forevermore."

And

Principle # 6 Turn from *wicked* ways:

Make up your mind to *purpose* to stop sinning and doing what displeases God. *Yes,* we all *have* (past tense) *sinned.* That does not mean we all "*continue* to *sin.*" Fall down; get up (quit falling).

Principle # 7 *Then I will hear them from heaven*!

Then I will hear then from heaven:
God will hear you after you meet the requirement. And God will speak favor to you and on your behalf. Expect God to move when

you meet the ***Kingdom*** rules. Let these fifteen to twenty-one days change your life and your mind-set.

Principle # 8 *I will forgive your sins*

Sins will be forgiven: God wants to forgive us; as we truly *repent,* we must stop and come back to God if we want the blessings of the ***Kingdom*** on our life. Stop and go back to His plan and purpose for you.

Principle # 9 *I will heal your land:*

Step 9—believe *healing will happen:* healing in your *mind,* body, spirit, soul, family, finances, church, social network, and extended life cycle. *Total healing will happen.*

Principle # 10 He will know who you are:

Know and believe God sees your heart and your change toward him. Know that God's eyes and ears will be open (2 Chron. 7-15) The Father will hear you as you stay in this spirit; the eyes of God and the ears of God will be toward you.

Expect your house to change and your environment to be cleaned.

Principle # 11 *Receive that He will sanctify the house* (2 Chron. 7:16)

A different spirit of relationship will live with you, the grace of God will abide with you, the spirit of refreshment will embrace you, and He will "sanctify" and set you apart with a different ***Kingdom*** agenda and determination of victory.

Principle # 12His presence will be established in you, and miracles will come to you.

Know that His name, His throne, and His ***Kingdom*** *shall be established in you forever (2 Cor.* 7:18). Now expect a miracle to be revealed and manifested to you!

Know this will produce an assurance and a hope; therefore, my life will produce miracle after miracle because I am in his ***Kingdom*** and his ***Kingdom*** is established in me. I am in his plan, and his plan is operating within me. I am at his throne, and his name is stamped on my forehead; therefore, I am the child of the King. I am a princess or a prince, I am the future of the ***Kingdom***, and I have an inheritance. I have a miracle because my father provides miracles. He will not skip me, he will bless me, he will give to me his best, and I shall wear a crown.

What a promise! And yes, you've got to do some Kingdom work to get it!

What is Kingdom Work?

HAVING FAITH, BELIEVING, HOPING, EXPECTING, and RECEIVING!

But it is worth it. To have the ***Kingdom*** established in you and with you is to have favor with the King forever. Wow! *Favor is fair!* Yes, favor is *fair*; I would not trade favor with the King for anything.

And once I learned the rules of the "***Kingdom*** rules of engagement" to my miracle, I found favor and favor attached itself to me, *so learn these ways today and enter into* ***Kingdom*** *favor. Learning and believing in the current* ***Kingdom*** *miracles and breakthroughs of God.*

The ***Kingdom*** *Never fails*

Chapter 17

Expecting Miracles, Miracles, and More Miracles!

Let's Look for the Miracles, and the Miracles Will Come!

*Seeing Miracles in the **Kingdom***

Should become a regular thing for you

The ***Kingdom*** Never fails

*God's **Kingdom** never fails, God's Word never fails, God never fails!*

If this is a true statement, I hear many of you saying "Then why are so many 'prayers seemingly unanswered'?" I submit it is because *the "purpose of their request does not have a **Kingdom** agenda"* attached to it.

When your *prayers* and *requests* line up with ***Kingdom*** purpose, "*heaven* is obligated to fulfill and deliver." *The angels only obey **Kingdom** assignment and instructions.* On the other hand, they cannot "cross or disobey" instructions that have been preassigned by God. Even if you pray for them too, remember they work for the King. They obey his instructions; to get them to obey, we must be in agreement with the Word.

So our ***Kingdom*** *commandments* (orders and prayers) must line up with the divine will and flow of the ***Kingdom*** *constitution,* the Bible.

Create a "Cosmo Clap"

When we come into this strategic assignment with faith, purpose, and order, we cause as "*a cosmo clap*" of agreement to take over in the atmosphere—this "clap" that will create a divine lineup of order. *The angels get the order, and the answer is released from heaven to earth on your behalf and in your favor.*

Therefore, it is important to get in agreement with your ***Kingdom*** constitution, your ***Kingdom*** assignment, and your purpose—with clarity and understanding.

God's Kingdom never fails, God's Word never fails, God never fails!

God wants to grant you the desires of your heart as long as they *do not violate **Kingdom** principles.* He really does! *Stop thinking God is* *against you* because you ask for "foolish things and he does not give them to you." Would you give your child a loaded *gun* just because they asked for it, cried for it, begged for it, over and over and over? Of course not.

Even now that our children are grown, we would not give them a loaded weapon, allow them to drive drunk, or give them drugs. There are just some things that good parents do and things good parents do not do! *The same is with our Heavenly Father.*

There are some things that *Abba* will *not do*: No matter how we whine or beg, he knows this thing that he would grant us would be like giving us *poison*—"pure sin."

So why are we then "mad" when *Abba, our heavenly daddy, says no!*

We must realize that our god has our best interest in mind and at heart always. Always! Always! When we trust our *King* to rule well over us, we do not have to pout, stomp, jump, rant, or rave; we can enter into ***Kingdom*** *security* to understand that *our King* is a good, solid, fair, living King who only wants the best for us!

Breakthrough and miracles are what our King does for us best, yes, even today! He is the god of breakthroughs and miracles. And when His children need a miracle, He does just that, and He always comes on time!

God's Kingdom never fails, God's word never fails, God never fails!

In *our ministry,* I know many times He (the Spirit of the Lord) has gone in "*like a roaring lion and commanded a breakthrough.*" And then there were times we experienced the "*breakthrough of the lamb.*"

We have seen the miracles of God! We have seen God's hand move one minute before due; we have seen His hand "stay the time," and we have *felt the favor of his love.*

This all leads us to know one thing. "*God still does **Kingdom** miracles, signs, and wonders.*" He does still perform and that our Father in heaven still *cares for us*!

Testimonies Are Still Important

It is important to believe in, know, and *testify in and about your current **Kingdom** miracles and breakthroughs constantly!* Because this will lift your faith and the faith of others, this can cause additional miracles and breakthrough in your life, and cause you to become a giant overcomer "by the word of your testimony" and create an atmosphere of hope in your life.

This is why *the church and* ***Kingdom*** *need "testimony service."*

I mean *real transparent times* where "the people of God share with the people of God how God has brought them out and encourage them to believe more in our god."

We need to rehearse what God had already done and is still doing for his people. So when other things arise, *we already know that God will do it for us.*

The people of God can be encouraged *to know God will do it for you,* and when He does it for you, *their faith is ignited again*; and they know if He did it for you, they will see that *He will do it for them.*

"He will work it out. He will fix it. He will do it again! Just believe and receive it. God will perform it today!"

Singing causes Miracles

Learn to Sing Songs that Lift Your Faith and Lead You to Miracles!

All songs of hope and biblical words lift our faith and cause us to trust our God again as a god of breakthrough and miracles. I knew a lady (Big Mama) who had cancer *four times;* but each time, she would activate her faith, stir up her testimony, and she would say, "He dun' it before, he gonna do it again."

She would SING, sing, and sing praise-and-worship songs. Yes! She lived to be over ninety-three years and did *not* die of cancer. She just slept away, singing a worship song, "Wonderful savior, how I adore thee."

What a wonderful life of miracles and breakthrough! Did I also say that she never had chemo or radiation; she said that "stuff was the quick way to die" (her opinion). And she would say "*God's medicine was the only dose she wanted to take.*" (That medicine in your book was fasting and praying.)

Fasting and Praying Will Lead to Miracles

Big Mama *would fast for six months,* get detoxified, and healed. She would say, *"God's looking for some mess to turn to a messenger, a mill into a miracle, and a pod into a pond of blessing. Guess I'm his girl."*

Can you go through your trial and test to get to a real testimony, to let God create a miracle for you!

Big Mama would say, "I'm gonna trust him until my change comes. *My change will come.* I *trust him,* and my change can, and will, come. Might not come today, but God will bring it tomorrow, on a wing and a prayer."

What a warrior, a voice of hope! What a great example of faith! She knew God would make it happen. She talked to people about being healed, she prayed for people over and over and they got healed, she encouraged people by her *pep,* and she danced in the spirit *and looked grand* doing it. She believes in the god of breakthrough and miracles.

This is a ***Kingdom*** *pattern*: we all must have made a pattern of hope and faith. Beat the "lion, tiger, and the bears" so when your Goliath comes forth, you will know this is a small fry, and you will defeat it because you have defeated it before.

Take your time of being alone and *smile* because this is your time of personal faith development and personal conquest. As you personally develop this ***Kingdom****-conquering spirit,* your testimony will develop and you will *walk the faith walk,* not by talk, but by experience.

Make a Demand for Your Miracle and Watch Him Show Up!

Personally, h*ow do I know God is a healer? Because I have walked the faith walk of healed.* HE has HEALED me and has now given me the gift of healing. Yes, He anointed my right hand for healing because I came through sickness, and I now speak to the bodies of those who are sick to be healed, in Jesus's name!

How do I know God can do whatever I ask Him (in righteousness)? Because I walked the faith walk of him. He has healed me *many times. Many times,* I know the King cares for me; I know it! *Make a demand for your miracle,* and watch the King give you his attention. Watch the King give you what you believe for; that is in his Word and will.

You Must *Sow* to Reap a M*iracle*!
The miracles come to us by our sowing;
we sow for what we expect God to do.

When we *make a demand* on the ***Kingdom***, we must have first obeyed the ***Kingdom*** rule of *sowing! Many of us want to reap*; rarely, one is willing to sow, but it's the ***Kingdom*** rule—*you will only "reap what you sow, after you sow."* When you need a breakthrough or a miracle, you must sow breakthrough and miracles seeds.

There are times when we have prophesied to people about their finances and they get the financial breakthrough; then when they have the money, they do not fulfill the promise they made God about the money they received. Shortly afterward, they are in a worse state than before they got the money. Why? Because they failed to continue to be faithful and support the ***Kingdom***. In fact, they stop going to church and reject the very leaders who spoke blessing over their lives. Now they are "cursed, with a curse." Their health fails, and their money has run out. Instead of repenting, they recluse, and some even go back into sin. They cannot see themselves giving God a tithe off large money amounts; they cannot see themselves giving the church a BIG CHECK, so they squander the profit and they do not profit! You must stay faithful when you are blessed financially. God just wants to know that he can trust you. If he can trust you once, he can trust you twice. Don't stop the flow of money; pay your VOWS!

SEE Yourself WRITING The BIG CHECK TO THE Lord!

You Must *Sow* to Reap a M*iracle*!

Seeds of finances, works, faith, faithfulness, and gratefulness—these seeds must be *constant*, day and night, night and day. Sown and scattered upon the soil to grow your faith.

When there is something you need from the ***Kingdom***, *you must "go high and get low,"* and *look for it to come on the horizon.*

Celebrate Your Miracles Before They Come . . . . . .

In the month of February, I start celebrating my birthday. I celebrate before my birthday comes. I celebrate in advance before I know it's coming; personally and in church we all celebrate because my birthday is coming!

Get ready to celebrate; in fact, start early. *Celebrate it when you see it coming, and go down to meet it halfway.* Yes, effort must be made on your part to collide with your destiny!

Yes and amen! *As you see your miracle coming, you must prepare yourself to meet it.* Your miracle must not be delayed in getting to you. Your pathway (mentally) must be cleared, and *your expectancy must be great.* That is what we do when preparing for a newborn, God's (miracle) best gift to us. We "clean, paint, buy, fix up," all for an expectant miracle. We see the miracle in advance, we name it, and we expect it to *change* us.

WE have to get up early and stay up late. We (mentally) prepare ourselves; we prepare ourselves emotionally, strategically and physically—all for our expectant breakthrough and miracles. God wants you to experience his touch of breakthroughs on a constant basis; this is a wonderful gift of the ***Kingdom***. *Don't let anyone talk you out of your daily **Kingdom** miracles and breakthroughs, great or small.* Don't let people tell you the god of Israel is dead. Refusing to believe the god of Abraham, Isaac, and Jacob no longer brings fire down for a praying believer.

It Must Be the Same Type of Celebration for, Planning for, and with expectation for our Miracles!

God wants to show off for you; *you have to allow God to show off and give Him the opportunity to "bring the fire."* Let them laugh and pick at you; you keep praying and waiting on the fire! When you know your god, you know the fire will come, and the ones that are laughing will be put to a moment of silence. When your God answers with fire, yes, the doubters will hush!

When the fire of breakthrough comes to your life and *you walk out smelling sweet—no smoke*—they (all: everybody, anybody, somebody) will know your ***Kingdom*** *covenant is still working for you.*

Where There is a MIRACLE, *there is FIRE* and Miracle-working POWER!

So rejoice and expect a miracle! What do you need God to do for you? Stretch and pull up your faith; A miracle needs **faith to ride on**, *it is the gas that fuels the tank, to get you to your miracle. Let your faith RISE.*

I keep saying to you that *the* ***Kingdom*** *of God never fails. It never expires; it never lets you down. Because I want to build your faith up!* (Never will your expectations and beliefs let you down.) *Never, never* will it let you down!

You* are to go *up (and not down). That's what I said; if there was a letdown in your life, it was probably *not* the *divine* will of the Father over your life. So he, like a good father, said NO! He was protecting you from yourself. So praise God, delay is not deny; God has something much better for you. Your Miracle is still at hand. Believe IT!

Go Dancing in the Rain!

When our forefathers wanted rain after a long drought, they would do "a rain dance." When the rain came, they celebrated the rain. They danced in the rain! Some people would probably run from the rain, but those expecting the rain enjoyed it, celebrated it, and danced in it. To others, this was foolish because they did not know what they were dancing about. They were dancing because they had brought the rain down, they praised God until their miracle physically fell from the sky, and they did not stop until it manifested itself, it hid no longer, and it showered them! Their miracle and the blessing are the same things.

You have got to keep dancing until you see it physically in your hand, on your head, and surrounding you. Dance until you see your miracle happen for you, in you, and because of you and your faith as long as you know. If I keep dancing so that the rain will come, you are all right. Don't explain it; just dance. Don't talk about it; just dance. Don't question the sky; just dance!

When your blessings start to pour, they might look like a joke to some people, "just a few drops of liquid." Your blessing may even look like bad weather to some people, but you know what you have been believing God for, so when you see it, "dance in it, and dance about it!"

Expect it, and when the raindrops come, do a crazy praise! Celebrate some more; go dancing in the Rain. Live it, enjoy it, and let everybody know you got it; you will not have to say much because they will see you dancing, dancing, dancing. Yes! In the rain!

So let's grow up and realize the ***Kingdom*** has a purpose in our lives—that is, to give you *good and perfect* "gifts." So rest, relax breath, let it go, and rejoice that the Father loves us enough to say *yes* and to say *no at his choice! And both are OK.*

Let me tell you a secret *I found out. When God says no, He's got something better.*

He, our God, and if he says no, to small things, so that he will grant us greater things!

Our King knows what is best for us in this ***Kingdom****; He is the ruler who knows how to say yes and no!*

Watch the *yesses and noes of God* in your life, trace them, and see what he had done for us!

God says *no* to an apartment He gives us a house
God says *no* to a bicycle He gives us a car
God says *no* to a pet He gives us a spouse who is allergic to pets

God is working to get our ***Kingdom*** miracle to us when we are in "maturity" to receive it; here it comes! When we have the right motives to receive it, here it comes. When we are finally ready to continue to give him praise after we receive it, here it comes! Our miracle is sometimes in front of our face, but our eyes and our understanding are not enlightened to receive it.

You see, *our King* is truly working for the ***Kingdom*** citizens. Receive your miracles and breakthroughs with expectancy knowing the ***Kingdom*** never fails. And your miracle is just at the end of your words of *faith!* Yes, He can!

Chapter 18

Raising ***Kingdom*** Kids

(with Power and Authority)

Burgundy Hair and

Purple Lipstick

Featuring Eleven Tips for Raising ***Kingdom*** Kids

To all Ministers with Children, You shall OVERCOME!
This chapter will help you to keep your sanctified mind as you do!

Apostolic protocol for ministerial children and families' ***Kingdom*** Children

I would like to address this *chapter in three phases* to help you explain the transitions of the Levites, those called and born into temple work, and life. In it all you will see *the good, the gold, and the gracious.*

It is my prayer to encourage you with my experiences and cause you to know that you are not alone and that no matter what, you are in the ***Kingdom*** and so are your children. Smile, laugh, and love as you go through.

The Good	(life)	Part one
The Gold	(opportunity)	Part two
	and	
The Gracious	("thank you")	Part Three

Kingdom Levites

Raising Levites into ***Kingdom*** Citizens

Levites are ministerial children. These Levites are children, "graced to be born to fivefold ministry officers, especially pastors, bishops, apostles, and overseeing officers."

I could write a book on "***Kingdom*** *kids,*" and maybe I will in another session. But I needed to *encourage* those of us in *active ministry concerning our children,* youth, and adults.

Many of us (ministers) *have had problems with our children as we strive to do* ***Kingdom*** *work.* Some of us do not know just how many challenges we have been shielded from. (If we know, it might make our heart skip a beat a two.) The "angels" truly have blessed us and our children, for the enemy has been after them (our Levites) from the day of birth—from the day one of breathing. They were put in the fire just by our lifestyles.

I entitled this chapter as "*Burgundy Hair and Purple Lipstick" because of life lessons.* But I will also give you tips and thoughts to help you manage and inspire, actually raise your ***Kingdom*** kids to become joyful Levites, and move into their divine destiny. The subtitle of this chapter came with a lot of laughter and a lot of tears; I named it this after my oldest daughter, so let us begin a journey.

This was when I found out my oldest daughter—we will call her *Pooh*—was not living out her ***Kingdom*** assignment (at this point) in her life.

Just a short story of a rebellious Levite's life: At the ages of thirteen to sixteen, my Pooh *had a rebellious spirit* and was determined *not to fulfill* her calling to the ministry. She terrorized the school system. She was suspended various times; she cut school, went to jail, and everything else.

This one day, I went to her school. (At this time, I was a public schoolteacher—part-time.) And I was walking down the hall, looking for my Pooh. Seeing one of her friends, I asked, "*Have you seen Pooh*?" She said, "You just passed her," pointing her finger toward the way I had just come from. "*She has the burgundy hair and the purple lipstick"* (on today).

My expression was that of shock—*"Burgundy hair and purple lipstick?"* I remember passing someone "*looking ridiculous"* like that. When I passed that girl, I thought, *Her mama should be ashamed of her looking like that, letting her out of the house.*

Not only did she have *wild hair, fake eyes and eyelashes, but also had a mini-mini shirt on and hooker's high-heeled boots. I couldn't believe this girl was my daughter.* First of all, she *didn't leave* my house *looking like* that! And where did she get those clothes?

What was going on? *I ran up to this girl, screaming her name, and grabbing her arm at the same time. Yes, I do believe in "spare the rod spoil the child," so I did grab her. Why?* (See, I was mad, betrayed, embarrassed, and hurt.) "How could she do this to our image?" And the lies! Oh, the lies! *Lying about who she was to me!*

I was flaming mad! And I was out of control; she was taking my godly authority and control. She is supposed to do what I teach her; she is a ***Kingdom*** kid. Where is this leading to and why is she not just enjoying having a mother for a minister? And in fact, I was a teacher too. So what in the world was she doing, disrespecting what "we" stood for?

Upon making eye contact with me, *she knew the "wrath of God"* was at hand! As these issues would develop, we tried everything—punishment, whipping, crying, praying, reading the Word, putting her in charge, sending her to her dad—everything.

After a very negative situation, I felt it best to try something extremely different. You see, we (I) had run out of other options, so I said, "Maybe a change of environment will be better for this child. Only ten months of school to graduate, maybe we can get it done in a new location." *So I sent her to her dad's house.* What happened? She ran away from there! I was so shocked when she ran away from her dad's home after one month. She decided to go back to Columbia, but not to live with me; she was angry and thought I was supposed to allow her to do what she wanted to do *in my home* and just "take it."

Of course, in her mind *it was my entire fault,* so she said (at that time), "*But I used my **Kingdom** authority.*" I didn't buy, take, or sell her crap for one second.

This was my firstborn child, *my Pooh,* blessed and prophesied over to be a preacher and a prophetess, though I still wanted her to do well. *I could not let her wreck her younger siblings with her current stage of rebellion and defiance.* So she returned to Columbia and went to live with a cousin, the one she always wanted to be with, the one I wanted to steer her away from so much—*you guessed it, one who was not living a **Kingdom** lifestyle.* When I found her, however, I went into "mother mode"; I put her back in school. One week later, she got out of school, again. I went again and got her from the house she was in; she ran away again. She had been drinking and smoking "something." And she just ran off in the dark. Yes, I went after her. She was only sixteen and wild. I tried to get her to get back in the car, but they ran off into the woods.

At this point I said, "*This is crazy*. I am not going to let this little girl torment *me*!" So *I left her to work on her testimony*! Sometimes, moms and dads of the faith, you just have to let them go and work on their testimonies! *Stop interfering and trust God to keep them safe and work it out.*

See, everyone outside the church had told her *what fun she was missing* always being in church.

They (jealous family members) made their lives of sin look fun and great! Everyone was doing better than we (so they made her think). Even though we lived very well, in her mind she was not having fun!

It turned out the very thing I tried to keep away, she was running to—drugs, drinking, smoking, and all manners of evil. I thought, *This child has lost her mind*. To make it worse, my baby child (my son) was trying to follow her footsteps, picking up these bad habits of his "hero"—his older sister. At this point, my middle child was the only one to seem to have any godly sense.

No one that spoke to my child during these times of trying to make my standards of serving God look bad, they did not tell her (my dear child); the truth, however, was *that the wages of SIN is death and that they were introducing her to a life of death*. Can you see that Satan made her current life look bad and his life look exciting but it was a trick?

This is the same trick he is telling your children, so don't be moved; be firm with the Word of God and expose the tricks of the devil.

I spoke to other pastors and leaders at this time, and it seemed everyone's children were drinking the "same water." We were all under the same attack—some of their children as having to be put away by choice or by law for bad behavior. *This burgundy hair and purple lipstick (and green eye contacts)—the spirit of rebellion was working overtime!*

But I then woke up one day and *God* himself spoke to me and said, "*She is working on her testimony*." Yes, we all develop on testimony; even *born* (**<u>Kingdom</u>** kids) *Levites* must be allowed to work on their own true salvation. Just because they were born into the ***<u>Kingdom</u>*** does not mean that the ***<u>Kingdom</u>*** of God has been born in them.

Your *Levites* will come through and become great ***<u>Kingdom</u>*** citizens, despite people praying against them. Yes, some people are praying for our children's fall; they have a mandate to come against our children.

*Today Pooh is healthy in the **Kingdom**!*

Today, Pooh is a college graduate and teaches in school. She is wonderfully saved; she is a wonderful wife and a lovely mother.

She's a *granddaddy's/grandmother's* "girl" because my parents bailed her out (literally) of everything she got into.

How Pooh's story is a blessing, even today

I, while preaching and praying for others, *did not know how to reach her*; but God did. So my job was to pray and ask God to keep her, guide her, and bring her home (into the ***Kingdom***); and he did, however, while I was doing what he called me and told me to do: his will in the ***Kingdom***. Not to sit home and cry or run my blood pressure up, but to believe in the god I said could conquer all. After I had done, all I believed I could do, I just had to live out the Word of God for me and stand on his promises without wavering or doubting.

I quoted the promises of God to my children while they slept. *I anointed them while they were awake. I prayed with them, I kept them from the world* (at least in my home, so I thought). Yet *I felt they did not get it.* What was wrong with these people (my kids)?

I questioned God so many days, should I quit my ministry? Will that help my children?

Should I stop preaching and teaching others? And God would speak to me and say, "*Not so! What does this have to do with preaching the Gospel? Do not let the devil make you quit." He is trying to get you to quit and will use any reason he can to do it!* This is when I learned one of the tricks of the devil: that *he will use any means necessary to make you quit!*

Through these prayers and tears, I learned to rest in Him. I learned to rest in our God!

Who is this Living in my house?

While your children are *not acting* like what you preach to others about or seen not to be all that ***Kingdom*** children "Levites" should be, keep doing what God has called you to do; they are just working on their testimony.

Other ministers look at you as if you are crazy and look down their nose at you and would say, "*How can you be this if your children are that?*" And God kept comforting me.

One night, my daughter had an experience that landed herself in trouble. (I was on the third day of a powerful revival and had two more days to go.) I decided to finish my ***Kingdom*** assignment. (Yes! I went to preach.) In the midst of tribulation, I went to praise my god. I found my peace only in the service of His love.

(The Good)

My sermon that night was "*Peekaboo—God Sees You.*" I talked about seeming to be one person for other people while truly *not* getting it, "the ***Kingdom*** of God, true salvation, and true praise inside you." I talked about fronting for your parents, church, and leaders. I talked about playing church and not receiving Christ as *Lord*! I talked directly to the youth and the adults! I talked to the preacher and the leaders. *I talked to change somebody, and God did it. Yes, the power of preaching will change somebody!*

During the service, I stopped and gave *my daughter's testimony* (what had happened that day), how I was hurt, but I still had a job to do. I had a revival to preach and crusade to run and people to minister to. Yes, in the midst of my pain, I had to minister to others.

I needed and wanted to be real and to tell them how God wanted them to be real and *receive the good of life*, not the life of death that Satan was handing out. I told them the truth, "Seek God and his ways and not seek after the bad."

Then as I opened my heart, I gave and received an altar call. I told my daughter's testimony and the events of that day: I talked about my pain and struggles, even to come out that night, how I was criticized by my parents for going to preach that night, and some other making remarks to me (negatively) who did not understand my commitment to the ministry. I talked about my personal struggle in raising a Levite and how parents who really love their children but are consistent with disciple often get the raw end of the stick! I talked, I cried, I danced, and then I gave an altar call!

Seventeen *young people went to the altar because they were living a life of hiding and playing before God and their parents. (Three confessed being pregnant; four confessed to doing drugs, cutting school, and other things their parents did not know.)*

After confessions, ***twelve*** *of them gave their lives to Christ. This was followed by additional confessions and a time of healing.*

From the adults, ***twenty-one*** *went forward to confess they were not living true Christian lives; of those,* ***nine*** *adults followed suit to salvation. The*

pastor repented *to the church and said he could live a much better life. At that time, his wife fell out in the spirit, right from the pew.*

A true **release happened at this church.** *All because of Pooh's testimony. The next night, the church was in overflow, and God moved mightily again.*

What a sermon! My daughter was in *denial of* ***Kingdom*** *heritage.* And here I was bringing others to Christ on her story! It was after this night that I really saw God was in control. *I had to "rest" in Christ.* Relax and trust him to save my children. I had to go through and die to some things just so others can live! I found and rested in my purpose to the ***Kingdom***. See, others were going through and hiding their testimonies, but God knew he could trust me to help others and to tell them "Yes, you can make it!"

They are working on their testimony!

Yes, I have had conversations about my children with God, prior to and after this night; I would say often, "*God, you called me, why would you not save my children?*" Or "*God I need my children saved and protected while I am out here praying for others who are praying for my children to be saved.*" God himself spoke to me and brought my heart comfort many days and nights. He said to me, "*I have already saved your children. Where is your faith, your* **Kingdom** *language? Just say what I say and watch me work.*"

"*But what do I say to people?*" I would ask the Father. His response, "*Just say they are just working on their testimony.*" *The Father told me to rest, do not try to work it out, and to "let them work on their testimony" and watch them become* **Kingdom** *warriors.*

Now Pooh loves the Lord. She always did; she was just working on her testimony! I laugh when I hear her talk about *going to choir practice and taking her children to choir practice.* "*Ms. Trill-Ville*" is a school teacher! (Yes, the one who wrecked the school is now teaching in the school.) God can do it! *Praise God! See, the Lord will bring you out!*

He never fails! **Kingdom** *kids become* **Kingdom** *citizens; true "Levites" they come into their own grace and glory. When they do, God gets the praise, and God gets the glory.*

They will get it right; just wait and see!

Keep the faith, keep your language right, and watch God do the rest for you as you continue to work in the **Kingdom***. Your Levites will realize their heritage and go back to the* **Kingdom** *to serve the King! I spoke to* *her (Pooh's) pastor recently, Pastor Johnnie White of* ***Kingdom*** *Vision in Columbia, South Carolina, when I was there in Columbia for revival. I asked, "How is my daughter really doing in the ministry"; He said (with his big Kool-Aid smile), to me, "She is faithful, a hard worker at everything, never misses, she is a joy to the ministry, and she got it right in her. You put it in her right, and yes, she got it right deep in her!" I could only shake my head and say, "Praise God, her testimony is prevailing!"*

"She got it right in her" is an old saying meaning that she is "saved real good, the message of the Gospel is in her heart, and that the person is on the wall for Jesus." That's what every mother of the Gospel wants to hear about their seed—they got it right in them.

I have no doubt that Pooh will be one of the greatest gifts to the ***Kingdom****, a preacher and a prophetess, as God has already promised, very soon. Why? Because she got it right in her! That's the faithfulness of God to His servants. He will make sure our seeds, the Levites, get it right and do it right.*

Eleven Thoughts and Tips to

Raising and Nurturing Young Children in the ***Kingdom***

From the pulpit to the pew
Young children and the ***Kingdom***

Thought # 1
Where and when you are born do determine if you are a *born citizen.* When you are a minister, your children are *born "Levites."* That's a fact. Still they have to "choose to operate" as ***Kingdom*** citizens.

Thought # 2
Someone could have been born to the tribe of Levi; however, they can also *choose* to leave the tabernacle and go out to live with the tribe of Reuben. They can cast away their heritage as Levites. However, that's where they are born.

Thought # 3
Young Levite children do not have a choice of church, religion, or to be members. My children are the seeds of Greater Harvest Christian Center Churches Worldwide—*Levites*! Period! No matter where they are now, they can still return to reign at GHCC in any of the churches as God develops and calls them into full-time ministry. And when they come home, I/we will kill the fatted calf and put a robe on them and a ring on their finger. That's just the way it is. *Members have to understand this.* "God put his hand on them in the womb." He made us a promise, and we are expecting them to fulfill it with the help of the promise giver; we expect them to rise above, to do better, and be the leaders they are developed from birth to be.

Thought # 4
These Levites are taught young. They are poured unto and trained to rule and reign; they are trained early by observation, participation, and experience.

They are praise leaders, technicians, choir directors, media ministry persons, drummers, administrators, church assistants, pastor's armor bearers, setup persons, greeters, ushers, security guards, financial administrators, clerks, secretaries, and pastor liaisons. Yes, they do it all from a very young age; they learn how to operate in the ***Kingdom***.

Thought # 5
They don't miss church. They are never paid and are seldom thanked, but they remain. Young children begin to hear church drama, see tears often, and feel our pain. We must train our children how to maintain in service; let them be children at home and always remind them that they have a heritage that can never be stolen, lost, or denied. Teach them not to sell their heritage.

Parental Protocol

When we are raising Levites, they are cute and cuddly; they go from arm to arm and hand to hand. They are allowed special access, but this cuteness will wear off, and your children will become a nuisance if you do not discipline them early. Do not let your children do things you do not or have not allowed in other children, Do not let your grandchildren do things you did not, or have not, allowed in other children. Do not discipline other children if your children have free reign over the house. If your children go up the pulpit and play with the microphones, do not say anything to the other children if they follow suit. You get the point. Set order for everyone, and make your children respect the same order.

Thought # 6
Train your kids first! They are cute and funny; however, they cannot be allowed to run over the church, and the members of the church should not be subject to their foolishness. They should not be allowed to have behaviors that are not acceptable with or among the entire church family. People do not like undisciplined children even if they are Levites; the behavior that is cute will become despised. Have control of your children early.

Tip # 7
Young children *should be sat with nannies, armor bearers, or trusted assistants; remember, in the pulpit, you are on assignment, not babysitting duties.*

Do not allow your young children in the pulpit for any reason. If you must attend to them, leave the pulpit; it's all right, but do not allow your children to sit on the pulpit. It is a distraction to the Word of God that is being put forth.

I remember once this young couple went to preach for us; they had *three young children. Two boys ran back and forth around the church and across the pulpit.* The baby cried one-third of the service; *the mother found no need to correct the boys or remove the crying baby***.** By the way, they forced themselves in the front row (because her husband was preaching) even when being asked to take the second row with the children and the baby.

This seating was a disaster; the boys ran back and forth across the pulpit area, and they thought this was "*cute.*" This was a major distraction to the service and put distaste for their ministry in my mind.

Her seating also caused other visiting guest pastors to be *displaced* to another row because they took up seven spaces, with the baby, the bag, the seat, the other three boys, and her personal belongings. Even when we were a small ministry, I always required excellence, so this drove me crazy that she would be so rude and ignorant. I did not want to sit any other pastors or leader beside her because her children were out of order.

Tip # 8

Let me pause to say two things, well, three things, OK

1) **S*it* where *you* are asked to sit**. Please place young children on another row—*no offense, but not the first row. If you have to leave, you become a distraction, or the children will become a distraction as they squirm and wiggle.*

2) Your children are "cute to you"—*not* to everyone else; please *control your children (especially when you visit away)***,** even if you do not control them in your sanctuary. (By the way, when we visited them, the people with the three children, they is their local assembly were as well out of control.)

   Later, we tried to mentor them (because they were a young couple, we thought we could help them with this issue). *The wife "had problems with our ministry style."*

   You see, when they visited the second time, we made sure the house was in "order." She did not like this. *I saw it was no need to take this association farther, so we just let them pass us by.*

After raising seven children, I know how parental protocol should happen; but if they did not appreciate this wisdom, so be it. I will keep it for the next young couple who will.

By the way, the wife was so out of order that during altar ministry time, she was *ordering and instructing our staff to go on the pulpit, take our set water, and give some lady in the audience just because she wanted to have a drink*. You see, when you are out of order, you are out of order. When you do not rule your house well, how can you run the church well? We must make sure that we have our house in *order*!

3) If your children are energetic (overactive), *don't give them sugar before church.* Honor other people and their ministry; honor their altars and altar space, no matter how small it is; and honor the area of selected pulpit space.

   This area may be flat on the floor, but common sense should kick in and let you know it is the pulpit area and sacred to God. It may or may not be a cornered-off area or a small space or a high tower with nineteen steps and gold chairs—have the same respect. Don't let your children *help themselves to the pulpit space, the pastors' office space or any stuff on the pulpit; and please do not allow them to make church a playground.*

   People will respect your message better when they see your family in order. And please tell your wife (or mother of the children) *not to roll her eyes* or to get angry when people ask her to control the children or ask the children to behave. Your message will not be received fairly if your family is out of order.

Tip # 9

Please do not go to church *feeding* your children cookies and sugary drinks in the pews and seats. I once had a lady (a pastor's wife) go to church with food (a burger and drink). She was actually going to feed them, her children, on the front row of the church. I stopped her and *asked her to please go to the rear and sit at the tables to feed her children.* She was offended (go figure, but she was); however, this offense could have been eliminated if she was operating in respect and order and common sense! Children are children; they will make a mess. Yes, even the cute ones, they may make a bigger mess.

Church and worship service are not the time for food and drinks. If It is not in a bottle, they can wait until after church. All of us can wait two hours to eat. If you know your children cannot wait, then feed them in your car on the way to church a little snack, and let us not take for granted distasteful mannerisms concerning food. Anyway, this is foolishness. We should not have to pamper bad behavior, especially spawned by the adults. Let me be frank; this should not happen, since this is not *the Pizza Hut* or an eating event. But if they do, for some odd reason, just have to eat a small something, you should quietly take them outside, and then even there, clean it up.

I cannot tell you how many church furniture, carpet, and temple items are ruined by parents who have to protocol and allow their children to mess up God's house. They allow them to write in the Bible, tear up the envelopes, and poke holes in the chairs. This is wrong! On top of this, they *never* ask the pastor "*Can I pay for this?*"

We once had a light-colored carpet in our church (never do this); it was given to us as a blessing. I spend, however, hours scrubbing after services the red stuff off the carpet so many times. If you are going to give your little one something to drink, it should be clear, not red! And for God's sake, do not allow them to walk in it and make a track with it all over the place. Respect God's house better than your own! Please.

Tip #10

4) If you change your child's diaper, bring an extra bag and tie it up, and take it outside to the trash can. Do not leave it in the bathroom (just like you would hopefully take it out at home). Please show the church the same respect. Do not just put the stinky diapers in the trash for someone else to have to deal with.

Tip # 11

Again this is God's house; train your children to respect it. Go to the restroom with them and do not allow them to waste God's products or overuse them as trash. Do not send your children *to empty bathrooms alone;* protect them at all times and know where they are and what they are doing.

Teens in the Temple

Watch and pray, pray and watch, and then communicate: Communication at this stage communicates a lot; let them be angry and sometimes let them miss a "Sunday service to visit other services." Don't put them in church prison. I *learned* this is a *must*!

DON'T LET ANYTHING DISTRACT YOU FROM YOUR ASSIGNMENT NOT EVEN YOUR CHILDREN!

I missed a "lot of good, healthy, needy communication." *I thought we talked a lot*; however, my children did not think so. (So they tell me today.) *I felt we did a lot, but my children did not feel so. They were angry and hating ministry, but because it was fun for me, I thought it was fun for them. I guess I was in my **Kingdom** zone, trying to do what I thought and still think was BEST for them as to grow up in a safe and healthy environment, serving God and serving others.*

Many nights we had church when the school had an event. Where did we go? To church, *automatically!* Now I see, maybe we could have missed one church event for school activities. (*My bad)* I didn't know. I thought this was the only way "I was being sold out to God and establishing faithfulness in them." That's all I knew—was it right or wrong? *Maybe both*; did it draw my children closer to Christ? *Maybe yes, maybe no!* I do not have *the* "*stamped*" *answer. However, may I suggest to you to always remember to have a balance*; children and teens should not *hate* church!

So whatever we have to do as a minister to *better your children and eliminate rejection* to their ***Kingdom*** assignment, we must do it. I love my children (like you do). I want to give them the best of *everything.*

I wish I had a mentor who would have told me to "miss a night of church and go with them to a basketball game" at least one time a year that this was all right and *would not close down the ministry—it will survive! So I take this time to tell you what others did not share with me. Don't get distracted, but give a little bit more to family time that does NOT include the church family. Then next week, get right back on with **Kingdom** work.*

I have learned, even personally, we must have balance; *I have learned to balance now. I even take monthly vacations and refreshment times with God and my husband.* I sometimes cancel standard evening services as led by the Holy Spirit; I also encourage family times. I tell my staff to see, "really see," what their teens are doing. *Let's not blame the teens for everything.*

Don't let them escape accountability and bad choices, but let's build a foundation they will fight to stand on, not wait to jump off.

When I was rearing and raising children, I only knew one reaction then; that was to *"pray, speak to them, yell, cry, pray, discipline them, punish them, and start it all over."* No spiritual mentor told me to *listen, to them, play with them, and miss church once in a while for a football game. Especially as the pastor, if I missed, who was going to be there? Now I know to cancel service and live life with your Levites.*

I learned a lot; in hindsight, I learned even more, so that's why I am sharing this with you. I have now learned how to finally rest knowing and trusting my King will deliver all His children, even mine!

This is what I constantly said about my last child, "*He is truly working on his testimony!*" My firstborn son, Emmanuel, my child, did what only a Levite son would do to test my faith! Yes, *E-man* could do some "wild thing." *He just wanted to be "grown," no matter who it hurt; he had a problem with authority.*

Unlike Pooh, who rarely gave us challenges at home, this baby boy (after he turned twelve) was a tyrant everywhere—school, home, church, EVERYWHERE!

After the age of twelve, WOW! Did he bring it on. Ages thirteen, fourteen, and fifteen were crazy and rough times at our home, school, church, everywhere! If E-man did not want to do it, he did not do it! Period! And the fight was on.

YOU WILL SURVIVE, AND THEY WILL TOO!

At school, home, church, and wherever he went, E-man decided he did not have to listen to anyone. One Sunday, *I was in the pulpit, and the police went to church. My young man decided to call the police,* because he didn't like me "telling him what to wear." Of course, the police had "a fit" telling him he should be ashamed of his behavior. This carried on for three years: the blowing up, getting suspended, the wide actions that came out of nowhere. My son actually told us he wanted to be in a "gang." Satan had his mind twisted; he thought this would make him somebody big. He did not understand that he was already somebody big.

So we began a "cycle" with him: school, suspended, out of school, homeschool, back to school, to private school, suspended, to court for something he did at school or home, back to homeschool, suspended again and again, to DJJ, and the rest is history. It went on and on. Finally he began to be really disrespectful at home, which led to the big stopping point of torment.

It has to stop somewhere!

Soon after, there was a "big blow-up" at our home; we asked for our son to be removed at the age of fifteen years of age from our home because of his anger management problems, and he just did not think anyone should, or could, tell him what to do. It had gotten out of hand and out of the spirit, even coming to blows several times—yes, fistfights broke out in the sanctified home of the priest. For safety reasons of us all, my son was put into a foster home (several), group homes, and youth camps. Because the problem of rebellion was in him, it showed up everywhere he went; it was something he *would not let go* (afraid to be used by God, "He knows he has a ministry calling" in his personal life). He made *everyone's life* a "*head-shaking* experience" while working on his testimony, and he still is working on it at this present time.

What happened to your salvation?

One day, another pastor asked him, *"Son, what happened to your salvation?"* Being the comedian he is, he said, *"It rolled down the street, didn't you see it? It rolled right by you!"* He was always so cute, and everyone just laughed at this boy! Yes, he knew how to wrap people around his little finger; and boy, did it work, for about two weeks anyway! He could fool the best for about a month, then the real little boy would show up as a bear!

I was so embarrassed. *"How can you say this?"* I told him when he got back to his seat. Boy, you're supposed to say, *"I'm still saved! Thank you, Mr. Preacher."*

That would make me look good, and that's really what I wanted him to say; however, E-man was saying out loud what he was seeing other people living. He was saying many people are living a life that their "salvation had rolled down the street"!

Now he is a maturing young man who is coming into his position in the ***Kingdom***, thank God; but we had to learn to rest in God, and so will you. He is still working on his testimony, and we have not seen the final glory as yet, but we will. I can only advise you to keep hanging in there; it will come to pass. The glory in their lives will be exposed, and the ***Kingdom*** will benefit from their experiences and their growth! Every promise God gave you about your children will come to pass.

Stay with God, and he will keep you in Perfect peace

We, however, we are *not* the only *ministers* feeling the pressure developing ***Kingdom*** citizens and smiling and preaching through the pain (of the Levites).

> They did leave here looking like that! . . .
> Still working on their testimony

Let's see. I just don't want to give you only information all about my children; otherwise, you will think that no one else has ever "jumped" this parenting hurdle, so I will share some other victory stories with you to encourage your walk in Christ. These were *all personal stories told to me during counseling sessions.*

Fellow pastors, please know that your children are *not* the "*worst children in the world.*" Our children ***are just magnified*** *with every step they take and make or do not make.* Keep your faith up, and see the victory. They cannot get to heaven on your testimony; they will have to develop their own walk with Christ, so let them walk!

Other Testimonies of Levites, working on their testimonies!

—The "*pastor's*" child who went to a church and stole the camcorder from the media room denied it for two weeks and finally brought it back.

—The "*elder's*" son who, at age fourteen, had five different girls pregnant in the church ages twelve to twenty-one and threatened the girls he would kill them if they told because he knew where they lived. The twenty-one-year-old finally told when the twelve-year-old got pregnant.

—The *minister's daughter* arrested for prostitution.

—The *minister's* sixteen-year-old who cursed out the teachers at school and threw a chair at the administrator was expelled!

—The *bishop's son* who got killed while buying and selling drugs: He was caught, and while being arrested, there was a struggle for the gun. He killed the officer during the process, and the other officer shot him.
—International pastor whose daughter was pregnant by the (married) associate pastor.

They are all Productive Levites Now!

—Many, many, many suspensions and expulsion stories. Too many to tell.
—The *pastor's* daughter getting caught having sex outside school!
—The *bishop's son* and daughter growing "pot" in the flowerpots in the kitchen, telling Mom that they were for her, taking one to school and getting busted, causing the police to go to their house and charge the *bishop* (being unaware of the content) for growing marijuana.
—The *preacher's* son taken to foster care on a false report.
—The *preacher* arrested on a false report by his own daughter.
—The *preacher's children* who set the house on fire!
—The *preacher's three children* stealing cars and going joyriding with three other ministers' children every Thursday night for over one year (stealing and damaging thirty-nine cars).

And you thought all we had to do was to preach.
We need you to pray for our children and us as we are praying for you and your children. Stop talking about our children and their trials, and pray for us!
We pastors and leaders, as well as our CHILDREN, need to be prayed for by you.

As you can see, "Levites" have problems too. Our children are not perfect; they can give the leadership stress, even though the leaders are their parents, until they as well decide to become ***Kingdom*** citizens.

I want to say to you (parents) *not to take it personally.* I used to ask my children, "*Why do you despise me so much?* Why do you hate God so much? Why do you not want to live a good ***Kingdom*** lifestyle?" I would say, "I'm not an addict, druggie, alcoholic, *thank God!* However, you are acting like your parents beat you and treat you like 'gangbangers.'"

I use to say to them, "God has better for you! Receive it and live." Please know that this day will come and you will see your children bring glory to you and God. Just keep praying and believing, and let God draw them, and they will be drawn forever. The enemy is after our children; do not forget to pray for your children!

Why are they (our children) so angry with us? Well, this world makes it look like *we are the ones with problems, especially to our children.* They make them feel out of place if they're not doing foolish stuff. Our children have to be taught that they are jealous people in this world that do not want them to succeed; they (ungodly people) want what they (Levites) have—they want their inheritance. Keep your children away from contamination, no matter how difficult it may seem; you do your part to keep them pure.

In these stages, please know that you must know where these *Levites* are, even in church. There were many days I looked up and saw that "all of a sudden," my children were not in church, especially my Emmanuel!

Where were they? Doing something they were not supposed to be doing and probably encouraging others to follow them to do it!

One day, I overheard a lot of cursing outside. I sent the elders to see what was going on. Well, there was a problem, and who were involved? *All the preachers' children*! Yes, out on the temple grounds, cursing like sailors.

Our Children Can Get out of Order Fast!

Why? One of the boys in the church, a teenager who was also a shepherd pastor's son (in-house minister's son) *had stolen a camera* from out of the media room and took it home. It was missing for two weeks, and God gave me a message for the people after the message from the pulpit that was titled "*Getting the Accursed Thing out of Your House*" and how not to let your children *"bring on a curse in your house" while you stick your head in the sand.*

It was so funny how just after that message, the production camera was returned. *We did not know who had taken the camera until it was returned.* I was shocked at how the camera really did get taken, so we had to change some church rules for the sake of the ***Kingdom***! Until then we had an open-door policy. (Wow, how things can make you change!)

The Sunday of The Cursing Levites

One Sunday, I looked up from the altar and saw some of the teens missing—so these "boys" and girls had gone outside *during church. While we parents were dancing and shouting, a group had left and gone outside* (about nine to eleven of them).

Outside, the boys were trying to impress the girls (of course). Well, somebody was "shinning" on somebody else, and somebody said, "*Who would want a thief, especially somebody who would take from the church?*" And everybody laughed, including my son, who laughed really hard. When he laughs, he always laughs really hard, but I guess he went overboard!

At this time, the offender began to curse, and of course, my son was the *"chief curser" of them all,* threatening to cut his throat and a lot of other violent things. This is how my son is. You better bring it if you bring it. He didn't steal it; his parents are like that! We are just like that for God now; the ***Kingdom*** will take what you are made of your character and use it for ***Kingdom*** increase. That how I preach; I bring it and I don't play church. E-man has not quite brought this gift and talent into the ***Kingdom*** to be refined at that time. So with these hot-tempered teens, nobody wanted to back down, and their "action was on"! His sister got involved, and my children and others got involved, and they were all at it with this out-of-control teen group. The point is, *how did these children get by every adult and go into a warpath outside the church right on site?*

Another Church Policy is in the making!

This brought on a "new church policy." No one goes anywhere without a parent!

See, rules in a ministry come into play because of actions that were taken. They might have been taken before you arrived at the church, *so don't fight the rules*; they are in play for you and your families' well-being. Don't think these rules are crazy or too much. There is a reason; that will help us all if we can just obey the rules.

We have a saying in our church:

Sheep: "Swallow and follow"
Mules: "Fool and rule"
Wolves: "Holler and collar"
Goats: "Buck and duck"

Where are you in the chain? Can you swallow and follow? *Or are you bucking and ducking the order of the house?*

Do not stick your head in the sand; *know that your children are leaders, and they will lead early.* And people will follow them! At three years old, my E-man would tell the adult ushers to do something, and they would do it; when I asked them why, they would say "he" told them to do it. WOW! What leadership. This is why the enemy wants them, our children, out of the ***Kingdom***. Because they are born to lead.

The question often asked by leaders of the ***Kingdom*** to their children and their actions can be answered in a simple way—*it's not about you. It's about their testimony!*

The "Warfare" Is On!

The "golden" are those who are becoming truly grateful for the golden opportunity to parent!

Why do you despise me, God, so much? Is it really being despised, or is it my golden opportunity to help develop a Levite for ***Kingdom*** use? We must come to know the difference so we can learn to "rejoice instead of complain."

The golden years will teach you to be grateful somebody's story is always worse than yours. Getting to *the golden moment may take years in your mind and spirit and heart. But remember it is not about you, your image, or how you think you should look to other people.* When I found out *it was warfare* to kill the Levites, not against me, but against God to take our children out of their inheritance by *trying to put them to shame,* I went on the warpath to let the enemy know the warfare is on! You will never defeat a true Levite because God says no! Everything they go through will be for ***Kingdom*** glory!

The enemy thinks if he can bring this "shame," to them, they will never be able to serve God. That this *past life of mistakes and rebellion and a lack of hope* will keep them *quiet,* away from being a ***Kingdom*** *"declarer" of the Word*!

He wants to shut their mouths; he wants to silence them forever. But he devil is a liar, and using the mouth of the unbelievers to do it (tell the lies).

But we must *"loose"* their mouths by letting them know that "they are just working on their testimony!" Let them know God still can use them no matter what! Let them know God is still in control, and whatever they are going through is for them to go to their destiny in the ***Kingdom***. *Keep the hope alive in them*! Minister to your Levite; speak into their spirit often! "*Tell them you love them and remind them their Father, the King, loves them, that they were designed with purpose, and that they are a royal priesthood and a chosen generation, that they shall wear the rubies of life and inherit the promises of the* ***Kingdom***. *In the midst of their mess, tell them who they really are. Tell them they are only fit for the master's use." Then trust God, believe his promises, and stand on his Word!*

There are two types of Levites: those whether by "birth or by being dedicated by the parents." See, Hannah, in the Bible, this is an example of one who created her child to be a Levite; she created a Levite by dedication.

Some people or children are born Levites by their parental heritage (their parents are ministers), some embrace their heritage (love it and embrace it with joy), and others sell their birthrights (they hate it and cannot wait to grow up and go into other lifestyles and employments).

Some people, because of their love of the temple and ***Kingdom*** work, choose to be Levites by the call of God in their lives.

NO matter what, or how, they have become Levites, it is the job of the body of Christ to keep them in the ***Kingdom***, to do the service of the Father. We must encourage them to go back to their rightful place in the ***Kingdom***. We must let them know there is a robe and a ring waiting for them, and we must stand firm with others to make them accepted when they return home.

If They Can Lose Their Testimony Forever, the Enemy Will Be Happy!

I have found raising "*Levites*" can be a challenge and a blessing. *I also recognize that these are God's chosen ones. They have to earn their testimonies just like we did!* Let's really be transparent. Have they, do they, did they do any worse than *you did?*

I can see all my children in me and me in *all* my children—different pattern but same point. However, I know this! I know this; *just like God saved me, He will save them* and fully mature them into ***Kingdom*** dominion. That is my rest and my peace.

I instilled in them a love of God, and now they will not depart. Call your "*Levites*" back for ***Kingdom*** work. God will honor your request because you have a right as a citizen for your children to obtain their ***Kingdom*** inheritance.

The teen years may be hard, like myself; *you may have to express tough love,* but let them know you love them. Don't take down on moral or respect issues. Stand in love and *watch* God.

Who am *I talking to*? Anybody *here* (in your life right now)? SAY AMEN!

As a parent, if you are holding your head up, *keep saying what you stand for*; hold up the banner(s) of God. Keep the faith and live! Be the best parent you can be and watch God do the rest!

Adults Levites

When you have raised them for the ***Kingdom***,
Let Go, and Let God

Adult Levites

There was a song playing (on the radio) one day, after a visit with some people who were having "torment" *from her adult children*: it was so simple, yet so powerful!

It said simply, *"Let go and let God!"* This is a Word from God, a divine Word when it comes to our adult ***Kingdom*** children. Let go, and please let God!

We Must Allow Our Children to Grow up and Be Matured by the Spirit of Christ

We must breathe and let God have the victory in their lives.

There are additional issues that come with adult children, especially those who still have not gotten it or gone the other way. *My middle child*—let's call her *Ms. Dream Girl.*

This is the one who gave me no problems as a child or teen, a beautiful young woman, saved easily and greatly talented, working on being anointed because she was grounded. So we thought.

We gave her her first house as a graduation present, knowing she wanted to move. *One year later,* she lost the house because of "bad choice." She wanted to participate in a "play" as a "*dream girl*" (in which she did a fine job); however, she did not think it important to pay her living expenses. Oh, let's say it—her wanting to be a "dream girl" took front and center! (For real, she played a major part in a stage production and did very well.) But she forgot to pay the rent!

I trusted that she *had I, together, she had never given us any doubt or problems; she was a dream child! Normally, the middle child is the problem, but not Alaina. She had worked by my side, never left, never complained (well, not to me, anyway.* I believed that the ***Kingdom*** was in her heart, mind, and soul). *So we let her go, thinking, she has never caused us many problems, has been a joy to raise, and is in ministry. So we gave her a rope of freedom.*

You see, she was the one who stayed with me when everyone was going off the "cuckoo's nest." I thought she was ready to handle some ministry for me and the ***Kingdom***; I just knew it was her to take over the church and the work I had established.

As I slowly took on the office of the apostle, left the city, and began to travel to start a new work (as I went to establish other churches and had less of a local presence), knowing that my church was settled with my daughter at the helm of things.

To my surprise, however, *she was not rooted and as grounded as I thought.* Because of this, *she quickly "dropped" out of church, started failing in school, had half of a job, started singing in the club, and running halfway wild; and you guessed it: she was soon pregnant.* She now was working on her testimony; she had waited to be an adult to start forgetting what she had be taught and trained.

This "prayed-over child" had done *everything opposite* that I expected her to do, but I have to realize, *she is an adult!* I have to allow her as well to *make her own decisions, however difficult for me,* and to rest again in the promise for all my children.

Alaina is a gifted poet since the age of seven, a published author, and a noted singer. I am proud of her accomplishments, and I can't wait to see the end of her story, for I know the call upon her life. By the way, her baby's father is a Levite (*an undisciplined Levite), a preacher's (bishop's) kid as well.*

The sad news is this is not his first child, nor does he have *any apostolic protocol* from his parents who are also his leaders.

Did we try to tell our daughter this was *not the right choice for a relationship*? Of course. However, she must establish her own testimony. I will continue to pray for them as they continue to grow in the ***Kingdom*** of God into their ***Kingdom*** destiny.

There will be a lot of bumps for her *as a single parent* that I would have chosen for her not to have. Especially at this time in her life, her career has been delayed, but not denied.

A lot of people acted like the world would end, they she found out that she was pregnant. Even the father's mother, a self-proclaimed bishop, started withdrawing from her. Yes, believe that once she called her weekly to check on her; now she stopped called at all. People, especially other pastors, they were "so disappointed." My thought was "why are you so disappointed? *Did you ever call her to encourage her while she was not pregnant?* Did you ever sow anything good into her life? Then why the sudden "false concern"? Why the condemnation?"

They (these leaders of concern) have even told me to tell her "*how disappointed*" they are in her. I will NOT even entertain this spirit because your disappointment is a "lack of faith," and now she needs strength more than ever! Most of all, she needs prayers of support to be a great mom!

However, saying all this, *her ministry has now taken a new life and destiny, and she will be able to minister to others in the spirit of grace, letting them know that her life is still in God. No weapon formed against her will prosper. She is a Levite! I believe God!*

And she is an adult; I cannot live her life. *I must live my life and help her when I can; I can only assist her. I know how to let go and let God do it!*

I had to learn to praise in spite of spiritual disappointment, *"Burgundy Hair and Purple Lipstick."* I had to learn to hold my head up high. *I had to learn to live my purpose, not through my children,* but through my own ***Kingdom*** destiny.

I love my children; like every other parent, *I want the best for my children.* I pray for my children; I praise my children, and I have learned to not expect any more from them and any other Levites.

They will make mistakes, but *they will go back to the position* God has given to them by birthrights.

Outside Influence of **"Family Members" not in *Kingdom* Destiny**

Even when my *family* wanted to be *against* my decisions, I had to *keep God's promises* and my ***Kingdom*** destiny in front of me. *And you will have to do the same thing*; their opinions are great, but you cannot allow them to break you down. Yes, they will come with *strong thoughts* of you and your children; they cannot be given the *mental authority to break down your* ***Kingdom*** *assignment and what God has told you to do.* Don't let them make you feel bad about serving God, having standards, and holding on to God's promises.

I realized I could *not* take them (my family members) into my assignment; it was not theirs, and it was not—*I could not have them telling me what to do,* to separate me from Christ, or to cause me unnecessary confusion or delays as "the spirit of Lot" had done with

Abraham. Sometimes they (other people, even family members) want to go with you into your assignment. *Don't let other people's emotions determine what God has told you to do. When you bring others into your blessings, they can distract you.*

"Lot" *will attract immorality* to your door. Their immoral opinions, behind the scene, will cause you much sabotage. *You would be surprised to know* what and whose immoral information is affecting your children.

I had to stop several (ungodly) family members from speaking "*parental disconnection and rebellion*" to my children. They would say stuff like "*I don't know why your mama wants to do this or that*" *or* "*Why won't she let you go to the party?*" *or* "*Why won't she let you wear that skirt? I let my kids wear this miniskirt. It's nothing wrong with this*" *or the famous* "*Why do you all have to go to church all the time? Your mama is mean to make you go to church.*"

This "bad" habit of others interjecting their opinions (including family members) must be voided and kicked out, let out to another pasture. Stop people and family members from negative influences saying things like "It's nothing wrong with you doing this" or that "your parents (mama) are too strict." This will undermine your family protocol and ***Kingdom*** authority. Confront anyone who gives your children poison of any kind. Do not let your children become addicted to people who speak against your directions.

Can you see how this undermines your ***Kingdom*** *authority* in your own home?

Disconnect from these people, family, and friends. *They* will poison your children, and you need to demand them (these family members) to *stop such behavior.*

"It's all in love. I just care about you and the kid."

Have you ever heard this? Especially from those giving unsolicited information concerning your children and their spiritual growth? Most of the time, this line comes from grandparents, aunts, uncles, cousins, and close friends. I as well knew I was undermined a lot by my parents, who would whisper things to my children (that they did not like or understand, especially if I said no about something) concerning me. Yes, negative influences can come from everywhere. Listen to conversations. If people knew how many times I kept the phone up and heard their negativity, they would have been ashamed. But I made myself know who was really for me and against me.

Grandparents, step back—*never undermine,* rebuke, or disconnect your grandchildren from their place, from their mother. Know your place and respect the parents; you've had your turn. And if it's not life-and-death, let it go! It's not your turn.

Parents—do what God has given you to do and let it go. "Rest in the promise; it's OK."

Living in *Kingdom* Graciousness,

Experiencing "Levites" the *Kingdom* Children, Will Cause You to Become Gracious

The Gracious

> The promise will be fulfilled, just keep a glimmer of hope in your heart.

Keep going in spite of "*OPP*": *other people's problems. These people and their problems, thoughts, ideals, and opinions embedded in your Levites,* may try to undermine your ***Kingdom*** success; but it will not work! *You have the victory; remember that all this is designed to teach you something personally as well.*

Because you are doing good (you, your family, and your children are doing great) in their eyes, better than what they're doing, by their own judgment and assessment of your life and theirs, your close associates, friends, or family *may be jealous of your* ***Kingdom*** *success.* They may be jealous that God chose you.

They will never accept your blessing. They will try to cause discord in your house by pushing, interjecting, and letting their children and their lives become out of order. They will flaunt (ungodly behavior)—this behavior, flaunted to your children, may become like "candy." When they know you have a "no-sugar" policy. Explain this to your children early and stick to your principles, no matter how good the candy may seem.

Don't *allow* others who do not understand ***Kingdom*** citizenship to rule your home.

Remember to be the priest in your home; *take what you are learning* in church, bring it home, and apply it *in* your house.

If your neighbor doesn't understand, *so what?* You live it out. Use the blessing, use the word of God, and the promise will come to you!

Don't Take Lot; he is not delivered

Leave "Lot" home, and go on with your life (even if you have to go alone) to become that ***Kingdom*** citizen that God has called you to be. *Lot may not be delivered yet, so leave the undelivered home.* Please trust me, *the less you involve others in the call God has given you, the better it will be for you and your children. Then when you go back home, they will rejoice in your success.*

And now they say thank you!

Tips on Blending Families

Blended ***Kingdom*** families, simply remember, when you get married, try to keep the exes out of the picture as much as possible. You have a new spouse now, and it should be clearly discussed that your new spouse is welcomed at all events and that your former SPOUSE is not "X," means just that, "excluded" in and from a lot of things they used to be privileged to; however, their role has changed. To form a blended family, this is the first thing that must be defined and respected as a rule of boundary.

New blended "family" gathering *should not include* the *exes,* especially unannounced; this will make the new person feel uncomfortable and cause undue "family blending" pressure. Make the new spouse and new children (if any) feel comfortable and accepted. Do not let people buy for all the children of the past relationship and leave out a present for the new children, especially at gatherings.

Tell the truth (to your older children about the breakup). Don't let them, the current family, blame the new person in your life for the past breakups and fights so you can have a way to wiggle out, shine, and look innocent and look good to your family.

Step up and tell the truth; if the new person did not break up your home, say so. Do not let things be said about your new spouse that are not true.

Men, especially, tell the truth to your children, even about your responsibilities and visitations (do not let them hate their mother because you choose not to come around). Take the blame; do not let the new spouse suffer for your past decisions. Nor the past spouse suffer for your current lifestyle.

Do all you can to "*blend," but if you can't blend, don't force it; make a decision to make your new family happy, especially your wife or husband.* Remember again to be *happy* with the *new.* Expose the truth: if the problem was you, say it; if it was your ex-partner, say it. Expose the old, reject nonsense, and try to establish the ***Kingdom***. I can truly say that in all these areas of my life, having experience in them; a new spouse, especially a new wife, feels secure when others are not allowed to disrespect her.

Tell your Family the Old this is the New!

This may be difficult, but to have your new spouse sitting around years of old photos of the "ex and past, gone days" may not feel comfortable to the new spouse.

Sometimes we have to remind our family to embrace the new; we can start this by asking family and friends to discard old photos of your *ex* or place them out of sight and put up new photos of you and your new family. *Don't dwell on long memory stories that do not include your new family.* Discuss this openly with your current and (former) family, and let them know that you will not allow your new spouse to be placed in a position to be disrespected.

In the case of adult children, please do not allow them to let their parent—your *ex*—(their mom or dad) tag along with them to "holiday" and family events, unless there is total agreement and peace on all parts. This can make the new spouse feel very unwanted, especially if they are all acting like one unit with an outsider present.

Try to find out how to blend your family *between your children and your new family,* not between your *exes.* Instruct your children that your new family *will include your current spouse and that if they are not welcome, it will limit your attendance.*

If there are any strained environments, or actions, toward your spouse, you make it known that this will cause you to leave the event immediately. And do it! You be the one to fix the rifts and underlying currents. If they can't be fixed, don't attend. Do not assume it is OK for you to attend any event and leave your new spouse home because your children do not get along with your spouse. You must chose to "cleave" to your spouse, simple as that, especially with grown adult children, who may be spiteful and full of resentment.

Do not let them break up your new life, hoping and living out a fantasy that will not come to pass. There may be times, until they know that you are serious, that you have to leave an event because of disrespect to your new spouse. Well then, leave, state that you do not agree with the actions being presented and acted upon, and get your spouse and leave. SIMPLE, leave the drama behind and press forward. Finally they will get the message, or you will disconnect; it is their choice.

The blood-connective parent (of the children) or family *should also be the one to let them (the host and attendants) know why you are leaving when the event happens.*

Make it plain and do not allow them to blame the spouse (because you do not tell the truth and bring to light the hidden motives and ugly actions of others). This will cause future strife if you do not expose the truth. Anytime your spouse feels concern or pressure, "*leave*, and cleave to your wife," no matter what the children say. *Never* disrespect your spouse in front of anyone, *never,* especially, in front of your children of a past relationship. This will not breed good family morals and values.

Successful families and family dynamics take much work. In it all, raising ***Kingdom*** families takes a lot of prayer and work. We must not be easily offended, we must not be selfish, and we must bite our tongue (a lot)!

You Will Get a Gracious "Thank you"; Just Wait and See!

I find that it will all work out; and after all the tears and years, they grow up and realize you loved them all the time, and finally they say "thank you."

Yes, your children will finally thank you when it is all over; they will come to you with a smile and say "Guess what, you were right!" Look for the day; it will come. It has come to us, and we were glad to know that our children grew up. "Yes, you have grown up enough to see it, what we were standing for, and imparting in your lives. For that we are grateful to God and pleased with his hand on your life. We are blessed that God has been gracious to us." And we smile!

Children, when they grow up and establish their own lives and their own families, finally see that they have been out of order and need to change their ways. Whether they ever admit it or not, they do become grateful.

If you allow them to have their lives and cause them to respect your life, you will see the Levites go into the ***Kingdom***, and the ***Kingdom*** rejoices because of their testimony.

Sitting here in this room and looking out over what is one of the greatest creations ever touched by the finger of God, His ocean—I absorb the greatness of the four shades of blue, no green. No, I really cannot name the color God has created in his glory, and I marvel at the plan of God. Who would have known, not I, that within six months, your life can be as different as night and day?

Yet minutes ago, I found myself crying out to God, "Please, don't let me be a 'spiritual failure.' I don't want to do all this stuff and fail you."

Not doing your will, wasting time, and repeating mistakes (we will cover all three of these areas in later chapters).

Do any of you feel like you've failed God, missed the mark, or are just getting by? Are you are tired of "just barely surviving" in this ***Kingdom*** walk and Christian lifestyle?

Keep Pushing Forward; He will meet you at the Finish Line

Where are you in your spiritual walk with Christ? Where are you in the ***Kingdom***? Another meltdown, breakdown, cry out—yes, even the "strong" cry! (Those of us who know how to fix our face when we have to come out in the forefront of leadership, especially spiritual leadership, we can really fix up!)

We cry, we ask questions, we mandate an audience with God because we are "cloudy, off course, need a course of directions" or feel that the timing expected for our miracle has been delayed. We, as my granny (the late Janie Hipps Brooks) would say, "*take a fit.*"

Well, I just "took a fit" and felt overwhelmed, unprepared, undecided, and un______ (you name). I fell on my knees and said to God, "Help me . . . Help me . . . Help me."

Do you know what I mean?

"Father, help me to minister, to pastor, be a good wife, mother, friend. Father, help me to trust you in this major decision in my life that I believe you have led me into. *God help me.*"

I went on and on in this realm about seven minutes, and God spoke to me again and said, "Get up, daughter, and go to the bath area." (which I did.) There he spoke to me three words ***"all is well."***

What a calm that filled my sorrow, pity, and despair!

Three Words "All . . . is . . . WELL"

It's amazing when God speaks, everything changes! Everything is made new. Everything is *peace.* And finally he said, "Write, for now is the time to tell the story of 'my glory' in your life and how to survive in the ***Kingdom***."

"How have you made it to here?" I heard the Lord ask. "*With you,*" I answered. "*No,* "he said. *"Then how?"*I asked. "*By faith?*"I responded. "*No,* "he said again. "*How?" I answered.* Then he slowly spoke to my spirit and said, "*One step at a time. You made it here by learning the way of the* ***Kingdom****, the character of my heart. You have learned of grace and glory, the administration of my* ***Kingdom****, the spiritual government, and you have embraced your* ***Kingdom*** *orders. You believe when I speak, and you still keep believing that I do what I say I will do and that I can still do miracles and breakthroughs. You made it to here by learning to worship and praise. You made it here by saying no matter what people chose not to go, even your family or your children or friends or whoever, you have said 'I am going on, matter what!'*

"You made it here by continuing to speak, and say what, I told you to say to the people, no matter who did not want to hear my voice. You stood on the fact that you knew you could hear from me. You made it here by standing on my Word and the Holy Spirit. You have learned that 'it's a process that you what you expect to grow will produce a crop. That is how you made it here, and yes, that takes, faith, hope, trust, patience, and believing that I would not fail you.'"

I said to the Lord, "Yes, you are right." He said to me, "Great and that's what you tell the people." If I can make it with the grace and Glory of God, so can You no matter what!

Simple and plain

It's a process. Growing up and receiving the grace to operate in the ***Kingdom*** to an expected end are processes that we all must take and go through!

"One step at a time"

But we must take the step(s)

Chapter 19

Kingdom Connections

A "***Kingdom*** connection" is one that has been directed, assigned, established, purposed, prepared, instructed, and blessed by the King. It is where the *King* has *said* "Go there! And this person has been positioned and prepared there to bless you, and you in turn will bless him." A ***Kingdom*** connection can be seasonal or lifetime. However, this connection is definitely a "*mutual blessing*" experience.

Most ***Kingdom*** *connections* involve "priests, ministers, prophets, apostles, bishops, and pastors." And the demand is always made first on the person to *give* something to the spiritual connection to open the ***Kingdom*** connection.

You see the order of God, the King; and ruler of our *Kingdom* has a law.

This Law is to "*give,* then it *will be* given *unto you.*" Sometimes, often, most times, we in the ***Kingdom*** get it backward; we *want something* from our leader—a Word counseling, prophecy, blessings, time, attention, prayers. *But we don't want to, haven't been taught the rule is to give first,* and after we give, *then we can plan to receive.* So the connection is jarred or disrupted because we are not following ***Kingdom*** order.

So sadly, the regular way or the way we view as "the normal" is quite the opposite. The world tells you to give first and then you get—we see this at our doctor's office, food stores. We pay for something first, then we receive. So we know how to operate in this principle; we just have overlooked it as a ***Kingdom*** truth. Because this is what happens, it hinders the ultimate blessing. *The person is not getting the fullness of the miracle or the Word of God; the enemy fools them that it is not import to give,* so we see the person goes, gets, and leaves.

The "***Kingdom*** stealers" will never be the first in line to bless the prophet, are far from giving tithes and offerings within the church, and do not covenant partners with the ministries that they say *bless them* (especially TV ministers and those we all glean from, other than their local assemblies).

At least once a year, please bless those whom you have eaten from all year. Please send at least one check a year for those you receive from!

Never leave the church with your pocket full of seed faith. Never let the enemy fool you to keep. The "faith seed" is taken back in your hand or is stuck in their purses or wallets, and there it dies; it's just eaten up by the cankerworms and dies. It is so sad to die, and especially to die with no multiplication.

It cannot multiply; it will not increase because where it should have been put in the ministry, sowed to be blessed, watered, and grow. It did not have the dirt of faith to adhere to and grow in. Your faith seed must be allowed to leave your hand to bring you back a harvest.

Naman (1 Kings 5) knew to bless the prophet. He knew what he wanted and was willing to invest to get it. "Plan to invest. Let the ***Kingdom*** gardener (the prophet) decide whether to take it or not."

Would you get dressed, go out to the finest restaurant, sit and eat, and not plan to pay for your *meal* on any occasion? Of course not. No matter how many times you eat. You would not even go to McDonald's or the waffle house and not expect to pay. You would be considered a crook or a robber. In fact, at some places we pay there *before* we eat, play, and entertain; we buy before the curtains go up!

God sends us a "personal coach, a spiritual enricher" for our lives, and we treat them like trash; we abuse them and never invest in them, the good of the land. We are robbers and will find ourselves under spiritual arrest, with God holding up our assets.

When we expect God to send ***Kingdom*** connections into our lives, we must understand the value and expect to pay the cost (invest), bless, give, support, uplift finance in our

Kingdom Connections

From 2000-2004, we spent *four years of our lives* (Bishop, our staff, and myself) traveling across the United States, teaching churches how to get their ministries registered, form incorporations 501(c)3, and train elders, advisory, and board of directors.

To our surprise, we found fivefold ministries to be the most offensive in ***Kingdom*** connections. What do I mean? We charged *other people* in the private sector thousands of dollars to do all *their administrative services for one week*, and these companies paid gladly! We only asked the *ministries* for *$499* for a weekend experience, and you guessed it—excuses, excuses, excuses! Many of them even asked for our services for "*free*." They disrespected the fact that this was our ministry, that years of time had been invested in our learning, that thousands of dollars had been paid for our knowledge, and that we were sent as a ***Kingdom*** connection to bless them.

When other nonprofit agencies discovered our classes, they were packed with a three—to six-month waiting list; they would travel for hours, stay in the hotel, and then many of them would bless us financially, above and beyond, because they were so *grateful*. By the way, they only paid $799 (pastor's special was 40 *percent* off). And again, *guess* what? Guess who complained. So we went where our anointing was appreciated, valued, and our gift was appreciated; and *God* truly blessed us.

We understood those *who complained* about cost, were people who did not value "***Kingdom***" connections." *Most of them did not really want to be a blessing.* They came to *rob and steal the anointing* of wisdom and education from us, and had *we allowed* this to happen, it would have been a *shame* on us! But because we knew what we were "*giving*" and that the value was great, we did not back down!

Don't stop your blessing from flowing because you are cheap!

We know we had a right to make a demand from those *seeking information.* "The prophet told the widow, 'Bake *me* a cake.'" *Why?* He knew what *he had* to share, the connection he was sent to do, and the *demand* that had to be made to receive it. So he could not back down! *You do it, and* I *can release* it—but not until you do something.

The Choice is Yours

You can get a true ***Kingdom*** *connection*—the *connection* that pulls your *destiny* into *reality*. It causes you to catch the *seed*, nurture the *seed*, birth the *seed*, and finally *live* in the reality of *receiving* what God has said to you, what you are *believing* God for, and what you are expecting from God. *Sometimes* we miss our *push* because we refuse to invest in our ***Kingdom*** *connection.*

What about the conference you were supposed to attend and you thought the *registration* fee was too high? Is it really ever too much to invest in education, relationships, and networking opportunities?

We spent of $50,000 for world education but complain at the $250 registration fee to a conference that will cause our spirit to grow! WE must change our mind-set to grow.

The *seat you* were supposed to sit in had a "***Kingdom*** connection" for you. The person sitting to your left or right *was your next step in* *the path of your success.* But you missed it because you were too cheap to invest in yourself. I cannot begin to tell you of long-term friends made and networking doors opened to us because we were in the right seat!

It is important to invest in your future and your spiritual growth. This will take you to the next level in your ministry, in the ***Kingdom***, and your life.

God had designed "something" *you needed* in similar to be placed at *that conference, sitting next to you, that was designed in advance* to bless *you* and to create a "***Kingdom*** *push*" in your life; but until we see the value in ***Kingdom*** connections, we will continue to have unborn destiny.

I believe the most *valuable* ***Kingdom*** *connection* you will ever develop in your ***Kingdom*** connections is with your *pastor.* Yes, your local pastor. But you have to show them that you are worthy of investing in, and you sometimes have to plant a lot of seed for the pastor to see you really want a harvest. As wanting something supernatural, you must be willing to invest and plant seeds until you see your harvest grow!

First of all, let me say through years of pasturing, I have found out that most "members" are not true members **because they never *connect*.** They never have had or sought out to have a "***Kingdom*** connection"; they really *never join* with the ministry, the vision, the team, the purpose, the direction or anything that will truly connect them, or make them accountable so that they can lock in to grow.

Yes, they come up front and shake the preacher's hand (sometimes that's the *last time* we see them—literally). Many of these "come-by-here members" do not even stay long enough to complete new members' class.

They lack minimum *faithfulness* for six to twelve weeks. They fail to receive their ***Kingdom*** connection, their assignment on ***Kingdom*** instructions; because of this, they are terrible ***Kingdom*** citizens.

They are "ever learning but never coming to the knowledge of the truth," yearning, they say, for the truth, but never receiving it. Many are now even going from town to town and from church to church, thinking they do the will of the Lord; however, if the truth be told, they are not even in *"churchdom. They are in dumb-dumb."*

The real fact is they are disconnected, a fallen part of the body perishing from disconnection.

What tree do you know, that can be repotted every two weeks and live, less more become fruitful?

This pattern will continue until they become old and better and finally fall off like a dead limb. They are like a plant; repotted every two weeks, it will die. Because of being transferred too many times. Our soul is this plant and must be left to take root and flourish.

It is only when you *stay completely connected* that you understand the value of the "trunk and roots." You will understand that as a branch, you can never live without good *roots* and a viable "trunk." So do not reject connecting to the root! This root is the Word of God and relationship with the Savior (Jesus Christ) and His spiritual patrol, the Holy Spirit. This is the "*root*" of your faith. The trunk is your local pastor, the prophet, and the apostle. If you fail to have a sincere ***Kingdom*** *connection* with these three gifts, you will perish, die, rot away, fade away, not reproduce fruit, and have no root connections to the plan God has for you.

Mealtime: Served at Worship Time
*Worship and **Kingdom** Connection*

The thought and action of Acts 2 and the Acts 2 church is a time for establishing a "parental time of nurture"; it is when the spiritual parent prepares, serves, and feeds the household.

In my house growing up (or should I say my parents' house), my father, Deacon Moore, was the cook, a divine *chef.* A great cook! And is still cooking in 2010 at eighty years old, and cooking great!

He prepared meals at least twice a day (breakfast and dinner). Dinner was normally at 5:00 p.m. *Dinner was served.* There was *not* a choice—"Oh, leave it on the stove, we will eat later," "I don't like this food" "I don't eat this or that," "I want to eat over here, and not at the table." *These* statements were not made in our home.

My father chose the menu, cooked the food, served the food, and we ate it; and it was good! Did I say he also paid the price—for the food—well, he did. When I was younger, my mother cooked, and it was the same thing. In my grandmother's house, it was the same; and as I raised my kids (all of them), it was the same. Mealtime means eating together at the table. I look in your face to see if all is well. I make a connection with you.

It was the matter of respect, honor, and trust to show up and eat the meal. You knew your parents were preparing the best for you.

In the church/***Kingdom***, we must learn to *show* up for the ***Kingdom*** *meals* (service times).

We must respect our ***Kingdom*** connections and spiritual parents enough to show up for family dinner. It is not our choice what our parents choose to cook. We must expect to eat healthy, balanced meals and receive our nutrition as served. "*Connection* time" or service time is not an *option.*

There is no other organization, company or group in which you can decide to miss 80 *percent* of its activities and still consider yourself a *good member.* Nowhere!

So why do we consider ourselves as members to the church when we have been disconnected for months, years, or weeks? We have not paid our membership dues, which we call tithes and offerings. And we constantly not follow the order of the handbook.

Why did you miss dinner?

If your ***Kingdom*** *parent(s), your spiritual* leader(s), served five meals per week (five services), yes, you are supposed *to be there.* Why do you think you can choose not to eat?

We work five/six/seven days a week, full-time and part-time. We give four to six hours a day to TV or computers. We go to the stores, do our hair, nails, toes, and whatever we want to do; we allow the enemy to keep us from making *our* ***Kingdom*** connections and mealtimes. Then we have spiritual upsets.

We say, "I have to go to work, school, and business appointment." We say church is too long; *however,* we stay up until 2:00 a.m. What is our real reason?

Is it because we do not prioritize and *value* our ***Kingdom*** *connections as a part of* our mealtime? Is it because we do not honor our spiritual patrol, and ***Kingdom*** coaches? Is it because we think we feed ourselves, because we think that we choose when, where, and what *we feed* ourselves?

Where do you get your grain to feed yourself? This cannot *be good* grain because it does not come from legal spiritual authority. No "*baby*" can feed itself; we need a *parent to* feed us, and 95 *percent* of the church is in a "baby mind-set."

You cannot afford to miss a "***Kingdom*** connection" time; you cannot afford to miss a spiritual meal or a time of worship.

Nothing will ever be more important than this time. In about thirty-eight years, I don't think I'd have *missed* over ten services (unless I was in the hospital or had a new baby). We must value the meals that have been prepared for our growth and our feeding.

What's your "***Kingdom*** *record"?* "What's your ***Kingdom*** *priority* to your ***Kingdom*** *connection?* Nothing should separate you—no height, depth, or any other creature. This includes and is not limited to boyfriend, girlfriend, ungodly spouse, children, family, anger, disappointment, lack of finances, home moves, tummy aches, backaches, headaches, "My toe hurts," "My finger hurts," "My life sucks," "My boss is mad," "My dog got hit."

I *have heard it,* over and over and over while I *prepare a wonderful meal,* and you don't show up to eat—not just one meal, but many meals that *you have failed to be seated,* to be *served.*

This is so frustrating for your ***Kingdom*** leader and the *fivefold coaches* and can often cause the one assigned to you to become disconnected from you as well. A true parent does not grain and good spiritual food on the ungrateful—"casting our pearls to 'swine' or careless people."

An opportunity to make a divine connection that will spear your destiny to joyous height cannot be treated like junk. Most of the time, *those "most disconnected" has the most problems.*

They fail to seek wise (godly appointed) counsel. Therefore, problems continue over and over. They are spiritually *vitamin deficient;* their iron is low, and they are *weak. They are a*lways *sick and tired.*

Remember—"*meals*" *provide nourishment* and *vitamins*

When you do not eat *proper "spiritual meals,"* you will not be *spiritually strong.* You will fail and fall short over and over.

Spiritual protocol must be administered in this area. When those preparing meals want to know why you are not eating and where you are at mealtime, don't snap at them; all parents should be concerned with their children's eating habits.

I believe because I cooked balanced meals—vegetables, rice, fruit, protein, dairy—in each meal and had lots of prayer.

Our children did not have a lot of childhood issues of health. However, I saw children (even in the church) who ate a lot of junk food, did not have a proper diet and were sick very often; the parents who did not cook meals daily, they had attacks of cold, flu, viral fever and missed a lot of days of school. They were always out of work and missing church with sick children; this let me know that prayer may have been missing in their homes or the declaration of healing scriptures may have been a missing element in their homes.

Kingdom Connections

Show up for the meal!

I believe because I showed up for the meals *my pastor prepared,* my children were stronger. I also had additional personal spiritual meals with times of prayer/fasting, scripture reading, praise, worship, and a lot of singing in my home. I took the meal home, I carried out lots of carryout plates, which included the Word, and continued to serve it to myself with the spiritual leftovers my spiritual parents cooked for me until the next mealtime.

Developing, appreciating,
and Maintaining

Kingdom Connections must be sought after and retained

I sought and continue to seek good ***Kingdom*** connections, and I believe this has been a success for our ministry. I went to prayer meetings, Bible study, praise services, choir practice, leadership meetings, revivals, conventions, Sunday morning and Sunday night. And everything our ministry offered in between times of regular worship. I love the Lord, and I love being in His house; I wasn't looking to *leave.* I was working to stay.

I wanted to be connected to my spiritual parent, and they could count on me, before and above everyone. I was faithful, not excuseful, and grateful to the *spiritual connection and the **Kingdom** connections God sent into my life to bless me.*

I honored them, even when I had to give extra for special projects. I got a second job and once took out a loan and repaid it for our building fund projects. I appreciated the work my spiritual parents did, and I believed in their vision. Now these seeds are returning to our ministry, pressed down, shaken together, and running over. It is coming back to me in full force.

I would like to think I imitated my spiritual father, *Pastor Darnel Williams,* in prayer and fervency of preaching; my spiritual mother,

Pastor Alma Joe Brown, with praise and worship; and others who have mentored me in the faith.

I grew because I wanted them to be proud of me. I was saved, and I wanted them to be proud that God was using me; in my life, I wanted them to say I was a blessing to them and that I had became fruitful, a blessing to the ***Kingdom***.

Work the work of Evangelism!

I loved our ministry, and it showed. I talked about our church, brought people to church, a lot of people; see, I did the work of an evangelist and I ate what my pastor fed and grew, and my bones are strong today because of these meals. Are you a person your leader can be proud of? Are you sent to help them advance the ***Kingdom***? Are you willing to go the extra mile to see the ministry you are planted in grow? Do the work of evangelism, and take the yoke of evangelism and help the ***Kingdom*** and your local ministry to grow.

Making and Keeping "***The Kingdom Connection***"

Finding your seasoned lifetime ***Kingdom*** assignment is paramount to keeping your ***Kingdom*** connection! This is the first great effort of your survival and satisfaction.

You are sent to "Elijah," but can you leave the crowd and truly connect to your spiritual ***Kingdom*** connection?

God intended you to "*connect*" with the right person (and people) to develop your "next-level" ministry. But can you see it when it comes your way to be able to make and keep the right connect?

Everyone wants to have a *life of* "*signs* and *wonders,*" but we are not always willing to drop our lives and follow the person sent to develop our ministries. Rarely will a person leave their town, city, or state to go to another town, city, or state and serve the person they know is supposed to develop them to their next level in ministry. But they are stuck in the now and not in the spiritual connection.

To keep your ***Kingdom*** connection, to meet up with your Elijah, you may have to travel. You may have to be like Paul and go to a street called straight to meet up with your ***Kingdom*** destiny.

What are you willing to do to get connected to your destiny? Where are you willing to go to be trained and become dynamic? You connection will determine your destiny.

Are you an Elisha?
Or are you just in the school of the prophets,
with the other students?

Are you just talking, or are you willing to truly move with God? If I told you to move to South Florida today to be trained, would you drop everything and go to the destiny God has called you to walk in?

It may not be our ministry; it may be the ministry of Pastor Paula White or Pastor Bill Winston or another person we have never heard of as a spiritual general of the faith. But would you drop your net and follow the call of God? The question is, however, would you be willing to attach to your destiny and your ***Kingdom*** connection?

In my beginning pastorate for *about five years,* God sent *me people* who were supposed to have transitioned to our ministry and make a ***Kingdom*** "connection" with our ministry.

Weekly they would go to our home and get blessed, prayed over, and delivered; they would receive counseling from me daily and always wanted my opinion. I was their *pastor.* However, they had membership elsewhere.

That's where they showed up with all my information and told others "what God showed them" without giving us any credit; they wanted to appear seasoned, as if they were actually spending time with God. They paid their money and sowed their time, talent, and gifts at these other churches, which they always complained about. But we were little, and these were big churches, so they were not going to leave them. They needed to look big. It didn't matter what God said; they needed to be seen by lots of people to feel like they had gone to church.

Whenever we needed them, "their church" came first. Every week there was some kind of drama, problem, or issue. As *I, "we,"* grew up and began to see this was not good for anyone, especially us, *we made a demand of loyalty and financial commitment to our ministry.* You know what happened after all this praying and laying hands on these people—them keeping me up till all hours of the night with their issues. When we required something of them, they stopped showing up.

After *years* of praying for them, running spiritual interference with God for them, and when God told me to tell them to make a "full connection to the ministry," they ran the other way. I was shocked;

they chose to stay at the church they were so-called members in. Did they really have "membership"? I did not understand their mind. But today I do; they were "spiritual whoremongers." They were married but sleeping around with our ministry. They were also transferring "spiritual STDs."

I learned they were disloyal to the church they were involved in and to our ministry as well. I felt betrayed, used, and abused and that my *time was wasted,* pouring into a "leaky vessel."

"*Who am I talking to?*" I learned three things from these types of "leeches" connections.

1. I do not *counsel people* who are *not my* members unless they are under my professional services in which they pay for *counseling services.*

2. If you *value my* "leadership" so much, join the church and go to dinner, spiritual mealtime or church; eat what is prepared and grow. I don't need to talk to you every day, all day, "wearing me out with repeated drama"; and if you value the connection, you will *sow* into my life to keep the "connection healing."

3. My *sheep will* hear my voice; if I say something today, I should not need to repeat it tomorrow. My sheep will embrace my values, the mission God has given us, and embrace our ***Kingdom*** assignment.

I do not need to "pastor other people' sheep." If there is to be a "connection," this connection must be drawn to by the heart of the people.

I *prewarn* you all, sheep and lambs in this season of "false" fivefold. *Do not connect to* anyone who says he is the ministry of the evangelist, elder prophet, teacher, missionary minister, preacher (office) that does *not have* a *local pastor,* and (*or*) an *active* apostle that they are submitted to; these people are spiritual death traps, subverting the Gospel, and going about to feed their own addenda.

These *seven* offices must be overseen and *submitted* to the office of the local church. They are supposed to be in "connection," not in *renegade* status. They are not to counsel you without pastoral leadership and Godly insight.

If and when *you meet* someone with one of these "titles," ask them, "Who is *proving* their gift? Where are they an active member? And who is their local covering?" We must call these officers back into ***<u>Kingdom</u>*** connection. Most of them will say, "God called me," "*I have got to be free,*" "*I can't be bound by any man.*"

Watch these people and run from their words, *for God will not cross his order.* Jesus did not disconnect himself from the Father; he always said, "I do what my father says to do, say what he tells me to say, and I serve my Father." If Jesus was then under authority, connected, why do we think anyone else can just "be free"? I often ask them, "FREE FROM WHAT?" You will then see, they want to be free from being "accountable and under spiritual order"!

There are No "free" Agent Evangelists!

If an evangelist is to go out and win souls, where are they expecting to take the souls they are winning, in their evangelism duties?

They are supposed to be *bringing them into the local church they are a part of and continue to work with them under the guidance of their pastor. Wow!*

There is order; an evangelist with "no home" cannot bring sheep out of the storm.

It is the same with other gifts in the church. So question people who assume *nonlegal* spiritual authority with you and over you. And if someone tries to connect to you and become your personal minister, by all *means,* tell your spiritual leader; if it's of God, it will last as you bring your covering into the knowledge of this relationship. If they are not real or any good for your spiritual growth your shepherd, your "pastor" will "howl" and *run* the wolf off. Allow it, embrace it, and trust that your spiritual leader has the best in heart, for you.

Remember the "ladies" I was "counseling" *for five years*—I went to their pastor and told him I was meeting with them before and many times as the meetings started and continuing to grow, with other people as well because I believe in "order." I am no sheep thief; I told him I was praying with them and that they had sought me out to meet with me for mentorship and as a spiritual mother and asked for his permission.

I informed him regularly of their progress. I even *asked* him to release them to me for a year. When they did things I knew was wrong, I let him know. You see, he was their "spiritual father," but I was their "spiritual mother."

We communicated and birthed *five daughters* in the ministry. However, in the end, like I said, his church was large; we were very small, a storefront start-up ministry; and they would not leave for "status's" sake. As you know, the time you spend praying, grooming, and directing others are soon forgotten; and the truth of whom you've helped may never be recorded or remembered.

Learn to be ready to drop your net and follow—

When you are on the up-and-up for Jesus, you do not have to hide or be intimidated when you are doing things God's way, so what you do? For the right reason will last. I counsel you to stay in season; however, prepare to grow up. Also be prepared to go to the next level and *leave gracefully when your season is over.* Take it all as "*experience.*"

When in a ***Kingdom*** connection, love people in spite of their ways or faults; remember you are there to learn something, so laugh as you enjoy the journey of meeting people and gaining the best they have to offer.

Practice being a good friend and learn—learn to love them in spite of their challenges; *laugh and grow with them; and when your season is over with them, do not let it turn bitter; depart prayerfully and with love. Keep friends forever; keep connections for eternity if you do not speak for then for years in between passing.*

Your ***Kingdom*** Connections will lead you to new places

There will be those of you who must be ready to drop your net and follow the person God has truly assigned you to. This is a lifetime assignment.

You are finally ready to be settled for the endurance of the time. God has granted you with favor this person life. "Your spirit must be settled, your wandering is over, your sorrows have passed, and you are truly ready to be satisfied at last."

Like the *disciples had* to make a choice. They had to "drop their nets." If you are to make a true ***Kingdom*** connection, you must "*drop* your net," as well and be prepared to follow others who have been sent in your life as a valuable connection.

Drop your net means to get you out of the way. "Drop your plans, drop your ideals, drop your thoughts, drop your desires, drop your current location, and begin to follow the person with your ***Kingdom*** *connection.*"

If you have to *move,* move; it's a big world. Maybe that's why things have been "tight" for you "where you are." God is trying to "nudge" you toward your ***Kingdom*** *destiny,* "push" you toward your ***Kingdom*** *connection,* and develop you in ***Kingdom*** grace and glory. But you are stubborn, fearful, faithless, and connected to your past instead of your future.

Anybody there, here, now! Take a deep breath and be ready to move into the next level of ***Kingdom***; learn to leave the crowd and follow *true* ***Kingdom*** connection.

Stop being a Crowd Pleaser and be a God Believer!

Wanting to be a crowd pleaser, or to be seen by many, can often deter you from your ministry. I met a "minister" (Minister W. M.). He served with us for two years. He had one terrible fight "with the enemy of pride." The pride demon made him often want to be seen, even if he had to been seen doing something wrong or acting out of order. In his life, in the church, and in the spiritual battles he often had facing him, he made the wrong choices, very often not being influenced by our wise counsel to be temperate in his ministry. If the right choice was to be quiet and *do the assignment and let God be glorified,* or the wrong choice was to be *seen, talking loud, being a spiritual joker, and parading around like a chicken rooster, clucking and making no sense at all, displaying true* ***Kingdom*** *immaturity, he would choose to be seen in the clown suit.*

The problems and spirits of ignorance he chose to cling to finally caused us to take him out of the ministry program, and his pride led him to leave the church; this unfortunate behavior led him farther into a downward spiral and eliminated him from his ***Kingdom*** connection. He had the spirit of *needing to be* seen by the *crowd*! We *were trying to groom him* (to be a bishop of a GHCC branch). But every assignment we gave him would be unaccomplished because if the *crowd* wanted him to do something different, he would go his way every time.

I ran across *some books* (from Bishop Dag Heward-Mills of Lighthouse Chapel International), and I began the study of the "*spirit of rebellion*". I found he had eleven of the fourteen signs of disloyalty to watch out for when a person is on their way to becoming openly rebellious. We were shocked at this learning experience because we had seen all these signs come to pass in him and many others as they went through our ministry.

We had just experienced this with one of the others ministers whom we had also just dismissed about two months prior to asking this minister to step down from ministerial duties. He had a bad, awful, and contagious demon on lying and would not repent; this often came to my ears, and when we asked him what was going on with his ability to tell the truth in simple things to us as leaders and to the members, he said it was not our business to ask him anything, and left. Storming out of the church and never came back. Both of these ministers, we later found out, talked a lot and often rode together to various locations unaware by us.

The demon that took them over very often was a "spirit of wanting to be seen" to a "*spirit of rebellion.*" He was defiant and seriously off course. His mannerism changed often, and his name was constantly in much confusion with Minister M. The end to the matter came when we gave him *a simple,* clear instruction, which was openly violated. He went and did the exact opposite to what we asked him to do. Of course, this involved a controversial issue (that needed the utmost delicate handling). We asked *him* "not to *give anyone* any *information* on this *situation,* especially to those who had previously left the church."

This "*Pastor Joab*" spirit caused him to directly disobey us because he wanted to be a crowd pleaser; when rebuked, *this rebellion caused him to leave the church nonrepenting; this minister had broken his divine connection to please the crowd.*

If you are to see yourself in the upmost areas of <u>***Kingdom***</u>, we must forget *the crowd.* The sad news is—guess where he went when he left us, *BACKWARD*—yes, he went back to the church he came from, after citing to us several times that *"after eleven years of being with them, he grew more with us in eleven days."* Why go backward, with all the up and coming ministries that can speak life into you, go forward, and gain more, never go backward, especially to a place where you did not learn or grow, in the first place.

Why go backward?

WE go backward to familiar places because we can be comfortable. He went backward because he was comfortable; no *one there would push him to grow.* He was stuck. This type of being stuck and is not good, this type of sticking in a bad place just because will probably make you miss the <u>***Kingdom***</u> of God. Because of pride, rebellion, stubbornness, and the other spirits of Satan, you will have a failure to repent!

Yes, this minister was a good person (as far as deeds of service to the church, especially if he could be seen doing it, were concerned). But these pride and rebellion spirits had overtaken him, and he refused to repent, so he went down, backward, and out of the area of the ***Kingdom*** connection what he was assigned to fulfill.

How many times have you chosen to stay at a place in your mind or walk out of your assignment with Christ to do the minimum and not the maximum because no one is going to challenge you to do better? *I would strive to be at the best place in life and go up to God than to go backward to a place of mediocrity.* No matter how my feelings were turned in the time of correction, I would never throw away a slice of pizza in exchange for a box full of dirt.

You must ask yourself these questions if you think you are ready to walk in a ***Kingdom*** connection!

- If you have to go alone, can you truly walk alone?
- Or can you walk with your leader alone?
- Can you truly accept and be guided by a leader? Or do you still have a lot of your own opinions?
- Can you desire to grow in the shadows and support the one who is up front without taking on credit or becoming offended?
- Can you truly follow without holding a "secret dagger" to stab and defeat your leader?
- Can you be trusted with the sheep to protect them and not try to steal them or their hearts?
- Do you act the same way in your leader's presence or out of your leader's presence?

Do not come into Spiritual Connection with an "Absalom" spirit!

Many leaders are burned out with trying to mentor, coach, and pastor "*Absalom*-type spirits" and "*Joab* spirits." Your time will come to lead if *you prepare, serve well, wait on God,* and be faithful. Stop trying to steal sheep, start your ministry off "church crisis," backbite, and defame your pastor, waiting on them to "sleep" so you can gain ground; stop waiting, planning, and expecting to kill the leader and gain ungodly power. *Shame* on you! Wait on the Lord, *birth* lambs; develop *a vision*; leave with a blessing; and keep your spiritual parents and ***Kingdom*** connections—you will be glad you did.

Bring something to the table when you go—"good experience" always helps! In addition to this experience you must also bring these:

—Loyalty
—Passion
—Compassion
—Resources
—Time
—Vision
—Humbleness

True Loyalty

To be a help to the ministry and the leader you serve in the ***Kingdom****, you must bring something to the table.*

Loyalty* is so important that it must be *mentioned twice—most "church folks" are not *loyal,* most staff people are *not loyal,* and most ministerial teams are *not loyal.* We stay in other positions for years (socially) and serve faithfully. We must bring faithful service to ***Kingdom*** *work.*

We must serve with passion, compassion, resources, time, vision, humbleness, and true loyalty to the ***Kingdom*** connection; and trust your leaders to lead you. *Leaders do not* want to hear how *bad the other pastor* was.

The question in our mind is, *how were you*? What did you add to make it better? How were they blessed by your service? That's true ***Kingdom*** connection, when both people were a blessing to each other, not just ask, what can my pastor or leader do for me!

What is change? (Look up the word in the dictionary; it will do you good.)
Change: ____
____
____

Why is change so difficult? Think about it.

Why is my change so difficult?______________________________

____

____

The *Kingdom* Is about Change! "Change and Power"

But you must *change* before you receive this *power.*

Kingdom
Connections
TRumpet Man!

We've got to have them . . . .

What's next for me?
Get a ***Kingdom*** Connection

Leadership and Prophetic Development

If you have a call from God, connect to a prophetic ministry who is able to develop your gift and talents.

You want to desire a spirit-filled ministry that can serve, guide, and correct you as you attend to walk worth of your calling. You are to be a part of *InterGlobal Association of Christian Churches Worldwide* (or some other association of growth).

Because our apostle and bishop are "called" with that special calling to grow and groom ministers and yes, prophets, we recommend this association.

Leadership should be your desire in the body of Christ because you have something to share that can truly help someone.

Whether this is praise and worship; teaching the youth, women, men, or seniors; or being a greeter or host, missionary, or indeed even the prophetic calling, yes, an association like *IGACCW* can provide training and covering for you and your ministry and a ***Kingdom*** connection that will cause you to be accountable and to grow in the ***Kingdom***!

Associations can help train you to be that special *star* for *God* and the body of Christ. Connecting to these types of global ministries can cause your ministry to expand and to network with others that are growing like you are.

Ministry, whether local or abroad, will grant you this gracious leadership training. After you are saved and spirit filled, your next step is to lead others to this place of fellowship and networking in the ***Kingdom*** as you grow to your next place. Seek to lead as others follow to associations that surpass your local ministry. *This is a **Kingdom** connection.*

Why Do I Need A Prophetic Connection?

Being connected to a prophet has always been the will of God. God said He would always reveal His plan to His prophet first; *yes, God still speaks to his prophets,* all the way to the end (Revelation).

The prophetic voice will always be active. You need to connect to this voice for your directions as well. Do not despise prophecy, but learn to appreciate the real prophetic voice. If you do not have a prophetic ministry, seek one as the Lord will speak first to his prophet. Raise house prophets to enhance the ***Kingdom*** of God and allow the prophetic move of God in your ministry. If you are not a *prophet (but over see a ministry),* you should open the door and invite prophetic gifts into your ministry to have a prophetic insight; only invite those that are under authority into your ministry. Often, their coming will create a revival and an excitement with your people to all this flow of ministry; this will cause you to begin to operate more prophetically in your life. This will bless you and your people and will bless you, creating prophetic connections for your life. Even if you flow prophetically, this will confirm you ministry in front of your people.

Kingdom "Mentorship and Coaching"

There is someone in the ***Kingdom*** assigned to train you; you just may have to find them.

Learning how to be *trained of the Holy Spirit* until your *Elijah comes and* learning how to follow Elijah (your spiritual mentor) when they do arrive can be difficult. But are you ready to be stretched out?

Yes! *The Holy Spirit teaches us all things*—however, we are still responsible to have *spiritual leader to help us* discern, clarify, and activate through confirmation, information, and inspiration the Word of God and the teaching of the Holy Spirit. What am I saying? I am saying we need people to teach us as well. If we do not need people and just the Holy Spirit, Jesus did not need to ever teach the disciples. He could have left that job to the Holy Spirit. But He spent most of His time teaching, healing, and showing them the ***Kingdom*** of Heaven.

No Man (Human being) Is an Island

God has placed you inside the body of Christ to be *led, fed,* and *even bled* (yes, we must give our life, sweat, and blood for the ***Kingdom***).

So God will send you someone to teach you. In the meantime, I want to give you a few ministerial tips to help accentuate you until you find your leader.

Until you are sent to your spiritual parent or coach, learn these simple steps to help you to grow in ministry.

How Do I Take on the

Vision of My Leader

Seven Simple Traits of a Good ***Kingdom*** Citizen

1. No gossip.
2. No backhanding.
3. Learning to pray prayers of understanding, wisdom, and guidance for the ability to serve faithfully and loyally.
4. Ask for ***Kingdom*** finances to sow into the life of your leader.
5. Belittle, know, show, and accept that God sent you; then submit to being sixty.
6. Know that it's Satan's job to make you doubt step 5; shake it off and stay planted.
7. Dig in, plant yourself, and get to help the vision grow.

SESSION

II

Chapter 20

Eighty-nine Points to

Kingdom Success

Eighty-Nine
Points to ***Kingdom*** Success

These points will be defined and discussed in seven sections total under the following subdivisions to help you better understand each area that the Father wants us to have victory in. Each section has a note section in the end and may be used for group studies, circle-of-power meetings, workshops, and Bible classes as well as individual growth.

S Skills
U Understanding
C Creativity
C Choices
E Educational enrichment
S Supernatural energy and health
S Spirituality identity

An eighth section has been added to discuss financial management and success in money and business matters; this section is called ***financial empowerment*** and can be used to lead you into financial savings and becoming a money magnet. As you forge forth, you will become powerful and have the spirit of SUCCESS.

Eighty-nine "Points" to ***Kingdom*** Success

Eighty-nine "Points" to change your life and cause you to eat the fruit of the ***Kingdom***

May you have ***Kingdom***
SUCCESS

Practical, Real, and True Application Points

Developing yourself with the
Eighty-nine practical points to ***Kingdom*** "success"

Seven Sections
(plus a bonus section on financial empowerment)

Skills

Understanding

Creativity

Choices

Educational Enrichment

Supernatural Energy

Spiritual Identity

Bonus Section

Financial Empowerment

Eighty-nine "Points" to Change Your Life and Gain

"The Mind-set of *Kingdom* Success"

Kingdom Success Starts with Y*ou*, Yes!

|The Road to Success Starts with **You!**

This will take planning, determination, and a creative mind-set toward improvement. And most of all, it will take *you*! Being in agreement to your success!

Do not plan to shortcut or evade pertinent lifestyle changes. *Instead, embrace growth and newness.* At first, practical application will seem strange until it is put into practice and becomes a common practice.

You are your biggest help to your future of financial freedom and family enrichment and life empowerment.

So let's start on the road to success!

You are on your way to success

Empowerment and Workshop Session 1
Points 1-10

Skills :

Skills is defined as "proficiencies in an art or craft." This being the basic definition of skills, we must acknowledge the point of first becoming proficient.

Then we must develop this proficiency in the art or craft. So you just don't "fall" into being skillful, but you must work passionately in a defined area or areas until you become good in it.

This factor of "good" should then be made great and then excellent.

Make up your mind to *develop at least one new skill per month.* What skills are waiting for you to start developing this month?

I will develop this skill this month:

____

I will develop this skill next month:

____

Skills

Session 1

Point 1 Access the hidden

You have "hidden and open skills"—skills you have not yet forced yourself to tap into. Acknowledging this is the start to a new mind-set.

To change or challenge your old mind-set, you must tap into your higher skill levels. Don't be a pansy—do something new—challenge yourself to learn and do something new this week to access your "hidden and open" skills.

You will impress yourself with your new ability! If you are afraid to try new things alone, enlist a partner to row with you on this journey, and both of you will grow to new heights and fulfill many of your dreams.

Point 2 Motivate yourself

Motivation of oneself is the greatest tool to finding your new skills.

Talk about yourself positively! You are not a failure!

If there is something you do great, talk about it and purpose to add to the list of these great things every day, every year, and soon there will be a lot of things you enjoy and are passionate about and are skillful in.

This will change your inner worth and job/society worth, guaranteeing you a greater paycheck and an overall well feeling about you and yourself.

Point 3 Bargains in life versus cheap life

Learn to seek out great bargains versus being cheap. A skillful shopper/investor is a gainful person. When you use the word *cheap*, this is only a loud way of saying "I have no shopping skills and no bargaining power"; when you are skillful at shopping, it says, "I have the ability to select great products and a minimum price."

Point 4 Try to do it yourself first

Instead of paying someone for minor jobs, try to do it yourself first. This will greatly increase your skill levels. Take a "how to do it" class/book if you need to. There are many classes available that will save you thousands of dollars: "how to paint a room," "how to change a doorknob," "how to plant a garden." You can greatly be rewarded by doing small projects yourself. And your confidence level will never be the same as you review your great work and others will admire your skills.

Point 5 Operate in new things

What are the three things you do well?

____

____

____

What are the three things you would like to do well?

____

____

____

______Can you learn how to do these things now? __Yes? __No?
Where? ________ How? ________ Cost?
Time?______________________
Well, get started. We all can learn to operate in new things; this is called additional skill development. Every year, you should have two new skills that you wish to develop to continue to allow your mind grow and enrich your overall well-being.

What is your new skill going to be this month?

____

____

Point 6 Dare to go where you have not been before

This mentality is the greatest of all mental skills—having a no-fear mentality to try new things and develop new skills. You are never too old, young, short, or tall.

Disabilities should not stop you either. Look at every person who could use every excuse that you have used, yet they now developed skills and conquered every fear. And the end—victory! Don't let your lack cause you slack. God has empowered you to succeed. Now go for it!

Point 7 Be teachable

Over the years, I have encountered several persons who said they wanted to learn something but were very unteachable or who lacked the ability to be taught.

When you lose the ability to be taught, you lose the ability to learn new skills. You must have an open mind to learn new skills. I knew a person who had been in the nursing field for over thirty-five years and retired for more than twenty-five years. We were talking about a new medical practice, but this nurse was unteachable, saying she knew more about medicine than we did.

She was right, but we knew more about this procedure than she did You see, this procedure has only been around for seven years, and she has long since retired, failing to go back to school and enhance her skill level, which had made her past levels of experience null and void.

You must remain teachable. Every day, something new is revealed to us that seek to know new things. Yesterday's knowledge is sometimes void; becoming teachable will keep your skills sharp and your mind-set open for higher gains.

Point 8 Trigger a new mind-set

Triggering a new mind-set means to make your mind do something that it has never thought of or done before.

A trigger is something that makes your lightbulb come on, like this book. Thinking on a "new meal" or going to a "new place" or experiencing a new adventure can trigger a new mind-set.

A mind-set is what you have set your mind to do; sometimes this is very limited—limited to what you can see, hear, feel, taste, and your personal experiences. When you challenge your personal senses to experience a new thing, your mind-set shifts, elevates, and expands if you will.

Prepare to trigger a new mind-set for yourself. Read a new magazine and try to embrace a new thought; this will also trigger a new mind-set for you. These new mind-sets will challenge you to greater skill levels.

Point 9 Get a bigger ruler

You cannot measure yourself by yourself; this practice of judging oneself by oneself can only bring a reading that is untrue and unmerited. If you are to assess your skill level, you must find at least twenty-two other persons with whom you can be measured by. This will give you a fair point at which to access yourself. Always remember, you could be the fastest runner in your town, but your town only has ten people. This will not make you the fastest person in the world. When measuring your skill level, be fair to yourself and others. Find out who and what is out there, and measure your skills fairly by a bigger ruler.

Point 10 Be teachable

Many people say they are teachable when in actuality they are "stubborn and rebellious." If you try to teach them something, before you start your sentence (or try to tell them something), they say, "Oh, I know" or "I know that already." They cut you off and continue down their path of limitations.

What about the people who ask you questions but never want the answer? They just want to and love to hear themselves say the problem over and over, and they love to hear themselves talk. I have had many people who ask me questions, but before I can complete my first sentence, they say they already "know that."

Sometimes, I stop them and say, "You do not know what I am saying. Because if you knew this, why are you having your problem, or issue, and bringing it to me? But if you listen, you may learn a real answer you can use."

This may be you—if it is, practice listening, especially in a conversation. For at least ten minutes before you say anything, listen, hush, be quiet, stop thinking about talking all the time, and receive *teaching*.

Teaching, experience, and open opportunity will thrust you into another level of success.

Summary

Embrace every new possibility with passion, grace, and enthusiasm.

Maximize your time and increase your skills!

Do not put yourself in a box; you can increase your skill level daily, weekly, monthly, and yearly. Your mind-set must be changed to "open" to continue to grow and embrace new things, ideals, and skills.

You have "hidden and open skills"; tap into them. Creating new skills will increase your life, health, mental views, and family stability.

Be teachable and be determined to experience life learning new skills and doing new things.

You have great skills; resharpen when necessary to stay on the cutting edge. A dull knife is no good.

You are created by the most skillful god, and great skills are in you. Do not fear—develop your skills.

Empowerment and Workshop Session 2
Points 11-15

Understanding:

The Bible says that "above *all,* that you get getting an understanding is paramount—get an understanding" beats everything and vital to your success.

This famous quote of Proverbs is most said and seldom understood. The word *understanding* being two joined words with different meanings forms to make a powerful statement.

Under = "beneath, covered by, the subject of"

And standing = "to maintain an upright position or attitude, a designated position."

When combined, it means to *"stand under.* "This makes us search ourselves as to what we are really standing under, or submitting to in our beliefs and directions in life. So above all (rephrased), "Make sure to agree with and can support what you are standing under." This will enhance your ***Kingdom*** growth and directions of life.

Understanding = "to comprehend, to believe to be the case, to support, to know the nature and character of." Having said this, understanding should be the essence in which our lives can be developed and groomed. The ***Kingdom*** soars when you truly move in the spirit of understanding.

Point 11 Get to know yourself

Yes, get to know (get knowledge and understanding of and about) yourself. To be better, and do better you must ask yourself; *do you really know you?*

List three things you really know about yourself.

____

______________________________.

How do these things make you feel about yourself?

____

______________________________.

____

Do you understand your ways? (How you react to things and why?

Who in your family do you act like?______________________________
______________________________ and ______________________________

To whom do people attribute your character? (Who do others say you act like?)
______________________________ Why? ______________________________

What are your greatest fears? ________________, __________________
____, __________________________

Do you now see that when you understand yourself, you can help others understand you better, and then you can create a "happy" atmosphere for yourself and others to enjoy.

Point 12 It's a new day

Understand that every day is a new day; start free today. Hope is new today, dreams and goals are new today, and the breath of life is new today. You must embrace the newness of the day to receive the best of the day, from the ***Kingdom*** and from life. Learn from the mistakes of yesterday and move on. Only embrace the positive, blow out the negative, and *breathe again.* "This too will pass"; you will do better tomorrow than you did today!

Keep living; it will get better!

Point 13 Get the answer; become the solution to the problem!

Learn the solution to whatever you want to change. We must answer the PROBLEMS in our lives with solutions, not in the problem. Everyone can talk about the problem, but who can find answers? These are the people who make big money. Problem solvers are few and far; if you can understand that you are here on earth to solve the problems and *not be a problem,* then you will have great success.

Everyone will not like you as a problem solver, but you will sleep great at night. You will also *get rid of lots of negative people* who only want to talk about the problems of life. The "woe, it's me" people will soon fade out of your life, and you will understand that the greatest good you can do for anyone is to speak the solutions and not problems.

Point 14 Understand the real meaning to work

You must understand that the real meaning to "work" is the ability to learn "new and promotion things." You must *work to learn, and not work solely for the ideal of gaining money*. The more you learn, the more you will understand. The more you understand, the more you will become valuable; the more valuable you are, the more your increase will attach to you, and the money will come.

Your purpose of going to work is to learn. You must pick up additional understanding and skills to be successful in life.

Understand that life presents opportunity every day for you to grab a better life and more fulfillment.

Point 15 Understanding the real meaning of friendship

Many people do not respond, respect or understand friendship. They do not know how to be a *loyal friend*. In a basic community and social activities, they formulate "no nice" thoughts and sabotage good relationships for toxic ones. This leads to failing and actions of death and wholeness, thrust against the principles of friendship. They lure people to emotional death, have sex with their "friends'" partners, steal their "friends'" promotions, kill their "friends'" dogs and kick their "friends'" cats; they molest their "friends'" children and steal from their "friends'" homes. *This is not friendship*. The Bible says "a *friend loves at all costs*," "*a friend is closer than a brother*," and "*a friend will do no harm*."

Are you a true friend? Do you understand friendship? Do you need to practice being a better friend? *Becoming a friend will draw a friend to you*. This will lead you to a greater level of success. Good friends will push you to greater levels of success.

Once I was in our friends' home for dinner (the Raines). I went to their refrigerator to get some water; while standing at the ice maker, I noticed a saying that said, "Bad people only talk about bad people, broke people only talk about broke people, and If all you have time to do is to talk about people, you have no time . . . ." The essence filled my heart. The next Sunday, I ministered on this "thought." My point is if I had not been in this positive environment with something challenging me to think differently, so many people would not have been blessed by this short thought on a refrigerator door. Thanks, Brother and Sister Raines. Good friends will push you into a positive place just by their surroundings. I like to visit people who have good saying and pictures on their walls, creating a calm and positive atmosphere. This helps me to be better.

I often wonder about people who do not have positive friends in their lives. I wonder about people who only live drama and trauma in their lives. *People who do not evangelize are often people who do not have true friends.* They have not invested in the other person enough to see anything positive, so they do not receive anything positive.

These people often think of themselves "more highly than they ought." They attract people, but not people of any successful statue. (Do you know anyone like this? Is this you?)

Friendship does not mean forfeiting your principles or morals or standards or just to have people around you. You do not want to gain "people" who do not respect you at your level of growth or people who push you back into old habits and lifestyles. People can come and go, but *friends would want to help you to be better.* They will help you grow and gain better ***Kingdom*** qualities.

True friends want you to succeed; they do not want to bring bitterness, old bad memories, or heartbreak to you. They want you to be *great*! If you have poisoning people in your walk, *change those people*! And get people that become better friends.

This week—let's review:

1. How do we treat people whom we consider friends and that consider us as friends?
   Let's purge "people" who are not friends from our circle.

2. Let's break new friendship grounds (step out of your circle) and find new friends.
   Find a new person to see if he would like to become your friend.

3. Find out what the Bible says about friendship.

4. Reaccess people to add to your road to success and others to delete from your walk of success.

Understanding friends and friendship will enhance you to become a better person and have greater success.

Summary—Session 2

When you set yourself up for greatness, you must add understanding to your arsenal of learning.

You must know yourself better than you do anything and anybody. You must be honest with yourself and your vision.

Understand that you are sent as a solution to the problem. You are an answer to the situation. See yourself as an answer.

You are called to cultivate your spiritual reserves and tap into your potential to understand and to be understood.

The spirit of understanding is the constant refining to your future.

The greatest gift is *the gift of understanding.* Love it and embrace it, and you will have success.

Empowerment and Workshop Session 3

Points 16-21

Creativity:

See these wonderful flowers behind this picture. Guess what? I made them, and they are proudly a part of our sanctuary. Someone quoted me a price of $300 for this type of flower arrangement plus the cost of the container. Well, I made this arrangement for $37 total including the cost of the container.

Am I a flower designer? No, but I do have creativity, and so do you.

Creativity flows through our veins; just trust yourself to begin your journey of creativity and see the dynamic results. You will impress yourself—I did!

Creativity **Session 3**

Point 16 A clear vision brings creativity

To be creative, you must have a clear vision and a direct flow to see yourself in the blossom of life.

To have a clear vision, you must be a seer; vision is the ability to *see* clearly and directly, and you must be able to communicate your vision well.

This takes planning and development of your written skills and your verbal ability. Work on this and your vision will be expressed as you desire.

Point 17 Commit to excellence

To be creative, you must decide that "just enough" is not good enough. You must commit to be excellent and do the "best" possible you can. Creativity flows when things are done right; you cannot sidestep excellence and expect to be creative. You must decide that your product is the best and that you continue to want to be the best.

Point 18 Maximize time

Don't be a time waster; use your time wisely and efficiently.

Really, get a day planner or a sheet of paper and see where the time in your day is going. You would be surprised at the area where you can pick up valuable minutes that will turn to hours and weeks, months, and years.

Time really cannot ever be regained, but it can be retrained.

Start being fair to yourself today and learn to say *no* to invaluable time wasters.

Point 19 Remember to dream!

Dream big! The sky is truly the limit. If you can see it, you *can* do it; there is not a lot to it! Seeing "it" allows creativity to begin—and grow!

Meditate on the "project," "goal," or "dream" you want to accomplish and do from the start to completion.

There is nothing wrong with dreaming. Without a dream, you will die.

Point 20 Focus on your "end result" until it becomes a reality

List five things you used to do that were creative, and enjoyable, and you stopped doing.

1. ____________ 2. ____________ 3. ____________ 4. ____________
5. ______________________________

Also ask yourself why you stopped.

"I used to . . . Why did I stop?" Ask yourself ____________________
____
____

Dream until it becomes a reality

Point 21 Creativity is a flow

Think of being as creative as a "river." It is a flow and must continue to be active and effective. Get rid of "river stoppers" and beavers who hinder your process and success.

There are unwanted elements that might deter your "river flow"; these are "beavers."

Who/what can you eliminate first that has stopped your progress?

Summary **Session 3**

Learn as much as you can about your dream.

Ask questions, join associations, and improve your learning and knowledge about the areas you want to be creative in.

Dream again and dream big! Don't allow anyone to stop your flow of creativity. God has given you a dream, and no one has the right to change, deter, or stop it.

You have the right to *get rid of* all dream killers, vision stealers, and "beavers."

Take time to *meditate* and settle your mind to focus on *good* things. This will help you define and develop your creativity and skills.

Notes:

Empowerment and Workshop Session 4
Points 22-30

Choices:

To have things in your lives that have created a recycling, of wrong choices, *you must put yourself on a schedule to change your focus and choices.*

This is a practical plan that, if followed, will bring you to a point of positive choices.

It is your choice to get better, do better, be stronger, and live longer. You can change everything by starting today. You and God are the only two entities who have the ability and power to change your situation. *The choice you make today will determine your tomorrow.*

What is your choice? To change or not to change, that is the real question.

Mention one item you will change today:

____

____

How will you change this item? "I plan to . . . ."

____

____

Choices Session 4

Point 22 Learn to forget the old

Learn to forget the old, all negative situations and events, and embrace the new, all positive situations and events that make you smile and grow.

Tell yourself *every day* that you are made in the image of excellence and that nothing will affect or influence that image.

You must release all bad thoughts. This can be done by thinking on new, bright things. For five minutes per day, just close your eyes and focus on the color (yellow) or whatever is your favorite color and say five positive things about choices you made today.

Good *choices* I made today . . . .

____

____

____

____

Point 23 Retrain your mouth

Retrain your vocabulary constantly and get rid of negative(s): (1) people, (2) things, and (3) ideals.

You must reevaluate often, and don't be afraid to toss out the negative. It is important to have your choices, to learn what is good and what is bad for you. Only you can really make this powerful decision. When you know it is bad, get rid of it. If someone or something causes you to not have control over your vocabulary, they are probably negative in other areas and need to be "trained or tossed." Put three good things in your vocabulary daily that you say about yourself.

Learn Your Own Good Points—You Really Are a Good Person,

Really, You Are!

Point 24 Talk about you

You must take the choice to talk about yourself and say good things about yourself—you yourself. Say it to others and to yourself.

Also make the choice to stop others from saying negative things about you to you. You do not have to entertain people who are verbally abusive and negative to you. Neither should you buy into their negative comments about you. Talk about your goals and dreams, and yes, tell your audience that you "are great and there are good things about you." To do this, you must believe this yourself.

List three good things about yourself so that you can share them with others.

____

____

____

Point 25 Get a personal promotion "team," a "DREAM TEAM"

Get people to be on your *personal team.* Meet with them monthly and talk positively about the new you, where you're going, and your new goals and personal improvement; to motivate yourself, find *four people and share your dream with them. The team needs to be balanced; you will be the fifth person on your team of success.*

Have on your team the following:

T = talker, one with whom you can actually spend time talking to and tell about your dream, changes, and positive choices

E = educator, the person who will push you to obtain information and strength by new knowledge on your dream. This could be an Internet person with the same interest as yours and a desire to overcome in an area, who will research with you, and help you to change for the better.

A = active supporter. This is your cheerleader and your person who will always be there for your moments of greatness, who will celebrate with you in high order!

M = mentor. This is your coach, the person who will get in your face and say "Push"; they will correct you when wrong and see to it that it is done correctly before you move on. They have your best interest at heart, understand where you are trying to go, and will be committed to help you get there.

And *finally, your greatest team member is yourself,* when all other members fail you must be able to count on yourself. Cheer yourself on, and raise the bar of expectation in your own heart, mind, and will. *You must tell yourself you can make it* and continue with great strides; you must even know how to "take one for the team" and be a great team player yourself.

Point 26 Life is like a refrigerator

Clean your "life refrigerator" often. Make a choice to get rid of "old, cold, dead, spoiled, depleted, contaminated, rotten, freezer-burned" areas in your life.

Clean out the old to get the new . . . .

Quick Points:

Point 27: Use spiritual disinfectants to rid yourself of spiritual germs

- ✓ **Pine-Sol** = praise and worship—find a good, joyous song to sing and sing it; it will brighten your day.
- ✓ **Bleach** = the Word of God—find a good, positive scripture to enrich and brighten your choices. You will feel so much better about the choices you make when you know it is the will of God.
- ✓ **Air freshener(s)** = Read and become refreshed with other good and positive books that help you to make good solid choices.

Point 28: Make up your mind to make good choices about yourself and for yourself.

Not a lot needs to be said here, JUST do it and it will be done! It's that simple.

Point 29: Reapply this principle: "Get rid of *beavers* in your life." These are people who will clog up your dreams and river of flow and stop you from getting the full benefits that God wants you to receive.

Point 30: Pray every day and refresh your mind and vision

Summary **Session 4**

Life is full of choices—good and bad. We must reprogram our thoughts to secure good choices in our life.

When cleaning your life refrigerator, use good cleaning products that disinfect and kill contamination.

Good disinfectants

Pine-Sol = Praise and Worship—find a good joyous song to sing and sing it; it will brighten your day.

Bleach = The Word of God—find a good positive scripture to enrich and brighten your choices. You will feel so much better about the choices your make when you know it is the will of God.

Air Freshener(s) = Other good and positive books that help you to make good solid choices.

Refresh yourself daily in your mind with prayer.

Notes

Empowerment and Workshop Session 5
Points 31-39

Educational Enrichment:

"Education is about control, and control is about education." Education allows you to make better choices and decisions, which will give you more control in your life and in the walk in the ***Kingdom***. This is a longer session and will take about two and a half months to really complete. Put it down and pick it up, but finally you will complete this section with pride and a happy sense of ***Kingdom*** accomplishment.

Take *Seventy-one Educational Days* in This Process
to Change Your Life.

This is the plan of learning to "make the best choices."

You are never too old to learn, never too sad to smile, never too young to die, never too stubborn to change, never too dumb to learn, and never too shallow to swim. "Go for it. There are bigger fish in the sea that have never been caught." Let's start on this plan today we can review it weekly to see our progress.

Do each point for one week, saturating yourself in the principles that will make yourself successful.

Seven Weeks "Plan" to Educational Enrichment

Educational Enrichment Session 5

This will take a *little longer to accomplish* because it takes education, a short course, a seminar, a workshop, something you must attend and participate in to improve yourself.

Point 31 Plan to educate yourself; Yes, Learn Something New!

Educate yourself; pass where you are today to where you want to go! Take one week to enhance yourself with new educational goals. Plan to take a short course or a semester to enhance your knowledge in one area: something that you want to learn for fun, work, or promotion. Something to do in the ***Kingdom*** is also nice. Plan to bring a new skill to your church or ministry; plan to increase your value. Remember, it is up to you to succeed.

What are you going to learn? ______________________________
Where are you going to learn it? ____________________________
When will you pay for it, (cost)? ____________________________

When do you start?
____
____

Point 32 Educate your family (children/spouse)

Tell them your plans, goals, and directions. Tell them your dreams and how they can help. Tell them your expectations; give your children/spouse and immediate family your goals, your dreams, and your visions for the next two months. Tell your family how they fit into your educational concepts. Give your children/spouse/family a part in your dream and goals (if you can) or give them additional responsibility to help (household-wise) so you can gain your new educational goals.

Point 33 Educate your inner circle/friends/society

Train your friends; tell them your goals and see who is willing to help in your *success*.

Point 34 Educate your target market

Educate yourself to your target market. Learn who's out there, who does what you want to do, and who you can partner with. If planning to start a new business, then ask others who have already started that type of business to even help you to plan to start your new business. Again ask yourself, what do you want to do? And when do your start?

Point 35: Education is ongoing; you must continue to educate yourself.

Take short courses, seminars, workshops; go to conferences, conventions, and empowerment clinics; go to book signings and library speeches; go everywhere; and do anything to enhance your education. Most of all, read, read, read, read.

Remember that Education Is Ongoing,
If you have not already learned anything new today, you are already a month behind somebody else who has!

Point 36 Educate the world

After you educate yourself, find out how to send yourself to the world. Develop yourself as a business person. Get some type of business started. Develop your business cards, Web sites, and invest in personal development classes. Learn how to speak properly and discuss your business and other ***Kingdom*** and world issues without debating or becoming overly aggressive.

The world is ready to hear about you. But if you do not go to the world, at least go to your family, friends, and social friends and introduce your business.

The World Is Waiting for You!

Point 37 Invest in continuous personal enrichment

We cannot stress this point; personally enrich yourself. Your clothing and hairstyle should reflect your upcoming life better. This personally will enrich your life. *Spend money on educating yourself.*

This must be added to your budget and not seen as a maybe or possibility but as a mandate for your future growth.

Point 38 Get legal

Take ten days to learn the practical business applications that may apply to your new business. Do not be afraid of legal counsel and legal advice. Your attorney is your friend—well, a mentor in this area. Choose one you can talk with about any questions, clarity, or concerns; choose wisely and fairly to your direct needs. Also take a short legal course yourself; you will be surprised how easy then some things will become.

Educate yourself to what you need to be legal; get your appropriate licenses (state and federal), if necessary, and all city licenses.

Point 39: Take a business start-up class.

Find one, and if you are serious about changing your future, take it. *No* excuse, *take it!*

Get a business; everyone needs a business—a personal business will enhance you, increase you socially, and bring you into a new mind space. It will also give you additional ministry opportunities. "Take a leap" and start your business today.

Start small, with something you can do easy and with limited time. Then you can add elements each year or start a bigger business; go for it. And you will see business is easy! Get help, ask questions, and you will grow.

Summary Session 5

Education is the force that will enrich your life, your happiness, your dreams, and your goals.

You must love education, and education will love you.

Embrace change and strive to learn something *new every day*!

Educate your family (immediate and distant) as you educate yourself.

Plan to know more next month than what you knew this month.

Invest in continued personal-enrichment courses and classes. Attend seminars, workshops, and school to enrich yourself and challenge your mind-set.

Use your new education to start a business. Plan it, believe it, and achieve it. A new "you" starts with an educated and expanded mind. Plan to stretch your mind today!

Empowerment and Workshop Session 6
Points 40-43

Supernatural energy and health:

You cannot be the best if your health is not the best.

For years, I went my merry way "constipated and loving it." Yes, I said it—*constipated*!

My colon was a mess; therefore, my body was a mess and my mind and energy—yes, you guessed it—they were a mess too.

You see, if your colon is not working properly, then you are at risk for low energy, low focus, low everything; and eventually, everything else goes bad.

Why? Next to our skin, the intestines are the next largest organ in the body; and when it does not function properly, you have other problems. Some people are on medicine, and they really only need a good cleaning out; go see a colon specialist (I prefer natural health specialist) and find out what you are really full of.

Supernatural Energy and Health Session 6

Point 40 Feelings do matter

When you feel good, you do good. No matter how you try to trick others, only you know if you really feel good. Some of us have settled for poor health so long that we really do not know when we feel good.

Take me, for example, I rarely talk about me, but I felt bad for so long, I did not now that I felt bad until I felt better. *I started with three colonics,* and then I realized that I felt bad before I had them. *Afterward, I felt light, energetic, and raring to go.* Then I began an intestinal-health revitalization program for myself. After six months, my waistline dropped three sizes, my breath was "sweet," my eyes were better, my joints hurt less, I got out of bed quicker, and I was a much happier person.

I firmly believe *I helped the Lord add fifteen years to my life.* I never knew I was supposed to go to the bathroom so much.

I encouraged everyone to check on their colon health and add years to their lives and happiness to their family.

Point 41 Skip at least one full meal a week—

Yes, fasting twenty-four to forty-eight hours hours is better! Going back to Eden, biblical eating of fruit and vegetables for your meal, will not hurt you at all. Try to eliminate one meal from your regular diet a week, giving your intestines a break to catch up and digest other foods.

Add vegetables, fruits, nuts, grains, and whole wheat to your diet. This will increase your health and your life. *One handful of nuts a week* will help your digestion and health. Also consult the Bible. Deuteronomy chapter 14 and Leviticus chapter 11 may add to your healthy eating plan. And please give your body water and proper rest (especially fivefold ***Kingdom*** leaders)! Do not neglect sleep and lots of water; help the Lord, out please.

Point 42 Add salt to your ministry (self), not to your food!

Try to use a *lot less salt now than we ever have; it is really not good for us. Please cut back on the salt!*

Salt is used as a preservative, and it allows excessive fluid to build up in your body and inhibits your ability to release toxins as you should. ***Kingdom*** people should be wiser concerning our health and bodies. God should give us wisdom on more than just speaking in tongues.

Extra salt affects blood sugar and our pressure and causes many other physical elements. So why is it so hard to lose the extra salt? I do not think God intended for us to have extra salt, but man made us thirst after it by using it in preservatives. We really don't believe salt is killing the human body, but it is.

When I was recovering from a major surgery and finally started eating, I could taste the natural salt in everything—even in eggs. I would say to my beloved husband, "Don't put so much salt in the food." To my dismay, he hadn't added any. I learned recently the amount of salt in a packet of ketchup and other condiments. I suggest to you to get the flyers from restaurants about their individual food preparations and learn the salt percentage. This will be your beginning to a healthier life. OK, pray for me as well in this area that I may use less salt, and be more healthy, with you in the ***Kingdom***.

Point 43 Water is Life, and Exercise is *power*

Drinking *water* is the beginning of great health; after all, your body is mostly water. When you are dehydrated, you are not giving your body the needed water to survive on.

This does not mean soda, energy drinks, or other liquid additives. Your body needs water and exercise.

Exercise will strengthen your muscles, your mind, and give you supernatural energy.

My godmother (Mother Ruff) is seventy-six, an avid exerciser and is in great health and shape (really great shape). She attributes this to water and exercise. I believe her and strive to reach her exercise routine; as a role model, she is tops to us young people, babies, as she calls us! She wears heels, she walks with a brisk pace, she dances in the church, and she is a glowing healthy woman. Truly she is crowned with beauty and wisdom. She has taught me by example as well: less salt, no sugar, lots of water, sunlight, exercise, praise, and prayer make Ms. Martha a fine lady!

Summary Session 6

We all want to live longer, so we must do something to create healthy habits—these habits include water and exercise.

Water is the *spring of life*, and exercise will strengthen your body to get you to the water you need.

Make sure that you drink water and do some type of exercise.

You must eat better; healthy eating is a key to supernatural health. Skip one meal per week and give your body a chance to catch up. This will increase your life by ten years.

Make sure you pay close attention to intestinal health. Keep your colon clean and fresh to help process food, give you energy, and brighten your day.
Get outdoors; do something outdoors at least once in every nine days (once a week is better). Rake the yard, plant a garden, and sit on the steps and read a book.

Doing something outside will increase the oxygen in the lungs; go to the park, take a nature trail walk—just get outdoors.

Empowerment and Workshop Session 7
Points 44-54

Spiritual Identity :

When you know the *Creator,* you can understand the *creation* better. The *Creator* is God and the *creation* is you.

It's planned and simple. We did not create ourselves or come from a big bang theory.

We were not an accident; we were created by a loving Creator who did not make a mistake or error.

It is wonderful and great that God so loved us that He breathed his very breath in us and gave us life.

Therefore, knowing this gives us the power to succeed and become a *success.*

Therefore, as we get to understand and receive our Creator, we understand and receive ourselves.

God is great . . . And so are *we*
God is love . . . And so are *we*
God is powerful . . . And so are *we*
God is abundant . . . And so are *we*
God is truth . . . And so are we
God is order . . . And so are WE
God is ***Kingdom*** . . . And so are WE

Do you get the picture?

As he is, so are *we* in his image.

Spiritual Identity Session 7

Point 44 "One" Creator makes us all valuable

I believe in *my* worth and the value of others. Therefore, I respect all life and every person and creation of the Creator, God. This respect will lead me to knowing other persons better and realizing that they have value as well.

It will lead me to conversations that will allow me to see this goodness in others. I will constantly try to find something good in others as I show them the good that is in myself, therefore showing the value of God, the creation, that He has created in me His creation.

Let us get a visual of who we really are. I am like the Creator in the five following ways:

______________________ ______________________
______________________ ______________________
______________________ ______________________
______________________ ______________________

Point 45 God cares for me

God is on my side. He loves me and cares for me. Yes, me—I have the embracing care of God. He cares for me, my well-being, my thoughts, and the direction my life goes.

It does not always make sense to me that everything does not work as I think or plan, but for sure, be certain that God loves you and cares for you. Be patient with the plans you have and meditate good thoughts, and you will begin to see the Creator's plan for you.

Point 46 It's in what you say

Confess positive scriptures about your health, well-being, finances, mind-set, and spiritual growth. You say it, you will do it; you do it, you will become it. You *will* achieve it.

Point 47 Get on a journey to go somewhere

Go from "I can" to "I am." It's a beautiful journey that will take you to your point of excellence.

You might be able to do a lot of things, but when you realize that the statement "I can do something" is an inactive statement of purpose . . . But "I am doing" is an active statement. Make up in your mind to change this statement at least two times per month.

I am now doing ____

____

I am now doing____

____

Point 48 I love to serve others

When I learned that the best gift is giving, I give more and, therefore, receive the best gift of all. Serving others has led me to be blessed. The greatest joy is the joy of helping someone else reach their destiny and their dreams; giving them what I have already learned enhances me with God and mankind. The ***Kingdom*** is about serving others.

Point 49 I love life

I am grateful to my Creator for my life and will not waste it for any reason. My life is valuable and is set for purpose. If I do not know my purpose, I will seek a counselor of God (a life coach or a personal adviser to help me find my purpose), a ***Kingdom*** mentor to help me find my path of Christian strength and destiny.

I purpose to live my life happy and with the joy of the Creator to whom I have gratitude for this—my good life!

The "Spiritual Latte"—
"Simple *Kingdom* Enrichment Points"
To meditate on with over a cup of tea/coffee or a glass of water

Point 50:

Read your Bible, start a study pattern "personally" in your own space, and read a Bible you can understand. I suggest the Contemporary English Version—this is a great read.

Point 51:

Join a ministry (church) and become active and supportive. Make friends and extended family with church members. Learn to be a good giver of time and talents.

Point 52:

Join a social activity: This will support your mind, body, and soul (just don't let it interfere with your church time); or join a basketball or bowling league or book club.

Point 53:

Enjoy each week by doing something great for yourself! "What have you done for yourself lately?"

Point 54:

Talk (call) or *communicate with someone something nice, everything. Take five minutes* to tell someone how much you appreciate them. *Drop a card in the mail* or reach out to a productive friend. This will increase your ***Kingdom*** gratefulness and your healthy walk in Christ daily.

Summary

Session 7

You are the best "you" the Creator has ever made.

He molded you for *success* and divine development; as you become one with the Creator, you will become one with yourself.

You have everything it takes to make it work. Meditate on the good points in your life.

Find daily thoughts and refresh yourself in his Word. These thoughts must become a pattern in your place in God and not allowed to slip away.

You will then see great things materialize for you as you pull out the good that is within you.

The ***Kingdom*** has need of the goodness that God has already placed within you.

Let the glory of the Lord rise in you and among you as you press into getting the best out of your life.

God cares about you. Yes, do not be deceived with negative images that tell you anything else.

Your life is about you, your growth, and development. Do not forget to give it back. It will continue to make you a better person.

You are God's best! He chose you for the ***Kingdom***; now let the ***Kingdom*** be shown in you!

Notes

Empowerment and Workshop Session 8
Points 55-75

Financial Empowerment:

Financial Empowerment

Everyone wants to be *rich*, to have money and wealth; and if you are a believer, you should.

But if you get it—*that is, money*—can you handle it?

Get out a sheet of paper and a calculator. Come on, do it! Now we will see; can you handle money, or does money handle you! *Add up all the money you have made in the last ten years and give an account for it;* this will let you see if you are really ready to handle wealth.

You will probably need another sheet to be honest about your spending, but after you deduct as much as you can, see what you should be doing differently.

OK. It will help you with future resources!

What are your highest-cost items, and how much of your ten-year income have you really spent on them? Now *WHERE IS THE REST OF YOUR MONEY?*

List here the year, the total income for the year, and where you spent the money. Then total how much you really spent and how much you cannot account for. Then finally, how much of the money did you invest in the ***Kingdom***, or did you just blow it? I tell people if you are going to blow thousands, at least invest it in the ***Kingdom*** of God; he is the only one who has promised you a minimum of 30 percent on your return. Now that's a good banker and a great return!

Yearly (income made) Amount Saved Amount Spent Where you spent it

____
____
____
____
____
____
____
____
____
____
____
____
____

So, my friend, how much money did you make in ten years? How about in twenty years?
And how much did you spend in twenty years or ten years?________
And what is the balance of your savings for ten or twenty years?

____

And what have you paid off with the money God already gave you?

___________________ ___________________ ___________________
___________________ ___________________ ___________________

Based on your pattern, can God trust you with more money? Are you a good steward of the finances he has already given you?

Are you a ***Kingdom*** keeper? Do your finances reflect supporting the ***Kingdom*** of God? Good habits? Ask yourself these questions and then set yourself and your finances in line so that God can truly bless you!

Point 55 "What's your happy goal?"

You need to discover your financial "happy goal." What amount of money will make you happy? What do you consider as financial success?

Have a hot cup of coffee/tea and be real with yourself about how much money you do need monthly/annually to be happy.

Now process a plan to help you reach that goal.

First, get a business going for yourself: your business, your work, your money!

Let's answer this question, "What amount of money per year do I need to be happy?"

____

I can start my own business; this business will be ________________
I will start my business on ____________________________

Point 56 Learn Monopoly

Yes, playing the game with someone else's money will give you a better feeling of managing your own. When you play Monopoly, you will learn buying, trading, and selling property. You will learn simple banking and real estate principles. Yes, really, Monopoly will help.

Point 57 Money is your friend

Allow money to be a friend in your mind, want to keep it, and *hang around with your money. Hold on to it and value it. It is your friend.*

Point 58 Invest in Wealth Training

Take classes at least two times per year; plain and simple, you need to invest *(spend money) on your success.*

Often we go to a bookstore, buy books, and read on the other topics. Other times, we have to pay for courses as well to enhance ourselves in our current job or positions, but we need to invest and seek help to increase our financial empowerment.

Also joining specific networking groups that address your business and your type of produce can be a great way to showcase what you do for little less than a lunch meal; it can also grant you information from others about the business you want to be in. It is a good way to introduce yourself to others and position yourself in the financial position to be seen and to go into the financial status you wish to gain.

Point 59 Partnership is valuable

Don't try to do it all; in the beginning you will need help and training, so partner. The ***Kingdom*** is about partnership and lots of them.

If you have value, you can trade "value skills." And use a lot less money so make yourself valuable, and do lots of bartering your services for the services of others.

For example, if you can type, however, you need some food for a special event, maybe a partner will fix some food for you and you design a new brochure for them. That's partnership in the ***Kingdom***; it really works. Especially if people need what you have to offer.

"This is called bartering and will help you out a lot. That's why educational enhancement is a must. Otherwise, you may bring "no value" to the table. So who will pay you and you will end up paying for everything that you may need?

Point 60 Time is Valuable

Invest precious time in others *as long as they add value to your life.* Stop hanging out with people who are not improving themselves financially. Hanging around persons who have no interest in financial success will kill your dreams and visions of wealth. Add new friends in business and new financial positions to your life; this will enhance your ability to continue to grow successfully.

Point 61 Stop playing—get a business

Everyone should own a business. "Starting a business" will give you twenty-two major business deductions, and see why a business is a necessity for your future financial success. This will open more money for you to invest in the ***Kingdom*** of God and open up more giving opportunities for you. The more you give, the more you will receive. This ***Kingdom*** cycle of giving will bless your pocketbook and your efforts in more ways than you can name.

If you want a free business, go to this Web site and sign on: *http://www.cashthecheck.datanetworkaffiliates.com/.*

Now there is no excuse not to be in business for yourself. I just opened up an opportunity for you to have your own business, with a Web site, and it will cost you nothing. It is in seventy-seven countries, so wherever you are, you can join. *NOW what is your excuse?*

Someone will say *"it must be a trick."* Well, it's free, so how can you be tricked? Get away from the negative mind-set, and let's go father in the ***Kingdom***. The ***Kingdom*** is about business!

Learn how to *balance your checkbook and get a savings account,* so when you need a business account, you have a relationship with a local bank, and they can help you start a new business account.

Point 62 Get the money, honey

Meeting a human need will keep you in the "cash flow."

Pick careers where people will always need your services and you will always have a career and cash flow. Do not be afraid to ask to get paid for your services. Get the money, honey! God does not look at being unprofitable as a good thing (look the scriptures up). So plan to prosper, and do not let his (Christ) dying be in vain. Why did Christ come? So we could be broke? NO, NAY, nope, not so! But so that we could have life and have life more abundantly! The abundant life is here for you. Change your mind, and your money will follow. Yes, the poor and broke we (in the earth) will have with us always, but does it have to be you or your family? Does the spirit of poverty have to be your mantel? Or can you take on the spirit of abundance? The choice is yours.

Think about this ***Kingdom*** point; even Lot, the cousin of Abraham, had enough sense to follow "prosperity and leave poverty behind," and he was BLESSED. Other family members could have followed Abe. I am sure he would have taken them along as well if they had only asked. But they did not see the MONEY, the prosperity! Follow the money, leave those behind you still talking but not walking in the faith!

Only follow the family members, coworkers, and friends who are prospering. The others, leave behind and leave them smiling, clapping, and laughing as you are on your way to your wealthy place in the ***Kingdom*** of God. Let them say you are "all about the money." I tell them, "If you are not about the money, you are about being broke. Don't rob or steal, but, baby, please set your mind to get some money, to attract more money, and to gain more money along your way home."

Point 63 Mentality of ownership

Change your W-4. Manage your own money. Stop letting the government manage it for you.

What is a tax return? Your money coming back to you after you let someone else hold it and use it for a year!

You lend the *government your money throughout the year,* and they give it back at the end of the year.

No interest.

Would your budget be different if you could add extra $200-$500 to your budget a month? Would that help you to start a business? Well, go for it today. Change your W-4s, give yourself the maximum deductions allowed now, and you can keep your own money for success. After you change this paper, you MUST start a business. This will offset any money that you may have to be responsible for. *Also, give big to your church; this will offset the rest of the monies you may or may not owe.* And you may find yourself getting even getting a refund!

Pull that money out now, and use it to start a business. Start acting like a business owner; invest in *yourself and you can write yourself a check!*

Point 64 Business is work

If you plan to invest in real estate, learn about all the loans, including hard money loans and all other facts. There are no get-rich-quick businesses. You must work all business, and the business will work for you. Don't spend your money if you think you will get rich within ninety days; it *will not* work.

Everyone selling "I can make you rich" products is not telling you the many, many hours you must work to make the business pay off.

Do not look to get rich overnight. Stop it; this is not sensible and will disappoint you in the long run. Plan to be in business and achieve by hard work. Only constant hard work will cause you to succeed. No tricks, no gimmicks—just hard honest work.

Point 65 What is your "*Y*"?

Your why is "*Why you do what you do?*"

When you strive for financial success, you must make sure it's enough to push you into success.

Why am I in the business?
Why I do what I do?
Why I want to succeed?

You will not be rich in ninety days.
Plan to work and be successful in the long term.

Point 66 New things are coming

Make room for new things—throw away five old things and make room for new things.

1. Sell if you can.
2. Donate if you can.
3. Throw away things you don't need.
4. Make room for increase.
5.

List five things you are going to rid yourself of to get new things.

Point 67 Learn the tax laws

No one is going to tell you (for free) how to save yourself thousands of dollars. *You need to get to know the tax laws; attend a tax class and find out what deductions you may be able to get.* These new tax laws will increase your inner growth and business growth, and you will be able to help your friends and family save money as well.

Point Fourteen There's Plenty of Money

As we learned, in the election process of 2008, billions of dollars had been spent on electing a candidate. There was no shortage of money. Think about it. Where did the money come from? *People*—these same people are available to you if you bring them a plan they can buy into. Do you believe? Here, go get it. Someone will pay you for what you do or know. Well, you'd better. The money is out there; go get it!

Point 68 Make it right

Make your product in excellence all the time. Spend the time to do it right, and it will bring additional business to you.

I teach small business start-up classes.

In every class, I give the new students an opportunity to present their business and talents. Of course, I want to see *excellence*! Recently, one student wanted a catering business, so I gave her the opportunity to cater for the small class. "No big to do," I told her. *To my surprise, this student went all out getting her catering dishes, spoons, and chauffeurs;* the food was good, but the presentation was outstanding and made me want to immediately refer her for other catering opportunities from which she got and made $1500 the following week. You see, how you present yourself is a great deal and can make you or break you. Always represent the ***Kingdom*** well; it will pay off.

You see, everyone is always watching to see if you are as good as someone else they know that does what you do. I stress to you: *always represent how* great you are, so put out the best effort every time. You will be surprised how quick you succeed because of your excellence.

Point 69 Do it right the First time!

No shortcuts! It always represents you! Do it right the first time! It will save you money and the time of redoing it again.

Don't cheat yourself. *Add cost before ever giving prices, and add staff cost.* Then set your price to represent your services, and *you do not have to be the cheapest if you are confident you will do the best job.* Be fair with your ability to make and increase your business, and neither you nor your client should be disappointed when you use these strategies.

Point 70 Open savings account and start your financial accountability

Open a savings account at a local bank (only allow yourself to withdraw from it four times a year).

The Prosperity Plan

Phase One

Saving at least $3,000 a year should be your goal. Do this for three years; then invest on the third and sixth years, then save for three years (for the next twenty years). Alternating plans of saving and investing will bring you into a the second phase.

Phase Two

Just so you know, real estate never fails.

After phase 1, now you are ready for phase 2. When you have saved up enough money, invest in a small property, maybe in a rural town, and "rent" out the place. This will add additional income to you, bottom line: Use it all to create more income but only to buy more investment property. Save again for more property to be obtained.

Your goal should be at least ten pieces of property (houses, apartments, mobile homes, any type of living spaces). You should continue this process, and you will see the additional finances being made and turn over and over again until you reach your goal.

Once you have ten investment properties, you are halfway set. This real estate investment will be good for years and *should produce a practical income for your retirement and financial freedom. These years and saving and investment practices will bring you financial fruit.* After fifteen years, invest in something else that will bring you as much income and resources. Then God will call you a good steward because you have grown in the ***Kingdom*** and produced more than you had.

Watch your personal finances grow. Never invest all your money into one area; this is not wise.

Spiritual Latte

Quick Points: "Practice income instead of outflow." My daddy always said to make more than you spend. It's that simple.

Point 71:

Review your income weekly, make your money grow, and increase and move ahead.

Point 72:

Tell others in your circle to improve financially; give them the power to save.

Point 73:

Find a stock that you like and can afford to invest small amounts of money in.

Point 74:

Get at least two bank CDs and roll them over for at least five years. (Don't spend them—reinvest them.)

Point 75:

Plan to leave some money here on this earth for your grandchildren, church, charity, or for any other great social-service cause. Get a life insurance policy that can help with all your burial expenses. Do not leave your family in debt when you die.

Summary

You should really have a business.

This is your new goal for the next six months: to plan to have a business.

After deciding what this business should and will be, market your product—professionally.

Junk will get a "junkie" price. *Excellence gets a better price.* What does your product look like? Always strive to improve it, revise it, and revisit it for your success.

Truth creates money. Lies destroy money; be real to yourself.

Look at what you have, not at what you have already used.

Do what's right for you; it will create what is right for your money.

Invest for death (plan to leave an inheritance to your grandchildren).

Use your credit cards, but pay all charges off every two months.

If you can't pay it off in two months, don't use credit.

Empowerment and Workshop Session 8
Points 76-80

Mind-sets for Success:

Spiritual Latte

Quick Points:

Point 76:

Always pay yourself. Pay yourself at least 10 *percent* of your income, give to charity or invest in your church at least 10 *percent* of your income, save 4 *percent* of your income for emergencies, and use 4 *percent* of your income each year for vacations and special events for yourself and your family.

Point 77:

The other 70 *percent* of your income should reach this breakup value—50 *percent,* living cost and expenses; 6 *percent,* other bills; 2 *percent,* splurge money; 3 *percent,* investments (to make additional money); 1 *percent,* insurance and health; 2 *percent,* retirement fund (and don't forget to leave the government their part maximum); and taxes, 7 *percent.* The extra penny—oh well, buy an ice-cream cone.

Point 78:

Get a dollar's worth of change and do this distribution so you can really see what and how your money should be handled. Or you can get ten in ones, and to the save percentage breakdown, it will really help you to try and start a new pattern for wealth development.

Point 79:

You are in control of your life (with the Creator, of course), and you have the responsibility to take control of your life. And you have the power to do so with skills, understanding, creativity, choices, educational enrichment, supernatural energy and health, spiritual identity, and financial empowerment; using these principles will create for you and your family success.

Point 80:

Success is what you make it.

Create success for yourself, and others will follow you!

Empowerment and Workshop Session 9
Points 81-89

Spiritual latte:

Quick ***Kingdom*** Success Points:

Point 81:

Remember that your health and mind-set are as important as your financial goals and business dreams.

Point 82:

You must embrace the *mind-set* of **tithing:** doing good and paying back and paying forward. These thoughts will cause you to become a "financial current," and good things will always come back to you as you sow good things out to others.

Point 83:

Turn everything that is not valuable in your *life into an asset, or get rid of them.* If it brings no value, it must be done away with. Declutter your life and see the good things God has already blessed you with.

Point 84:

"Faith without works is dead." Take active responsibility for your financial success. Set reasonable financial goals. *Start the seventy-one-day plan to retrain your mind, thoughts, life patterns, and business goals.*

Point 85:

You decide how much "wealth" is drawn to you; join networking groups, social activity groups, and money groups to enrich your knowledge and make new business contacts.

Point 86:

You must become healthy, wealthy, and wise. Read new materials, enhance your skill levels, and seek positive environments. Purpose in your heart and mind to attract wealth.

Point 87:

Life is worth living, especially when you make it worth living. *Life is great, God is good, and His mercy is enduring forever. Say this every day, and create good things to come your way!*

Point 88:

You have a divine destiny to help others. You will do great things in the ***Kingdom*** when you put your mind to it. The ***Kingdom*** needs you! Whatever has been your test created your testimony and is now your victory. Help others get through their struggle and challenges by sharing how God has brought you through your struggles, showing them that now you as well have the victory in Christ Jesus.

Point 89:

Meditation is a *good principle and a calming factor in your life.* Mediate on good thing for five minutes every day. *Keep a journal of good thoughts and points in your life.* Maintain positive thoughts as much as you can during the day. Invite the purpose of the King to be the center focus of your life. Laugh as often as you can, and be a good person to other people, and it will return to you. A great book to meditate with, besides this one, THE BIBLE! Yes, that's the book for me. I stand alone on the Word of God, THE BIBLE!

Final thoughts

Practice these *eighty-nine points to* ***Kingdom*** *success in your life,* and you will see the glory of God daily. At the end of this journey, you will be stronger, wiser, and more complete.

*Start a "**circle-of-power ministry**" with twenty people like yourself who wish to change;* ***meet every month*** *and see where you are in one year.*

You are on your journey to complete success. You are on your way to ***Kingdom*** *growth and* ***Kingdom*** *citizenship. This journey will require change, and you must be willing to change. God calls us into a realm* of *change;* the truth of this ***Kingdom*** *reality is to embrace change!*

People who really embrace the ***Kingdom*** embrace the fact that they have to change!

Chapter 21

Secrets to the "Thirty-one-Day" Turnaround

A Developing a Mind-Set

of

Kingdom **Success**

Thirty-one days to a ***Kingdom*** turnaround!

I want my life to line up with God's plan for me!
I want my life to reflect the perfected and divine will of God!
I want my life to show *I am a certified* **Kingdom** *citizen*!

Five quick Steps to Change

1. Confess positive energy every day.
2. Read a positive thought three times a day.
3. Realize something you want to change about yourself and know why you want to change.
4. Give others permission to hold you accountable to the change you so greatly need.
5. Log your changes for forty-five days.

We have another challenge for you to take that will bring change in to your life.

Take thirty-one-day turnaround challenges

Take the thirty-one-day challenge to change your life (in the next few chapters).

The King Wants Us to Change to Impact the ***Kingdom***

God wants us to always focus on *change*. There are many times in your life when he will request you to review your life and *change*!

I pray in Jesus's name that
Somebody will invite this life of change to happen today.
Someone will want to know God better and deeper as the King of kings!

Somebody's mental lightbulb will come on today, that they need to change!
Someone will become a certified **Kingdom** *citizen!*

I pray today . . . and forevermore.

That this will be your lightbulb? And that it will shine brighter forever!

The Truth Is You Have to Help Yourself with Your Change;
You Have to Want to Change
and
Practice Change!
YOU must want to become a *Kingdom* citizen
This Is a Section That Will Help You to Change in Thirty-one Days

CHANGE CAN ONLY BEGIN IN YOU! WITH YOU! and BE FOR YOU!

During this season in your life, you are about to go into a real spin of things; everything may feel upside down. It is good to shake the bag up and see what's really in there.

Your Personal Prayer Must Be This:
God, help me change some things in my life so I can be a "***Kingdom*** changer."

Thank you, Lord. I am on my way to my change, and I am on my way to my blessing, my turnaround.

My mind of

***Kingdom* Success is**

*I want to become a true citizen of the **Kingdom**!*

Make Up Your Mind to Start This Section Today *for Thirty Days*!

This section will help you focus on your success in the ***Kingdom*** of God; it will help you to maintain and become aware that the success you need is already in you!

Thirty-one days of prayer will train you and enhance your time with God to have and develop a mind of ***Kingdom*** success, a mind to help you to turn your life around, and a mind to help you become a bold lion in the ***Kingdom*** of God. Let's get our mind on ***Kingdom*** success; failure is not an option!

"Lord, Certify me as a *Kingdom* Citizen" Is my Prayer!
Four Quick Steps to Change!

*I speak a lot about change because when you go into the **Kingdom**, expect to change. You cannot keep the old way of thinking or doing things and say that you are new. Change is a part of changing into a **Kingdom** citizen. These are four quick steps to help you to change!*

Step One

- Declare a thing, say it, and find a scripture to back up what you have just said; then begin to pray the scripture with the thought of success, turnaround, and victory in mind and see God brings it to past.

Step Two

- Believe God to turn it around; believe God to change you and give you a mind-set for ***Kingdom*** success; and believe God to instruct you and guide you into good ground, good thoughts, and good success.

Step Three

- See the hand of God in the midst of this situation of growing being there to provide your request. He wants you to learn to be a ***Kingdom*** citizen and He wants you to establish your faith and purpose in Him.

Step Four

- Expect a miracle to happen for you. If you are looking for good things, they will come. You change, and you can change fast; you can do a lot of it within thirty days! *That's all it takes to break a bad habit or to pick up a new one,* thirty days! In thirty days, you can make great changes. You can do it; make up your mind first and your body will follow. Expect yourself to become a believing, receiving, prophesying, faith-talking, action-filled superpowerful ***Kingdom*** citizen for Christ.

All in thirty-one days to a turnaround

The "Thirty-Day" Turnaround Prayer

For ***Kingdom*** Success, Citizenship, and Mind-set change

Welcome to the glory of God

Thirty-day turn to a turnaround miracle, breakthrough, and change!

Welcome to ***Kingdom*** victory!

Rules to ***Kingdom*** Victory!

My dear partners, let us first establish some vital facts; shall we say rules!?

God wants the best for you.
You must meet God halfway to establish your blessing.
You must not quit on day 29.
You must make the thirty-one days of confessions.
You will no longer settle for seconds.
You will gather the best of the grapes of the land and eat them.
You will be obedient to God's voice as he establishes you.
You will hearken, obey, and have strength in Jehovah-jireh.
You will prevail against your enemies and have *victory* in *Jesus.*
You will follow the path of your blessing all the long days of your life.

To establish a thing, you must first decree it.

God has given you the authority to decree a thing with your mouth.

That is why it is important to *pray out loud.*

See what area you need to make a change in, and let's place it before the Lord.

"I am waiting on a great change in my life so God can be glorified!" This must be your mind-set going into this. You must have great expectation to receive great *favor*!

There are some qualifying *factors, however, to any blessing! These factors are important and must never be forgotten.*

You must first "qualify" to decree and see His great turnaround power! And you must show a seed to see God's favor find you. "Obey, and you shall prosper."

This ***Kingdom*** *breakthrough is not for everyone.* Only you and those who still believe in ***Kingdom*** breakthroughs and ***Kingdom*** miracles must take action now and receive what you believe in thirty days. This is a good way to begin to restore the glory back to God and His church. You may even set a ***Kingdom*** precedent in your life. Your change may just change everybody and everyone around you. Your change will bring the knowledge of the glory of God in the earth realm.

Please be a Part of the Prophetic Connection
Every Thursday Night

7:45 p.m.-8:45 p.m.
Call 1-954-603-7729 or 954-483-8617
Tue-Wed 12:00 p.m.-5:00 p.m.
To request number and access
Do you qualify for a change?

Who prays: Not everyone is qualified to ask God to bless them; you must make the qualification to be able to ask God to bless you. The qualifications are easy, and everyone should be should they qualify before join this thirty-day turnaround and doing this section.

Qualifications for this prayer:

While we would want to think that everyone can get a thirty-one-day turnaround, this is impossible unless you qualify; I want to make sure everyone is qualified to receive this blessing, and then we can be one accord.

Brother *William McDowell* sings a song, "I give myself away, and draw me close." I highly recommend *you purchase his CD for a great worship experience.* I met him personally at TBN in South Florida, and he "sowed his CD into my life." I listened to him on this CD, and it took me into the presence of the Lord. I want you too to *listen* to the words and allow yourself *to experience Jesus and the Holy Spirit* like never before.

Then *ask Jesus in your life as your personal Savior*; ask Him to fill you with His precious Holy Spirit and guide you through these thirty-one days to a miracle and a turnaround. We can do nothing without the presence of God, His Son, and the Holy Spirit. He must help us to truly change.

**YOU MUST BE BORN AGAIN TO QUALIFY TO BE BLESSED!
IT's A FACT!**

How Do I Qualify?

You must be born again (accepting Jesus as Lord and Savior is a *must)*!

- You must acknowledge the power of God through His Son, Christ Jesus.
- Read Romans 10:8-16
- You must acknowledge the power of the Holy Spirit, singularly, corporately, and through the mouth of His prophet(s).
- You must believe that the power of God is activated through agreement (two or more in agreement) with the will of God.
- You must *not pray against the Word, will, or essence of God*—this would be *witchcraft,* and we'd cancel its assignment and work of darkness *right now in Jesus's name.*
- If you do not have a scripture reference for your request, you must *seek one. Find a Word of God to stand on for thirty days* and *agree with* it and believe it to see the power of God manifested in your life.
- You must be a *tither* and an *offering* giver. To whom "much is given . . . much is required."
- You must covenant to pray for Apostle and Bishop Rice as God is leading them in this prophetic movement and will return to you the prophetic blessing through their prayers.
- You *must trust God* that this is the divine will and direction for your life.
- Then you can transform as a vital butterfly in Jesus!

Chapter 22

Kingdom Sowing, "Giving and Living"

**We give you the opportunity to
Sow in your field of Expectation!**

**Sowing is the beginning of every good crop
Sowing Leads to Flowing
Sowing Leads to Growing
Sowing Leads to Growing
Sowing Leads to Knowing**

God does not use Trickery to Bless you;

Stop looking for a Trick and do it God's way!

Do not be fooled or tricked; God does not hear everyone's prayers. It is a choice to put yourself in position for God to hear and respond to your prayers.

Answered prayers start with right relationship with God!

Any born-again believer, covenant faith partner, and ***Kingdom*** citizen qualifies for a blessing; if you are in ***Kingdom*** living, I agree with you. If not, I come into agreement with you to become qualified for a blessing right now! Yes, I touch and agree with you to meet these qualifications.

Now we meet the qualifications. Let's believe God for something big!

How Do We Do This? By Prayer!

First We Must Be Committed to Pray!

First step to starting is you must select a time to pray; you must be committed to pray, and you must know "when to pray."

Prayer is going to be the foundation of this change in your life.

Everyone does not just get a blessing—no, not so. *You must qualify for God* to stop and hear "the cry" of the righteous and bless you, so let's make sure you qualify. It's easy; call us if you need help.

You must be committed to *pray at least three times a day for thirty days.*

This prayer that you are going to pray *must be* uttered *out loud*!

- (First *watch*—pray): Before 10:00 a.m. (time to pray)
- (Second watch—pray): Before 6:00 p.m.
- (Third watch—pray): Before 12:00 midnight

Second Step

Second, We Must Be Committed to Sow, What to Do Next?

You must sow to grow . . .

We want to give you a growing opportunity by allowing you a *sowing* opportunity.

If you sow on this promise, you will see the face of God. You can lift up your offering and tell God, "I am giving this toward my change!"

Since we are in agreement with you, we are going to ask you to sow into this ministry for thirty days. Every Friday, we are going to allow you to sow in covenant with us for your change! We expect change in you, and you will have a team to pray with you for your change. So let's get ready to SOW A SEED TO GET A HARVEST.

Sowing a seed for my "change" starts your process for healing and change.

You must step out in faith; faith without work is dead!

Do not try and get something from God without sowing a seed; it will not work!

Stop trying to sidestep this principle; this is the first step in your change!

He (our King) will not break His constitution—the Word, His Word, in His Bible!

In expectation we must plant to reap a harvest
Third, We Must Be Committed to Sow, What to Do Next?

We must have a direct contact with someone who is believing with us and for us, and we must plant a seed in their ground of faith to produce a harvest. Your seed on the ground of faith, where two have touched and agreed, will produce a atmosphere of fertile reproduction.

We are "faith farmers," and we must sow the seed of faith to get a harvest in return. Two must touch and agree; as we receive your miracle request, we come into agreement with you immediately.

We offer you the opportunity to use our ground, our proven fertile ground that has produced much fruit, to sow your seed of faith in. Then we together believe for a great harvest to be returned to you within thirty days. We believe God is with you as you fast and pray and do a thirty-day turnaround in your life, that the power of God will direct you to a greater harvest of miracles, finances, health, wealth, and mental renewal.

Yes, we believe God is with you, so come into partnership with us as we expect a mighty harvest for you. Follow these instructions carefully, completely, and wholeheartedly; and believe God our King for more ***Kingdom*** living!

How to Sow to Grow?
Sow a Seed into This Ministry on Friday for Four Weeks

Let's say in faith:

"I'm ready for a change"

Now let's plant a seed of faith on it!

I call Fridays seed-planting day. Friday is the day we keep our seed planted in the ground so we can keep our harvest coming back on every wave. I have seen people plant on Friday and be eating off the crop by Monday morning. People all over the world plant their seed in the harvest field every Friday; and God restores, creates miracles. And we see and hear testimonies of what God is doing in their lives since they have become faithful seed planters.

Bishop and I want to give you the opportunity to become a part of seed-planting Fridays!

- *Every Friday, mail your* ***Kingdom****, faith, and covenant seed to:*

Mail to**: Rice Ministries InterGlobal (RMI)**
P O Box 87-8485 Pembroke Pines, Florida 33084
Attention: The Prayer Covenant Team Ministry

Seed-Planting Fridays
Planting My
My Turnaround Offering

Please *make checks or postal-money orders (from the post office please)*

Payable to *RMI* (or *Rice Ministries International*)

You will find a *form to use for your sowing* (next); *make a copy and mail it to us today***,** and let's start our walk together! *We will walk with you to your miracle! Thirty days to change: miracle breakthrough and turnaround and change.*

Please copy this form, tear off, and mail it with your pledge; also, include your "action pages" for prayer and agreement!

Mail on Fridays! FAVOR FRIDAYS!

Four *Fridays* of each week: four Fridays of favor or eight Fridays if every week!

Remember to get on the ***Prophetic Prayer Line***
Every Thursday night 7:45 p.m.-8:45 p.m.
(For more information, call 954-603-7729)

Yes, I am your covenant partner! I believe God for my miracle, breakthrough, and my change!
I sow today my Friday night "breakthrough seed" offering.

Name: ____________________
Address: ____________________
____________________Apartment # ________
City____________State____________ Zip Code: ________
Phone Number:____________________©
____________ (H) ____________ (o)
E-mail Address ____________________
Prayer Request: ____________________
____
____

Amount of my *"turnaround"*
I will mail in on Friday's offering: included today: Amount $____________
I Pledge every Friday $ ________ Amount (spell out)____________

Please deduct my pledge from my credit or debit card (each Friday)
Type of Card ________ Card Number ________ ________ ________ ________
Expiry Date ______ ______ three-digit code on rear of card ______ zip code of card ______
My Signature ____________________
I also want to sow a special "one-time pledge" of $ ________ included today!

- Please send me a bottle of **free *Exodus* Anointing Oil** because I am coming out!
- I want to join the "one million prayer warriors"; sign me up and send me info.

Welcome to Faith

1) PLEASE TEAR OUT THIS PAGE.
2) MAKE COPIES (for yourself).
3) AND MAIL IN TO US (weekly)!
4) Mail to: **Rice Ministries InterGlobal (RMI)**
PO Box 87-8485 Pembroke Pines, Florida 33084
Attention: The Prayer Covenant Team Ministry

The Action Page

Faith without work "is dead." Let's activate our faith!

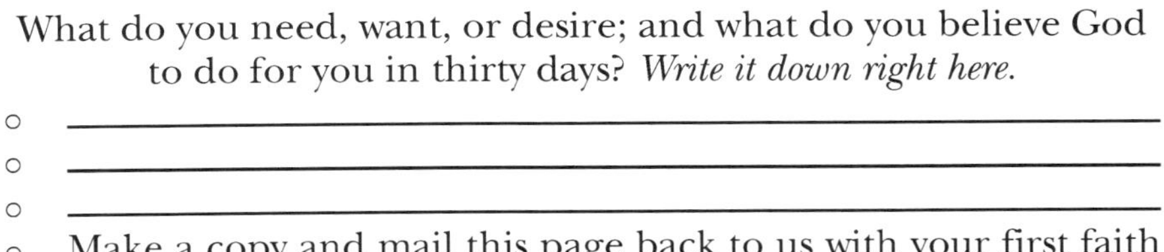

What do you need, want, or desire; and what do you believe God to do for you in thirty days? *Write it down right here.*

- ____
- ____
- ____
- Make a copy and mail this page back to us with your first faith seed so that we can be in agreement with you and your family with your turnaround.

Do it quickly so we can get in agreement with you.

- Next, call **954-603-7729 or 954-483-8617 and request to receive the phone number and code for *Kingdom covenant partners*.** You can only join us on this line after we have received your partnership and seed offering; you can then get the codes to join us for ***Thursday night prophetic partners*** **prayers and prophetic breakthrough!**

Do it today to start your thirty-day turnaround!

*After you finish, you will receive a certificate from us signed, certifying that you are reformed from this world, connected to Christ, a true believer of the King of kings, a "certified **Kingdom** citizen"!*
Are you ready to believe God for your victory?

YOU will receive a FREE *Kingdom* Citizenship Certificate when you have partnership with us

SAMPLE CERTIFICATION

of

Kingdom Citizenship

Be it hereby known to all men that ____________________________ has successfully completed the course to a "thirty-one-day turnaround"! This course has prepared __________________ in prayer, fasting, ***Kingdom*** *authority, and mind-set change. The* ***Kingdom*** *ambassadors has spoken in and over their lives for thirty days, and mind-set change has become evident in them. It is through this time of fasting, prayer, and meditation that ______________________ has submitted to the will of God in their life and has committed to become a* ***Kingdom*** *citizen.*

We hereby grant all rights and privileges and respect as is due all fellow citizen of the Cross of Christ. May your walk with Christ continue to reflect the grace and glory of God, our Father Jehovah the eminent King, through his son Christ JESUS. It is this day of that we seal this covenant of faith, power, love, joy and victory.

This sample certification is rendered under the hand of Chief Apostle Rice, so let it be sealed.

This date of ____________________ is my completion of thirty-day turnaround.

What I turned around in my thirty days __________________________________ I know God worked in me the work of ____.

Third, We Must Be Committed to "Connection," What to Do Next?

We want to have a personal presence in your life as you go toward your change. We would like to help you to have success in this area.

We would like to have a connection to you long after you put this book down, long after the reading is past. This book will be one you refer to many times in many occasions, but we want to connect to you prophetically as well. Please call and become a part of the Prophetic Connection Ministry. Our Prophetic team will keep you lifted before the Lord and will speak into your life weekly. Also, as you are going through your thirty-day turnaround, we want to be a covering for you during these thirty days.

So do not fail to contact us. Include all your information when you mail us your pledge and sow your seed in to FAVOR FRIDAYS! And we will call you shortly; getting you connected with the men and women of favor, grace, and glory is our pleasure.

And seeing you become a ***Kingdom*** citizen is our joy!

We are just a phone call away.

- **Every *Thursday night*, get on The Prophetic Prayer Line with us at 7:45 p.m.- 8:45 p.m.**

You must have access to this line; please call us early to get access.
**Call *954-603-7729* and *request* the special access code

or

E-mail us www.greaterharvestworldwide.com
ghccpray@yahoo.com **to receive the code**
or ghccstaff@yahoo.com

Please write your code here:

The Code #

How to Believe . . . for Thirty Days:

You can know that the "master prophet" Chief Apostle Dr. J. G. Rice and the Eagle Prophet (Archbishop Rice) are praying for you, and you can agree with them every Thursday night for a prophetic "agreement." It's your time for a change and a turnaround in your situation. Please, do not forsake to call in and get your ***Kingdom*** *connection; you will know that God is in your favor and that you have received.*

Believe for Uncommon Favor with God.

Let the Master Prophets speak over your life!
Believe that you will become the best citizen of the ***Kingdom*** God has and that you shall have ***Kingdom*** success. Believe, repeat, receive, rejoice, and be restored in Jesus!

Fourth, We Must Be Instructed On What to Do Next

Follow the above *instructions* carefully, and you will see "results."

This is the Word of the Lord from the mouth of the master prophet. You will hear the voice of God concerning the following.

•

A Word to Our *Kingdom* Covenant Partners

What is *Kingdom* Sowing?

*"**Kingdom** sowing" and seed connections are vital and important.* When you need is a special type of miracle, *you sow your "best" miracle seed.* This may be $50; $500; $5,000; $50,000—it has no limit (or minimum) because it is determined by you and what you really need God to do!

To receive a harvest, we must enact our faith. These "special offering seeds" are prayers overblessed and the prophetic words of faith water them (by our apostle, bishop, and special ***Kingdom*** breakthrough-and-miracles prayer warriors). We believe God is with you and for you every day as we expect God to do a miracle in your life.

Sowing seed is not an option; praying and believing God is not an option! Teaching over faith is not an option.

Remind yourself weekly to sow *special* seed into your miracle and watch God prove himself to you: how big of a miracle do you need? Make your first seed *a great seed.* Put your best in the *ground weekly* and expect a harvest special.

Just as important is keeping the prophetic connection call every Thursday night; it is designed to have a ***Kingdom*** *faith,* building time and connection with you. It, however, is only for those who really believe *God can* and *will* and press in every week to get it!

We believe "if you obey the prophet, you shall receive a prophetic reward." So together let's join a great ***Kingdom*** opportunity to see our God move.

Tithes and regular offerings shall *go* to your *local church,* to the set apostle, or bishop. If, however, *you are not tithing to a local church, we will cover you as a covenant partner until you find a local assembly to join; you may send your tithes with your special seed offering to our ministry to activate your **Kingdom** obedience and **Kingdom** fa*ith.

Just get it out of your hand into the hand of the ministry that is feeding you. To rebuke the devour! If this is us for right now, OK, But seek to join a local assembly.

(We will allow you to plant your seeds, offerings, and tithes with us. Until you join a local assembly, you will receive our covering, prayers, and blessings, teachings, and other ministry information; and you can even join our daily prayer line.)

We have a special "outreach" ministry of accountability, we would like for you to become a part of our *covenant partnership ministry family* and use us as a place to sow your ***Kingdom*** seed or as a place to keep your faith strong. *We will pray over your seed, and know this is planted in good faith ground.* We will believe for your miracle, change, success, and breakthrough with you. Let's go up together in our faith as we reach heaven with our expectations.

RMI

Rice Ministries InterGlobal
Mailing address: P O Box 87—84-85 Pembroke Pines, Florida 33024

Bishop and Chief Apostle Rice
PO Box 84-8785,
Pembroke Pines, Florida 33084

You may start a turnaround on any day!
Today is a good day to start, and
t***omorrow is a good day to continue to pray for thirty-one days.***

Chapter 23

Featuring

The Thirty-one Day

The "Thirty-one-Day" Turnaround "Prayer"

The Thirty-one-day Turnaround Prayer

Let us pray!

Heavenly Father, I come to you in the name of Jesus; and I receive your quickening in my spirit, heart, mind, body, and soul.

I ask for the *quickening of our spirits to manifest your will* in our lives. I bow and worship You and come to you with praise and thanksgiving, in fear and trembling, and in reverence to your desires in our hearts.

You are my only "reverend" and no other; *You are the* god that has bestowed great love on me. Therefore, I believe that you want me to prosper in every measure of our lives. Father, in Your holy name—the name of EL, the name of Jehovah, the name of God Almighty, the name of I am—you are the one and only true and living god. As "Abraham's seed," I ask you to *remember me* according to my tithes and offerings and the covenant of our fathers who served you as I now do. I stand on Deuteronomy 1:11. We receive it in the spirit of everlasting truth.

God, I *join now my faith* with others believing for a "turnaround, completely and honestly in every situation of our lives." Yes, we know You will come through on our behalf. I believe You for my miracles. So we confess that Your *Word is* over my life, my finances, my family, and my faith, our heartfelt bounty, our strength, our mental stability, and our cheerful and faithful attitude.

I am *blessed in the city and blessed in the field,* blessed in all my lying down and rising up. My day is prepared by You and filled with Your glory.

Your blessings overtake me in every area of my life; my leaf does not wither, *but brings forth good and godly fruit.*

I take *authority now in* the name of Jesus over my debt. I speak to You boldly and say "Be paid off and gone": notes, mortgages, and *bills are canceled, deceased, and dissolved* along with bad relationships and friendships that take my mind off the divine will of God in my life.

I declare my finances flow monthly in the amount of ______ per month. I need this amount to be happy in my life. You said you would supply all my needs according to your riches. I redefine this flow of riches toward me, unstoppable; my positive flow of life come to me now in Jesus's name, flow!

As *the water runs toward me* and my needs are met in abundance, I rejoice in my Heavenly Father's love for me! Therefore, I know Him as the god of abundance who richly restores in my life. Abundance is my grace, and *I walk in the committed authority of great abundance in my life. I renounce and rebuke poverty, nonprofit, and debt; they are not my friends, and I release them to leave me life forever. Take with you any ungodly spirits that you have brought in with you that are not of my Savior, Jesus the Christ.*

Evil spirits, *witchcraft*, *disappointments*, **and** *disarray must go* from my physical, spiritual, emotional, mental, financial, environmental, social, family, employment, church, ministry; and any and everything that attaches itself to me from this day forward will, shall, and does create a blessing to me, for me, and with me.

I am a ***Kingdom*** *citizen*; I serve the King of kings and the Lord of lords. He will not withhold any *good* thing from me! Never, so, good things, I call you my way today. I have attractive money, success, people of means, wisdom, knowledge, and purpose that can help me or are attracted to me.

I am on track with my ***Kingdom*** destiny; favor runs me down and overtakes me daily. The curse is removed from my life. *I attract abundance, gain, and overflow of good and goodness to my life.* I look for breakthrough and ***Kingdom*** miracles in my life. My god, the King, does "supply all my needs according to his riches."

I am not broke or broken, sick or tired; I am refreshed and renewed daily. I touch and agree with thousands who are reading/declaring/believing and are receiving their ***Kingdom*** breakthrough and miracle today, just like I am receiving more. So I am not alone. Our god is faithful and moving on our behalf. I agree with all legal requests and ***Kingdom*** agenda prayers, and I receive those who are in agreement with me. I am expecting God to give me a ***Kingdom*** *breakthrough* and a miracle in ______________________________ ______________________________ by or before ______________________ (put in date thirty days from today); and because *You* will, Father, I am already thanking you for it, blessing you about it, and testifying of it in advance.

My mind is strong; my faith shall not waver; and my mouth, head, and heart are in agreement with His Word over this in my life. My scripture is ______________________________ and I stand on it today.

Breakthrough, come now in Jesus's name. ***Kingdom*** miracle, manifest now, in Jesus's name.

I have done as Your Word has commanded me to; "I have sown my seed, and it shall come to pass." Hallelujah! And praise our god who pours wisdom, knowledge, and understanding on me today.

Therefore, I resolve *to restore my faith in my God* through evangelism and making soul winning abound toward the ***Kingdom*** of God. Father God, I need a turnaround in ________________, ________________, ________________, ________________, and ________________. These "bondages and oppression" of ________________, ________________, ________________, and ________________ must cease to exist in my life.

Strongman of ________________, ________________ *and* ________________

I no longer want you to be present in my life. I rebuke you by the blood of the Lamb. I personally resist you, and you will flee from me according to God's Word.

I bind you *away* from me, **by the blood of Jesus**, and *loose the presence of God to totally captivate me in every area of my mind, will, and emotions.*

Father, I receive your directions for this turnaround; *send a word our way by the prophets of God* to help us in our decisions and spiritual growth.

Now, Father, I praise you today; for this is your day, and I put my mind on Your Word to fulfill Your promise in me. *We pray for Apostle* and *Bishop Rice* and my leadership in your holy will for my life. Bless me now with *godly wisdom and send uncommon favor to me,* and your protection be over me daily. My enemies are defeated today in Jesus's name! I fret not myself and am not concerned with them, for no weapon formed against me shall prosper. I destroy the forming of the weapon by the power and blood of the Lamb, Jesus the Christ; all lying tongues shall fail, and all evil toward me or concerning me shall cease.

If there be any wicked thing spoken against me, it shall return to the sender with haste and shall fall foil concerning me: all roots, fruit, tentacles, and backlashes ceased toward me now at this minute in Jesus's name and shall never be formed again toward me. I hid behind the hedge of salvation and the grace mercy and love of Jesus Christ, my Lord and Savior. I declare God the Father, El-Shaddai, Jehovah, the Great "I Am" as my buckler and my shield this day and forevermore.

Any sins I have committed, I repent for them and seek your forgiveness as to not block my blessing. *Thank you, Lord, for forgiving me and taking any guilt away for any transgressions. I also forgive any others who have transgressed against me and that I have transgressed against.*

Father, *Your Spirit now overflows in me* and in my innermost being as living water now erupts. I praise you for exposing anything to me I need to know, including my enemies and all truth. My ministry is flourishing big in me and is effective to all I meet, I am a wise soul winner and evangelist for the ***Kingdom*** of God. I praise and worship for God is God to me. He is a lovely mountain in my sight! God is greatly to be praised and glorified and worshiped. God has full control of all my years and days, and therefore, they are long filled and with great joy. My body is healthy, my mind is alert, and my spirit is happy and full of hope! I have a great expectation of what God is doing for me right now, I received my miracle today and every day, and better miracle and gift from the Father await me. So I thank you, Father—God, ABBA—in advance for every good and perfect gift that comes from you!

I renounce all relationship that dishonor you, Lord Jesus, and break the power of ungodly soul ties over my mind and emotions. *I proclaim freedom* to be the child of the highest God. Jesus, you are my shield and glory. I fear no evil for you are with me, and you are the lifter of my head. *Therefore, my head is filled with praise and glory* as you turn my situation around. Holy Spirit, *you are my strength as you turn my life around for the glory of God.*

Father, *You are my salvation* as you turn my "spirit" around to line up with your *This is your first test to see* Spirit. You are my rock as you turn my faith around and toward your purpose for me; You are my life.

I live greatly and I live abundantly as you have died for me to do. I live wealthy, healthy, and wise; and I move in grace and glory. You are my El Shaddai; because of You and for You, in Jesus's name. I am used greatly in the ***Kingdom***. *I open my vessel to receive a miracle in my life and a breakthrough from the things I have named.* I believe you will do this for me and in me. *Money is mine for the sake of the Gospel, my goodness and great success! Prosperity lives at my door; wealth and riches are in my right hand forevermore! Favor is my friend and surrounds me. Goodness and mercy follow me all the days of my life! A table of goodness is prepared for me in the midst of my enemy, you anoint my head with oil, and my cup runneth over.*

I love you, Lord, and *I receive my turnaround.* I feel it now, and I know you are in me and I feel your guidance in me; so I become stronger in You. I will tell others of my victory in You and *that my life is better* because of Your promise.

Thank You, Father, for turning it around for me today! Yes, it is working for my good and turning in my favor!

In Jesus's name, *I have the Midas touch; everything I touch turns to gold!* Souls come to me!

They are attracted to me so I can bring them into the ***Kingdom***. I have the wisdom to win souls now in Jesus's name. Money comes to me! It is attracted to me; I have the wisdom to used money to multiply! Happiness is my friend! Wealth and riches live in my house!

My home is a happy home; my family is happy, saved, and free from the influence of the enemy! My children adore me; my spouse is happy to dwell with me! And I am happy to dwell with them. (If you are not married, say. "I believe, God, for a spouse that will be happy to dwell with me and I with them," and *life is anointed and appointed with* ***Kingdom*** *destiny.)*

My life is focused upon Christ and living for the ***Kingdom***. I establish the presence of God in the earth; the wealth of the wicked is mine, and *I am sold out for Jesus! I am a winner*! In Jesus's name, amen! Amen! A*men*!

I am a miracle; God sends me miracles every day. I create a miracle upon miracles as God has graced me to walk in miracle power for me today; I create favor for me today; As God has granted me favor, favor follows me; I create joy and peace through the Holy Spirit for me today.

I see myself getting better, stronger, and clearer in what I must do for my breakthrough. I strengthen myself, my mind, and my will to do it today. I am the best. God has in His plan for me and I come into agreement with Him for my *miracles* of life. "Angel of the Holy Spirit, be free *now* to bring me my blessing! Be free now to lead me to my wealthy place in Jesus's name.

"Holy Spirit, be free to *speak to me now* and to guide to all truths. I open my heart to you now. I am a better person today than I was yesterday, and I will be better tomorrow. I open my 'spiritual mind' now to increase in the will of the King for me in the ***Kingdom***. I realize I am *brought with a price and my King loves me*; I am not alone, and He will never forsake me. I am a child of the King, and

I am on my way to my turnaround. I turn as the Lord turns me for my success and breakthrough. I turn toward my miracle. Yes, my breakthrough is upon me, my greatness is at hand, my prosperity is nigh, and my miracle is on my lap, my hand, my mouth, and my life!

"*I have today and every day manifested success, prosperity, open-door opportunities* to preach the Gospel, and manifested riches in Jesus. I praise you now, Father God. I praise you now, my Savior Jesus, and I praise you now, Holy Spirit, for looking out for my well-being and for providing ways for my constant success." I am blessed today and forever in Jesus's Name.

Amen!
Copyrighted by Dr. J. G. Rice 5/10/09

Now Take Time for Positive Mediation!

After you pray, have a pen and paper ready (a little notebook or journal) to write down what the Father may say to you, after you pray. Expect him to speak to you as well, expect him to communicate with you, and expect to hear his voice!

Now spend ten minutes thinking of things to thank God for good things! Create an atmosphere of blessings and gratefulness.

Next, spend ten minutes sitting alone quietly and allow the Holy Spirit of God to speak to you. Write down what he says to you every day. And keep a journal of His Words.

Play a praise-and-worship song and end this time with good thoughts of success and see your miracle come to past.

Work on Your Success

Now after you pray, there is a section to work on each week that follows this prayer.

Work on your positive reinforcement to continue your miracles. We must pray and work; faith without works is dead, so let's work on our transformation together.

Everyday working log! Check off every day you pray!

"Thirty-one" days to a turnaround

Sun	Mon	Tue	Wed	Thu	Fri	Sat
				Call in *reminder	1 Mail ***Kingdom***. Seed "Favor Friday," we "sow seed."	2 Prophetic Connection 10:00 a.m.
3	4	5	6	7 Prophetic Line 7:45 p.m.	8 Sow seed	9
10	11	12	13	14 Prophetic Line 7:45 p.m.	15 Sow seed	16 Prophetic Connection 10:00 a.m.
17	18	19	20	21 Prophetic Line 7:45 p.m.	22 Sow seed	23
24	25	26	27	28 Prophetic Line 7:45 p.m.	29 Sow seed	30

Scriptures to Read Each Day

Matthew 18:19	Matthew 6:9-13
John 16:23	Philippians 4:13-19
John 14:14	Mark 11:23
Isaiah 53:5	Deuteronomy 8:1
Psalms 72:19	Deuteronomy 1:11
Isaiah 25:1	Gen 12:1-4
Psalm 18:46	Gen 12:7
I John 3:8 I	John 13:2
Psalms 3:3	John 14:13-14
Psalms 32:5	Proverbs 18:21
Deuteronomy 28:8	Job 22:27-28
Luke 6:38	Romans 11:26
2 Corinthians 9:8	Acts 2:4
Psalms 1:3	Acts 15:8
Proverbs 10:22	Acts 10:38

You may also add to this list, and read your "personal *promise*" scripture.

Other scriptures I have read and will read that help me to stand on my promise, I am expecting God to move for me, by his Word!

____________________ ____________________
____________________ ____________________
____________________ ____________________
____________________ ____________________

____________________ ____________________
____________________ ____________________
____________________ ____________________

SESSION

III

Empowerment Section

Chapter 24

Planning to Succeed in the ***Kingdom***

Let us bless, give honor, and respect to the Lord for something good every day! To gain more in the ***Kingdom***, God requires gratefulness! We must have a grateful spirit for God's presence to flow. Let us think on good and pure things for our spirit to flourish and produce good and pure things. Try to log something different each day.

Think of something good every day for thirty days **a**nd write it down, here. This will help to develop your *grateful spirit* in God.

Week 1
1.
2.
3.
4.
5.
6.
7.

Week 2
1.
2.
3.
4.
5.
6.
7.

I Am Truly Grateful For

Week 3
1.
2.
3.
4.
5.
6.
7.

Week 4

1.
2.
3.
4.
5.
6.
7.

Let's Plan To Have

Kingdom Success

"If you do not plan to succeed, you automatically will fail."

You should seek to know the King and his character.

When you plan to succeed in a company, it is good to know how the company will operate and what the president stands for. If you plan to visit a country, you may want to overview some of it laws. Many American women when visiting other countries must be subject to their laws; and like it or not, they must obey, or they will be arrested, detained, and punished by the law of the land. They need to understand the basic policies of a country before they go, and if the land requires total covering from head to toe, many times, even guests of the country must comply to be received. They need to understand the principles and how the government operates.

Our King Abba Father, our god, wants us to know how he operates, how he answers the questions we have, and how we can expect him to operate as well as to know what to expect of him as a father, what rights he has, and what he will and will not do! Let us review in a **"spiritual latte"** style, a short and quick type of review. How our God answers his citizens and his children, how he answers any of our request or questions that we may have at hand or requests we may have in the future as we go through our process of change.

How Do I Know When I Have Heard from God?

The will of God can be answered in many ways; however, the final word is the *Word* of *God.* God will never cross His Word.

If the scriptures do not agree with something you think you heard in your spirit, it is not the Spirit of God. No matter how good it sounds, it must be scripture to be God.

Be very sure that God's Spirit is tried by the balance of his Word. This word will always be tried and true and will always agree with Him! *We cannot pick favorites with people or what they say what does God say. He, our father,* God, is the final answer; and if the Word does not agree, then it is not the voice of God.

Do not be led by seducing spirits or games of persons who would lead you to believe differently. God will not cross His Word; after "rightly dividing the Word of God," what did His Word say?

What is My Purpose?

What is my purpose? Your purpose is to communicate *with your Father about His will for your life and the lives of those you are responsible for.* Doing this will enhance your spiritual growth and direction for you and your divine purpose. Make sure you are communicating with God constantly and continually as He continues to give you His directions.

How Does God Really Answer us, and what does he say?

God answers, vocally, through the reading of His Word, through the voice of His Spirit, and through the voice of his prophets. God answers through prayer, praise, worship, and prophetic utterances. God is answering more and more *through weekly assembly worship and through the teaching of your leadership.* God rarely answers through people who are *not* assigned to speak into your spirit. Your answers should come from godly appointed counseling.

What Are God's Answers? How does he answer? What type of answer does he give?

Yes: "You are in my will. I say yes, yes, yes!"

No: "No, no, no, this is not my will or plan for you at all, not now and not ever! NO!"

Wait: "I want you to have something better! Or I want you to have this at a later time."

Finally the Answer is Yes—but it is the "conditional yes"!

Yes (but with the conditional understanding), God says, "*Yes, I will grant it to you because it is your heart's desire. You have applied the faith principles and stood on the word of truth. I cannot go back on my word! Two or three of you have touched in agreement and have caused a 'cosmic clap.' It does not violate my word,* so I will grant it unto you by your constant request! *However,* it is not my best will for you, but wait. This is not My will."

Have you ever tried to get an answer from God? Contrary to popular belief, God does want to give you the answer on all things! Let's lay something on the altar and on paper and try to learn how to get an answer from God, Remember he wants you to communicate with him. As you go through this process, you will find you can now see answers faster and hear them clearer!

<table>
<tr><td>Week 1</td><td>Spend time with God. Tell him the answer you need, and wait for the answer. Do not receive any answer that does not a scriptural backing, or reference, that is the will of God.

My time is in God's hand
I will meet with him at an appointed time.
What time will you meet God?
____
____
What do you need him to answer for you?
____
____
__________________________</td></tr>
<tr><td>Week 2</td><td>WE must believe God for his answer and expect it to come into a seen realm of manifestation! While we are waiting, we must anchor our faith!

We must stand on the Word of God.
When you find scriptures to meet your need, please list them below and read them two times a day.

Scripture (s)
1. ____________
2. ____________
3. ____________
4. ____________
5. ____________
6. ____________</td></tr>
</table>

Week Three	Journal your experience and joys while you have been waiting or if you have already received the answer take time to write what happen that you received it! This step will help you to hold on to what God has done for you. I must journal my ***Kingdom*** *accomplishments* and my successes. ____________________ ____________________ ____________________ ____________________
Week Four	I must continue *guarding my mouth from being negative! I must learn how to hold on to my blessing!* I must retrain my mouth. My three scriptures about my mouth are these: 1. ____________ 2. ____________ 3. ____________ Other references ____________________ ____________________
Week Five	*Focus on praying and fasting and believing God for his changes in your life.*

Weeks 1 and 2: Make a plan for your success, journal a written plan for your success, and keep to it! Planning to have *Kingdom* success is just that—planning, making a plan, and doing what it takes to succeed. We do things by weeks to form good and strong habits, for a month (thirty days) of a consistent doing will bring change after you have spent a week or two in prayer and fasting, getting to know your Bible and the King. Spend the third and fourth weeks expecting to change!

Weeks 3 and 4 Mental and Emotional movement Toward a *Kingdom* Mind-set!

The *Kingdom* is about Movement

Pack your bags: mentally, emotionally, and (maybe even) physically. If you have to move, *MOVE*! It is hard to talk like *royalty* while watching rats move across your furniture and roaches having a picnic on your lap. It's time to leave the place you are in and go to another place. Make up your mind to move. Movement creates action, action creates faith, and faith without works will not survive. You must create movement in your life to wash away the bad and be able to allow the flood of the new springs and rivers of life to come your way. *Prepare to MOVE*! The **Kingdom** is about *MOVEMENT*.

Where will you go from here?
What do you wish to accomplish?

____

____

____

Write down three things you are leaving.

1. ____
2. ____
3. ____

Three things I am *unpacking* and leaving here

1. ____
2. ____
3. ____

Three things I am *taking* on my new trip

1. ____
2. ____
3. ____

Again, answer these questions about anything in your life or that you would like to see to grow and move even in your family, your job, your church—anything that you want to see move!

In the ***Kingdom*** of God, we have to have movement: *Praise is movement, prayer is movement, faith is movement, to speak is movement, to think is movement,* God wants you to have movement!

You must prepare to MOVE; now GO and get it! But realize that even to "*go and get it*" will take movement!

Chapter 25

Kingdom "Help Tools" for Ministers

Sermon Tips and Preparation Guide

Has anyone ever taught you how to put a sermon together?

It's really easy. Let me tell you that a great sermon is life changing, empowering, and needed in ***Kingdom*** growth, ***Kingdom*** class, and ***Kingdom*** schools. Yes, people want to feel good, but they want some substance as well. Prepare well, and the Holy Spirit will grant you favor in the rest of the areas you may lack.

Five *Kingdom* Tips for a Good Sermon

Tip 1
What are you trying to convey?
Tip 2
Find scriptures to back up what you are trying to say.
Tip 3
Write down how to say it best on small cards so you use lesser words and get to the points.
Tip 4
Ask yourself, can a child understand what you are really saying? If not, start again, and make it simpler.
Tip 5
Always give goals to reach and challenges to make a person better after hearing what you have said. Give them points and tips within your sermon to help them grow.

Basic Outline for Sermons

A.

I. **Introduction**—brief comment about what you are going to talk about—a statement that will be leading into your subject matter. This is the opening statement on your topic.

B.

II. **Focus point** from which the body is built:
This is the *main topic;* it will be based on scripture story and focus point.

- **Detail 1**:
    1. Scriptures or stories supporting your topic (examples from the Bible)
        a. (expounding upon that scripture)
        b. (expounding upon that scripture)

- **Detail 2:**
    1. Scriptures or stories supporting your topic (examples from the Bible).
        a. (expounding upon that scripture)
    2. (expounding upon that scripture)

- **Detail 3:**
    1. Scriptures or stories supporting your topic (examples from the Bible).
        a. (expounding upon that scripture)
    2. (expounding upon that scripture)

C.

III. Conclusion:
  A. Summary
    1. Restating detail 1
    2. Restating detail 2
    3. Restating detail 3
  B. Thesis (opening thought) reworded and repeated
  Make your closing fiery, something to remember you by!

D. Final words and a challenging statement. It should say thoughts *like*

"In closing," "I challenge you to, " "Can I pray for you about this?"

"Spiritual Latte"—

Quick Tips for your

Ministerial success

Ministerial Tips for Successful *Kingdom* work

Ministerial Tips for your success in *Kingdom* Work

Never embarrass your leader or your church! People are watching you!

*In a **Kingdom** connection seven things we must know*

- Get rid of the "burgundy hair and purple lipstick." (This is not the circus.) Some colors are nice, warm, and flatter you; however, your leader should not have to compete or explain your hair being purple or burgundy or bright orange or your clothing being too eccentric. If you want to be a leader, tone it down, please!
- You must "embrace change" to become a minister—even our apparel must *change.* Short skirts must become longer, tight pants must become looser, and most of all, your mind must change to be a help and not a hindrance.
- There are "holy garments" to be worn by the priesthood; don't let anyone tell you differently. Find them and buy them; invest in your proper apparel.
- Short shirts and skirts and low top blouses are not allowed and acceptable.

Here is the clothing test:

- Get in front of a mirror and stretch; if you see anything showing, like skin or flesh or this is too short or too tight, *take it off*!
- If you can't move in it, take it off. If you can't bend down with it on, please take it off! How can God use you if you can't move? Or if we have to pin you down in a sheet, how can you get your full breakthrough! This is not *old school;* it is respect for the people you serve and other ***Kingdom*** citizens who have to watch all your belongings hang out. Please, ***Kingdom*** keepers, cover it up!
- Bad teeth and bad breath—go quickly and get your teeth fixed. The ministry requires speaking and being in people's face; if you are a leader of any kind in ministry (ushers and deacons especially) as well, please get your teeth and breath in excellent order.
- If you want to be taken seriously; Always be on time or before time, but never late.

- Control your time and make sure that your appointments and everything else follow after your committee to ministry. Be on time; don't be late. Don't cancel the engagements once you have taken them to preach in. You made the commitment; do not overbook yourself! This is not the dentist. *Remember, you have a holy calling; don't play with God.* If you say you will do something, do it especially if you have taken to minister the Gospel and preach.
- Prepare to sow into your "divine connection" finances, time, and talent. If you are connected to a ministry, please pay your tithes and offerings.
- Be happy to serve; don't make excuses. Do what you say, when, and how you say.
- Be humble and honor those you meet with grace. Don't be cocky. *Humble* should be your middle name, *humble*.
- Bring people with you when you are invited to minister, and please have them prepared to be a blessing to the ministry that you are going to.

Chapter 26

Kingdom Keepers—"Armor Bearer and Adjutant Training"

Serving God's Leaders

God's Armor Bearers

Kingdom Soldiers
Called and Chosen to Serve

Workshop and Training Section

Featuring Guidelines

for Armor bearers and Adjutants

Serving ***Kingdom*** Generals and Admirals

"Those who lead the body of Christ" and those called to assist them in this journey are often called *armor bearers or adjutants, nurses, elders or personal assistants, executive pastors, and personal intercessors. This section should enhance your growth in being a blessing and a professional ministerial assistance to your leader.*

Thirty-seven Tips for ***Kingdom*** Keepers

God's Armor Bearers training, those who serve the in the palace

Tips for *Palace Keepers*, *Kingdom* Keepers, and Ministerial Servants

It's a blessing servicing in the palace

An armor bearer, a palace keeper, a ***Kingdom*** *keeper and adjutant, the person staff of the leaders,* ***should be graced with extra blessings whenever they are available****. Not that they should expect them, but they should surely not be withheld from any "palace blessings" when they are in overflow. They should be the ones to eat of the fruit first after the leaders. They may also at times have extra fruit available to them just because they take good care of the leaders. There should be no bountiful restraints ever if the harvest is available, especially if they serve you full-time or part-time with their thereon taking over or about twenty-nine to thirty-five hours to give* ***Kingdom*** *support. Bless them when you can and however you can. When they only serve the leadership about nine to fifteen hours per week to assist the leaders, check on them, pray for them, and be available to assist them in any emergencies when you can; and if you can, try to bless them at least once a quarter with something special (sometimes more). Also provide for their gas expenses when they have been your primary driver, going with you nightly, driving for you, and attending extra services with you.*

Your staff, "the A team"—armor bearers and adjutants and other personal ministerial team staff—should be supporting the vision and understanding that you are no longer your own but have been assigned to the higher calling of servanthood. They should also understand that it is an honor to serve in the king's or queen's palace and do so with the highest confidence and grace. Just a side note here: An A-team member who is chatty will probably not serve well or long; be careful and patient to select people who are not in everyone else's business.

The reward is more personal than public; however, the reward is great!

Many will not understand your dedication, some will be jealous, and others will speak evil of you for doing good; if you are doing a good work, do not come off the wall.

Do not let anyone run you away! They want what you have.

However, you are chosen and blessed to be in this position because of the greatest benefit that God wants to bestow on you, the face-to-face encounters you will see while serving your leader, and the benefit of having your faith grown and nurtured.

i. You will see miracles up close and personal.
ii. You will experience miracles beyond your belief just for servicing the prophets.
iii. You will be the first to eat of the fruit of the harvest.

iv. You will catch the "mantle" of the prophet.
v. You will become *great* as being a *servant* = *minister* to your leader.
vi. You will have great doors of opportunity open for you as you watch, learn, and serve.
vii. You will travel and see the great land of God!
viii. You will eat, sleep, and go to the best places as you serve your leaders.
ix. You will become a great prayer warrior and the greatest of intercessors.

These are the benefits of being an armor bearer or an adjutant; never forget the benefits—never, never, never!

God has given you a special assignment to take care of the pastor, the leader, and the vision carriers; *but someone must take care of the shepherds*, especially when they are wounded or bleeding. The leader has taken a hit for someone and is bleeding. You must know how to restore your leader, cover them, not allow any additional hurt to come to them while they are wounded, preserve their lives while, in some cases now, having to defend the sheep.

You must be strong, agile, a quick thinker, and not afraid to be victorious. Then after your leader is restored, you must still continue to be humble. You are *not the leader* just because you help the *shepherd out when they were bleeding.*

You must know how to stay in your place without expecting to be celebrated when the leader arrives back to camp. They will shout "Hail our leader" and forget you carried the leader thirty-nine miles all the way home, killed three wolves, and slew nineteen enemies. That will not matter to them at all and may not even be mentioned to any one out loud ever. But if the leader can trust *you not to try to outshine their weakness* and seek the glory for yourself, your promotions, and potions in the palace will increase.

Just be quiet, pray, and smile; and praise God you were able to fill in and to do your job with great effect. You will be rewarded very quickly! If they never call your name, it should be OK. It is not your job to announce *that if it weren't for you, the leader never would have made it and would have died.*

Kill your flesh and do not seek vainglory; you should want no credit, because this is your job, your ***Kingdom*** assignment, and your ***Kingdom*** joy!

You are here to attend to you shepherd, You are here to stop the bleeding of your shepherd, and **You are the one sent to stop the bleeding! Be ready to act.**

When "Shepherds" Bleed

Who in the _Kingdom_ Can Help Us?

Taking Care of ***Kingdom*** Leaders

Anointed to pour the oil and anoint my feet
Opening Doors for
Your ***Kingdom*** Leader "***Kingdom*** Hookups"

1. Who do you tell about your leader?
   If your mother made the best pie in the world, would you tell the teacher at bake-sale time? Of course!

   If someone told you they needed a car, would you recommend your car dealer?
   Of course!

   If someone you know needed a new home, would you call your "cousin," the realtor, and hook them up?

   You open doors for everyone you know, but how about opening doors for your ***Kingdom*** leaders!

Simple Say:

To the pastors that you see that work with you, sit with you at lunch, or you communicate with, your friend's, brother's, or sisters pastor, the pastor that works in your office, let them know, "You need to get my pastor for your next revival because my pastor teaches the Word of God, and it has blessed me. I will bring you a tape, and you can hear why you will be blessed by our leader. I'll also give you a business card, and I will tell my pastor about your ministry, if you will give me a DVD, tape, or CD. My leaders love ***Kingdom*** builders and ***Kingdom*** citizens, so have my leaders come to your church soon." Now you are opening doors and being a blessing to your leader.

Become a door opener for your leader.

You are in a ministry (school) to be trained; you graduate to a ***Kingdom*** connection to serve (work).

Thirty-seven Tips to help Make You an Excellent "*Kingdom* Keeper" An Armor Bearer, and Ministerial staff

The Duties of an Armor Bearer

Thirty-seven tips to help you be an excellent Armor bearer

Basic Duties and Insights

- Must have *direct love,* compassion, and concern for the (leader) one they bear arms for. Without this spirit of true love, you are not called to be a *palace keeper. You will have to give a lot for the one you serve with little or no recognition; you must love what you do and love who you do it for.*
- Must be a help to the leader and not be a burden or extra baggage or problem.
- Must be available to the leader. Your life is to serve now; be available!
- Must understand the leader and preassist with any need and service things that may be needed or anticipated.
- Must *understand the basic workings of the ministry,* the vision, and the goals as well. Knowing this will help you to help your leader achieve these things as well.
- Must *assist administratively* (typing letters, phone calls), if you can't do it now, seek to be able to assist your leader full-time as requested with light duties.
- Must travel with the apostle/bishop to all functions, *no* exceptions; in fact, *you should drive your leaders to any event to take the pressure off them,* and they can rest while you drive. Please do not talk when on this assignment unless you are engaged by the leader in conversation; then please keep it short.
- Must *have a love for driving and assisting the apostle/bishop to events.* Don't complain, if you are the driver, about how you feel. Unless you can't do the assignment, just drive and be happy to serve.
- Must have a *spirit of protection* to the leaders from all others. Be ready to protect your leaders at all times. It should not ever get physical, but if it does, you must be the first to protect them in spiritual and physical war!
- Must *be watchful,* not playful and silly; must be matured, serious, and on guard at all times, watching the leaders and paying attention to what is going on around them.
- Must *know when to dismiss others from your leaders* especially after they have ministered; must give a barrier of strength for leader.
- Must *make and keep the appointment calendar* for pastoral engagements and visits if requested; must know where and

when you are going and must *remind the leader instead of the leader reminding you.*

- Must *handle and arrange financial honorariums* (payment for apostle) and collect honorariums when assigned and as assigned.
- Must *never reveal private information or conversations* with any other persons especially in-house members.
- Must *ensure the leaders look and sound good* at all times, enforcing public awareness (as to the microphones, instruments, and sound— *if the leader is struggling with sound; ask someone to fix it quickly and handle it).
- You *must as well be dressed appropriately* at all times to ensure continuity of all staff members.

Dress in simple suits and colors so as to not draw unnecessary attention to yourself and away from the Word. After all, it is not about you.

Wear shoes you can stand in without taking them off.

Be prepared to carry your leader's "stuff" (Bible, water, pens, notebook, whatever) even if this means *you carry smaller personal items yourself.*

- Do not accept engagements while on assignment with your leader without permission; remember, *this assignment is not about you; serve with loyalty.*
- *Do not be "chatty" with the other members* and other people's staff persons. No offense, but *act invisible*; smile and be courteous but not engaging to the other staff or leaders.
- Consider yourself like the *presidential CIA or FBI.* You are here to support, protect, help the leader, and not to be seen.
- *You must think smart, talk little, know much, and tell nothing; support the leader always and be minimal with your opinion. Always strive to promote the leadership and not yourself.*
- *Must be* **able to direct nursing staff, alter team workers,** *and direct willful with authority. The more of a help you are, the better you can be an assistant. Your duty is also to pray; you must be able to pray for your leader.*
- Must pray for the leader daily at least thirty minutes *(twice a day), if possible, more.*

During service, ***your prayers are always for the leader****, not for anything or anyone else; cover them—your leaders—in prayer. Stay focused on praying for them only.*

- Must make positive statements about the leader.
- Must have a servant's heart.
- Must be willing to dress in the ministry attire.

Tips for Bag Preparation

- Must prepack the ministry bag and care for its contents at all costs. Do not leave it for any reason; *refresh it* and have it ready at all times with needed items. Remember, these are *not items for you or your children* to eat and drink when in your care!
- But these *are temple items for the use of the leaders*—only for your leaders.
- (1) *Glass*-Hard-Good Plastic (stemware) is better for travel and safety, but if your leader wants glass, give him glass well packed and protected.
- One hard plastic coffee cup (16-20 oz.).
- One travel mug filled with hot water.
- Drinks should be supplied by you (find out what your leader needs and likes): juice (cran-apple), water (whatever they prefer, just make sure it's purified water, Aquafina or Desaine), Gatorade (lemon or orange).
- Vitaminwater or Gatorade (lemon or orange) and tea bags (lemon or green tea).
- Towels—hand towels for leaders (and spouse), at least ten.
- Kleenex and throwaway paper.
- Mints (hard)—spearmints, peppermints (or Tic Tac), and Halls of some kind.
- *Ministry cards and information (to give to others) that may be requested.*
- Paper and pen for other information needed to be obtained from others.
- Current *calendar (to book additional events on the spot).*

> *Always have with you seed offerings to give and to assist with the service as well as to make your leader look good.*
>
> *Do not expect to travel with the leader and the leader pay your way or accommodations; you should be in position to*

be an armor bearer, financially and spiritually. This is a giving position.

Do not expect to leech off your leader for accommodations, food, or offerings except to go and be a blessing not a curse.

Anybody can give water, hold the oil bottle and pray. You need much more to be an assistant to the leader and the vision.

Positions in service
Where do palace guards stand?

I know your leader may give you standing directions; however, you both must always comply to the leading of the house for directions on where the armor bearers should stand or sit. Always ask so as to not offend others.

- Positions should be without distraction and function to *assist* the leader and not to hinder or to draw attention to oneself. The armor bearer is always with the leader unless released. (This includes in service, before service, and after service.)
- Even though the armor bearers are always with the leader, they *must never position themselves equal to the leader.* They must be limited to reveal any information and always refer others to *not* become familiar with their leader.
- Pastor: Never assume another pastor is comfortable with your armor bearer and always assume that they may want to speak with you in private. Please allow them this opportunity and release your armor bearer to the other side of the door to engage in this *king-to-king* or *king-to-queen* conversations, especially before you minister.

- Armor bearers should position themselves on *each side of the leader* when they are ministering. At the altar time, please *do not post yourself in the rear of* (behind) the minister (never in the rear, unless assigned); let your leader see you in their side view at all times, never behind because they cannot see you and they may back up over you or trip over you. *Do not be in the way of the flow; pay attention.*

- *Do not be behind your leader, spacing out, not paying attention or chewing gum; act like the camera is on you, and do your best to be interested with good facial tones and expressions.*

- Always move quickly and swiftly when doing something for the leader; and when in service, move quickly and quietly, not bringing attention to yourself.
- Always have mints and give to the leader immediately *after preaching and before personally ministering to others;* before they minister to *anyone, give them a mint, please!*

    - Prayers should be for the *protection of the one you are assigned to* and not to the persons being ministered (unless assigned for a short time). Then you should return to the post quickly.
    - *Your eyes, your ears, and your spirit should be kept focused on your leader* as to spiritual attacks from others aimed at the leader. Must be prayed up and positioned for spiritual war.
    - Must be an intercessor *always praying in the Spirit* when on post with leader, not *overpraying your leader (verbally too loud)* or becoming a distracted force, but with power and demonstration being felt by your leader, not heard by the minister or other people around.

Tips on seating for armor bearer and staff

Positions (when seated)

- ❖ *Armor bearer sits on the outer right-hand side of their leaders.*

If there is a husband-and-wife team, an armor bearer ***does not ever sit between*** *a husband and a wife and never between the bishop and the pastor.*

Sometimes, for space's sake, we must sit behind our leaders. This is OK.

If you feel as if your leader is in danger, stand up on a closer wall to them and go into observation mode. Be able to protect your leader at all times, at all costs.

If your leader starts a "praise party" or has a moment of personal celebration, **you should shield them from any hurt or danger quickly** *and with as little movement as possible.*

If your leader is called up to be ministered to, ***you should immediately go and stand behind him to assist him from any hurt****. No one should have to call you or wave for you to go;* ***know your job****.* ***And be alert at all times****.*

If you must *sit behind your leader, do so with grace, honor, and humility. Remember, you are a guard and not in the service for showtime or comfort. You are on duty, and an important job has been entrusted in you.*

Rewards for Service

Other Assistants and *Kingdom* Workers

When on the altar, who ministers and who does what?

Armor bearers to the side attend personally to speaker
Lead/Adjutants (Second in command to chief armor bearer)

Adjutants
A. *Handles the oil and my covering cloth (lead armor bearer)*

B. Handles my microphone and towel(s) and other necessities

First Row
Nurses and intercessors on the *front watch*

Attendant/ Nurse
Collects apostle's (a team worker) belongings (armor bearers in training)

Altar worker/team is to handle the people being ministered to.

Minister/Team worker A. Handles the traffic flow

Minister/Team worker B. Handles catchers and directions

and

Other team worker
Missionary and Mother C. Handles intercessory for altar workers and special prayers (salvation and special deliverance)

Chief armor bearers, adjutants, and lead armor bearer team are responsible for the personal belongs of the apostle, bishop, or those whom they are assigned to service.

They are the chief intercessory for leaders. They handle all drinks for apostle and leader. They are not to be distracted and must always keep their eyes on the apostle or leader they serve. They are to provide personal items such as extra mints, flat shoes, Bible, pen/paper, and drinks are the direct duties of the chief armor bearers.

Appropriate Seating Tips for Leaders when Only Ministers Occupy the Pulpit

Armor bearers sit as close as possible in the front row or second row to access their leader.

Nurses sit on the outside of the armor bearers or directly behind the leaders for a rear guard or stand on the wall closer to the leader they assist.

Armor bearers may also be placed directly behind the leaders; when nurses are "preferred" to sit beside the leadership, the armor bearer staff will take the position beside them.

Deacons and ministers should also sit directly behind leaders when possible and will serve to assist the chief armor bearers and altar workers always.

- *To be an armor bearer is a great honor and a special privilege; not everyone can be an armor bearer.*

The only assigned persons to have an armor bearer are the apostle, bishop, and pastors.

No minister inside of another person's ministry should have a personal armor bearer since they themselves are, in fact, armor bearers to the leader they serve. This will confuse the persons selected to personally serve you since an armor bearer can only be truly loyal to one person.

All in-house personnel serve as armor bearers and will not have an official armor bearer until they are in "pastoral status"; until then they are considered themselves an armor bearer. We will all try and serve each other (as you are assigned to minister in their appropriate positions; however, we will not exalt ourselves higher than we ought). If you are serving in-house, you do not need an armor bearer.

Who cannot be an armor bearer?
Some people just don't qualify for leadership; especially to be an armor bearer!

Who Cannot Be an Armor Bearer?

- A *liar:* one who possesses a lying spirit, lies, or creates false statements.
- A *God robber:* one who does not pay tithes, offerings, and is willing to give sacrificial offerings.
- A *lazy person* who is needed to be reminded of things and is in need of special attention.
- *A nonthinker: one who is not quick on their feet and need to be reminded of their duties.*
- A *nosy person*: one who is always in need of being in others' business and needs to be the center of attention.
- A *gossiper:* one who tells others' business, situation, or concerns especially to other people.
- A *leech*: one who "sucks from the ministry" instead of giving their all.
- A *nonservant* spirit: One who is looking for someone to serve them and not become a servant, pay money for them, or provide accommodation for them; this is not an armor bearer, but a letch spirit.
- A *noncaring* person: One who does not have the leader care, front and center, must be willing to lay down their life for the leader, without any doubt.
- A *faithless* person: one who speaks doubt and unbelief often and moves out of fear versus faith and speaks a yo-yo conversation.
- *Those who are* short-term members: *"armor bearer" is a chosen lifetime position, not "seasonal."*
- One who "*crosses," backbites, and gossips* "behind the leaders' back about their decisions" *for any reason.*
- Those with *"nasty"* spirits, unclean motives, and terrible attitudes.
- Those who *cannot honor other leaders* (pastors, apostles, bishops, ministers) with love and grace.
- Those who cannot stay in their place and keep their tongues with honor.
- Those who love to be seen in high places and want to outshine the leadership.
- Those who are cheap and looking for a free ride!

Chapter 27

Kingdom Guide Section for "Administrative Protocol"

Kingdom **Strategies**

And

ADMINSTRATIVE

Working Information

Kingdom **Administration**

Tips for ***Kingdom*** **Administration**

Kingdom **Administration—We Must Have It!**

This guidebook section was developed for use at our church, the Greater Harvest Christian Center Churches Worldwide Inc. and for our Association InterGlobal Association for Christian Churches Worldwide. This guidebook was developed as a standard protocol and guidance for guests we invited to our ministry so that we could all operate the same way—in protocol and order.

The *financial protocol* was left out due to various variables that influence or connect financial accountability, in a personal way, at each individual church.

Legally check with your state for these financial protocols so you'll be in compliance.

This session is written in first party, as to address *our guests specifically*; however, this can and should serve as a general guideline for any and all visiting speakers and for yourself as you visit others.

Experience has taught me a lot, both hosting and visiting others; I hope this experience will help you as you grow in the ministry.

When I first started looking for examples as to what I should do to host other ministers, there were *none*. So I have included these helps and tips to assist young ministers and ministries in what they should or should not do.

Administrative Tips for ***Kingdom*** Success

Includes sample letters
and suggestive ministry tips'
for standard operations
and ***Kingdom*** protocol

Administrative protocol and tips for the ***Kingdom***

Every ministry and minister should be able to say who they are!

You should have an introduction for your ministry—some sort of page that tells who you are and what you believe; we send this in a packet to others we invite to our ministry, along with several of the next few example pages for the church to have a clear understanding of who we are, our flow, our policies, and what we expect.

We believe in having a good understanding between our guests (referred to as visiting ministers) and the ministers and ministries.

The following should be used as examples as they fit you and will be used as training guide to help you along your administrative way.

- This is what I have learned by experience over the years, and I want it to help you early in your ministry; again, these next pages and this chapter should only be used as a guide for your administrative setup and a guide to others who attend your ministry and a standard for you as you travel abroad.
- *These are excerpts and sample form to be used only as a guideline to help you in establishing protocol in your ministry; for more examples and formats, please consult with us directly and personally for your individual needs. It is our pleasure to serve you in your growth and directions.*

First Example of Administrative Protocol

This is an example of an introduction to your ministry

Introduction of our ministry

Greater Harvest Christian Center Churches Worldwide

Meet our Founders
Archbishop and Chief Apostle Rice

The ministry of Greater Harvest Christian Center was birthed in 1986 after our now chief apostle and then evangelist for seven years (under the name of Harvest Reapers) heard God say "*Go and help My sheep,* develop them in the directions of My ***Kingdom***, feed them, and grow them up in My statues. Shepherd them, and I will bless your works, shepherd, and know that I am with thee."

Our apostle started out on the journey, which has now lasted over twenty-nine years. *GHCC is still growing leaders with a **Kingdom** commitment, purpose, and direction.* Teaming up with Archbishop James Rice, the past pastor of Rice Chapel, in 1999 they have brought this ministry a long way. God has blessed them to birth *several works internationally and globally* in which they give God the praise. *We are now blessed to have our chief apostle and bishop with headquarters in South Florida.* And God is still growing Greater Harvest. In 2008, Chief Apostle was voted in as the head of the *InterGlobal Association of Christian Churches Worldwide (IGACCW),* and she is networking many ministries together under this covering (if you are a fivefold ministry gift, you are welcome to make an application to join).

The Prophetic Connection

The "prophetic connection" was birthed as a tool to *help connect prophetic gifts to be able to function globally as a combined unit.* It is rich in substance when five or more come together to proclaim the voice of God; a "conclave" is established, and God moves as a fresh wind and restores, rejuvenates, replenishes, redefines, and causes the people to rejoice.

We invite you to join and become a part of the prophetic connection if you have a prophetic mantle in your life, need training by a master prophet of God, or want to host a prophetic connection conference in your city or town.

We are God's voice for God's people, with God's mantle, and a Word from God himself. Under the direction of Chief Apostle Dr. J. G. Rice,
"the master prophet of God," we serve our community, our states, and
the world that our God has made, so formed for His glory and His goodness. Join us today!

Call 954-603-7729 and leave a message for our staff and you can become a part of something fresh, something good, and something great!

Excerpts taken from Prophetic Protocol (Rice 1995, "Serving God's Generals")

Second Example of Administrative Protocol

How to operate in the ***Kingdom*** as a visiting minister and Host expectations For Guest Ministers and How to Be a Great Guest

A Word from our leaders, visionaries, and host(s)
Chief Apostle J. G. Rice and Archbishop James Rice

Welcome to the ministry of the Greater Harvest Christian Center Churches Worldwide where we "let the praises ring." *This is a ministry of prayer, purpose, prophecy, and the purpose of the* ***Kingdom*** *of God in this earth to mirror the will of God in heaven.*

We are so delighted to host you here at GHCC on behalf of our great leaders, Chief Apostle Dr. J. G. Rice and Archbishop James Rice. Again, welcome.

Enclosed you will find some valuable information about how we operate here at GHCC under the direction of our chief apostle, the master prophet of God. *We believe in order, understanding, and moving in wisdom.* So this booklet has been formed to bring clear directions of our ministry to you. Please *read this entire booklet* and refer to it often as questions arise.

We hope you will find it enlightening and well received as hundreds of others have and said that "they too wish others would be upfront and make what they need and plan as we have done."

The booklet is updated yearly and keeps getting better and better as we address the ongoing needs of ministry and visitors and as we become visitors ourselves. We learn more about serving the leaders of God.

Ministry is also a godly business, and full-time ministry is no exception to the rule. We operate in excellence when we invite persons to minister for us. This comes in three phases in which we expect to be successful in them all: *first, spiritually; second, financially; and third, in a continued prophetic connection* that will bring years of prosperity to both our ministries and ***Kingdom*** growth. We seek to excel in all three areas of ministry while you are here with us and when we are graced to be with you.

Please *feel free to address any issues, questions, or concerns* you may have with our chief apostle or appointed staff person.

We strive to serve in excellence; if there is anything you may need in your stay here at "the Harvest," please feel free to ask for our assistance.

It is important that you *read this entire booklet and address any need early*. We will believe you have done so, and any questions hereafter arising will be referred by answers contained in this booklet. Let's have a great time in Jesus, and again, *thank you for coming*.

On behalf of our great leader and team

GHCC Administrative Staff
On behalf of our Chief Apostle
Dr. J. G. Rice and *Archbishop James Rice*

Third Example of Administrative Protocol

Time and Order of Service

This is an example of service times of your ministry

Our service times and flow

(Enter your specific service times here.) Remember, there is no time to be "fashionably late" as a minister; be on time, before time if possible, and NEVER late without notice.

Be obedient to ministry times, and always remember to enter quietly and without form or show, and have your staff to adhere to this as well.

1. Ministry time
2. Service flow
3. Cancellation policy

Corporate Prayer: fifteen minutes before service

Praise and Worship: followed immediately for twenty to thirty minutes praise and worship.

Immediately followed by Preached Word

* * *

Guests, please know that after this, we have no set flow; we move into preached ministry time *as the Spirit directs. This is why being on time is a must.*

(Refer to section above for instruction.)

How should you govern yourself with respect to ministry time:

Ministry time: It is usually not more than ninety minutes. This should include the preached Word, ministry time, and offering time. If you are with us for more than one service, please keep in mind that you may minister to others the next service. This will encourage the people to come the remaining time you are with us.

Some of our members do have small children and also go for work. Please keep this in mind as well for weekly services.

Fourth Example of Administrative Protocol

An example of cancellation policy of your ministry

Cancellations: Our commitment to you and your commitment to us are valuable. We do know, however, unfortunate or unexpected things (major things) may occur. We *expect an immediate notification* in any change of your schedule for the conference/event as soon as you find out or feel as *situation arising that may delay or deny you attending with us. And we will do the same for you* as we respect each other in the ***Kingdom***.

If, however, *there is a cancellation on your part* and *funds have been spent by us* (ticket/hotel and other arrangements), *we will expect you, as a* ***Kingdom*** *citizen, to reimburse us for any funds lost, for any reason, on your part* (if no funds are lost or a reschedule can occur and these funds can be transferred safely to the next event, we will do so if we can).

We try to be good ***Kingdom*** keepers with funds; this is why we *book tickets only one week in advance* and pay for rooms upon arrival.

Fifth Example of Administrative Protocol

An example of a general conference schedule of ministry

Conference ministry dates and times: TBA

Services times are ______________________________.

Night service 7:15 p.m.

Day sessions 11:45 a.m.-1:30 p.m. (Wednesday to Saturday)

Regular Weekly Service Schedule

Sunday services 11:15 a.m. and 7:15 p.m.

Tuesday night (Bible study) 7:15 p.m.

Others services and times will be announced

Fifth Example of Administrative Protocol

The following information we believe every minister and guest minister should know: it was first developed as a handbook, but I will release this information to you in this section as administrative protocol for the sake of ***Kingdom*** *training and ministerial development.*

This is an example of information sent to speakers out of our "Prophetic Handbook" and information for visiting ministers and guests of Greater Harvest Christian Center Worldwide.

What We Will Address in This Section

1. Time protocol
2. Musicians' protocol
3. Keynote speaker information
4. Eating and meal policy
5. Ministerial attire
6. Developing a protocol for reaching staff and leadership
7. Rules for visiting armor bearers
8. General overview and policies of concern
9. Anything you would want your guest to know (but don't want to be put in a position to verbally have to say what's not allowed at your ministry)
10. Media ministry and book table policies
11. Flights, transportation, and travel policies
12. Hotel accommodations and room policies
13. Guest and travel arrangement for their guest
14. Emergencies and cancellation policies
15. Prophetic liberties, addressing behavior (and ministerial liberties not to be taken on your watch)
16. House rights
17. Personal review of ministry

Examples of Administrative Protocol

This is an example of letters and rules you may wish to establish in your ministry.

Let's start with time

As our guest, we will ask that you please be on time.

Time:
Our services start on time.
All *guest ministers* are expected to be in service before service begins to ensure *information of the day and the flow of service is established.* We expect all guests to arrive at least twenty minutes *before* service begins. The set time for your arrival is 7:00 p.m.

In-town guest: Please be mindful of this and adjust your schedule to comply. This will also allow you to meet with Apostle and Bishop before service for prayer. Apostle and Bishop are a part of the service from beginning to end. Lateness affects them entering in service for prayers and praise.

Out-of-town guest: Should arrive on the first day of service forty-five minutes before service (to rest and change, if needed) and be able to meet with Apostle and Bishop as well (prior to service) for information and prayer.

Overnight guest: Should arrive *by 2:00 p.m.* to check in room and be able to rest and be on time. Also remember, a paid-for room unoccupied does *not bless* our ministry.

Any person arriving *over fifteen minutes* late will *not* be *allowed to minister* that service. Please do not be offended and make your travel arrangement to accommodate this.

Musicians' Arrival and Protocol

Musicians are to *arrive forty-five minutes before service to set up any equipment* before service starts and be in place when service starts and throughout service and *should not break down equipment before the benediction is over* (till the end of service). They should bring their own equipment, cords, pedals, and microphones as needed.

We are a *church that uses performance tracks and recorded music* and may not have what you need to accommodate your musicians. So please make sure *everything* your musician needs is supplied by them. *Musicians are to be placed where directed* and not where they want to go. (Please ask musicians to be courteous and to follow the house orders.)

No musician will be allowed to set up after service has begun. No exceptions. Please inform your musicians to adhere to this schedule. We do not want to offend anyone, so we ask you to inform your musicians of this house rule. *Finally, we do not pay musicians to serve in the house of God. If you select to bring a musician, it will be your financial responsibility to financially accommodate them throughout their stay;* this will include food and room.

Hosting Our Keynote Speaker

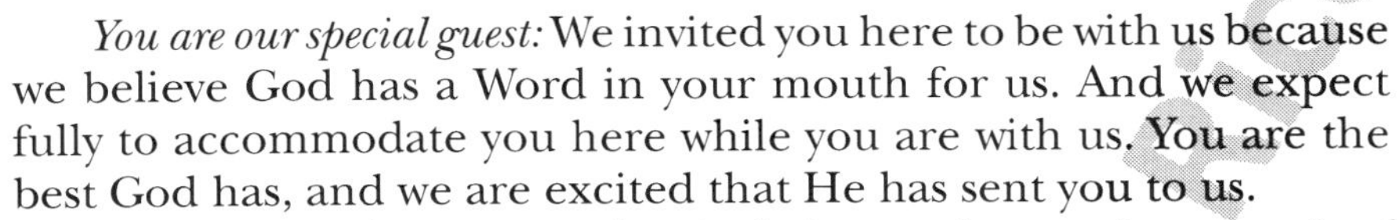
You are our special guest: We invited you here to be with us because we believe God has a Word in your mouth for us. And we expect fully to accommodate you here while you are with us. You are the best God has, and we are excited that He has sent you to us.

Hosting our keynote speaker includes meals, travel, room, local transportation, and some items needed to make your preaching more comfortable while you are with us.

Your guests are your guests: First be mindful that *we have invited you.* You have chosen to bring along others to accompany you. This is great, but *your guests are your responsibility.* If you bring anyone with you, you must take care of their hosting needs.

Eating out and meals

Please let others know when eating out, *we will not pay for their meals. Verbally ask them when ordering to request the server to bring separate checks for them* (so as to not strain the atmosphere). Your meal (only) will be paid for by us.

We prefer to have at least one meal/outing with our guest alone (husband-and-wife team considered as one). As far as outings are concerned, please, however, inform your armor bearers/guests/ and other members/persons that this may happen several times per week if your stay is a weekly one.

Normally, the hotel we will host/accommodate you in will serve some type of *breakfast.* Since revivals and conference time lend more to fasting and prayers, let us know your meal habits.

We provide one dinner meal at 2:00 p.m./2:30 p/m. (and will have you back at the hotel by 4:30 p.m./5:00 p.m.). Or we will pick you up for mealtime as arranged.

At night *a meal will be arranged at your accommodation* as you wish.

Other items provided for your stay:

Purified water (local brand): at room temp and cold, Gatorade/ juice as requested, hot water for *tea*—herbal or regular, *peppermints* (normally red, or by request), *soda* or other drink (by request), towels, and hand sanitizer; for any other request, *please let us know at least forty-eight hours in advance.*

Thank you, from the staff of RMI, GHCC, *Judah Praise,* and Wealthy Place Ministries.

Additional Request concerning children and members

If you have children, please control all children at all times.

Do not allow them in the pulpit or in pastoral areas.

Please escort them (all children) to restroom and other public areas.

Other members are not allowed in pulpit as a general rule of respect, thank you.

Sixth Example of Administrative Protocol

Ministry Protocol on Attire

Ministry Protocol

You may reach Apostle and Bishop Rice before the days of service, up until one hour prior or one hour after service if you need directions/information/instructions or driving directions; *it is best to contact them forty-eight hours prior to service. We do not answer the phone calls close to service times or when we are in preparation and mediation for service.*

Ministry attire for guest ministers of GHCC—please adhere to the house rules.

Men of God: Shirts and ties, please. Rounded collars also accepted. No blue jeans, open shirts, revealing clothing, shorts or tank-top shirts, flip-flops, sandals (open toe), and short pants. *Men* and *women,* if you must take your shoes off, please have some type of footwear on for health and safety reasons (*please*).

Women of God: No pants, short shirts, open blouses that reveal your breast, other revealing clothing, blue jeans, or garments too tight that will distract or not allow you to flow freely in the ministry. Please wear appropriate underwear. Again, *please, no pants for service.*

And have appropriate footwear at all times.

Robes and clergy attire are accepted. There are no color limits or style limits. Hats are *not* required but are accepted if you choose, ladies.

Ladies: ***If you wear pants to the church, you will not be allowed to minister*** (please adhere to this request). Outside the church is fine, but please not in the pulpit.

Armor bearers should dress likewise, appropriate for service. Please, no *tight, revealing clothing,* and they should have limited *pulpit* access. Please make sure they are ready to serve you. If you do not have an armor bearer, our *in-house armor bearer will accommodate your needs.*

Armor bearers should sit where requested by ushers and staff, please. We *do have* assigned seats for armor bearers, and our senior minister will be on hand to assist them.

Do not let the armor bearers sit or stand in the pulpit or allow the armor bearers to take the bishop's or apostle's seat. Thank you!

Seventh Example of Ministerial and Prophetic Protocol

What Is **Not Allowed** at the Harvest

We take ministry seriously. Due *to past experiences,* we find it *necessary to address certain issues* and concerns that past guests have caused to be addressed.

We do not allow married persons to bring other guests of the opposite sex (other than their spouse) and share a room. This includes all activities to be suspicious—*homosexual activity, bisexual activity, and any other ungodly activity. We will not condone or pay for such behavior.*

When you minister for us, please respect the following rules.

- *No parking-lot prophecy:* (1) Prophesying outside the sanctuary *is strictly off limits and outside the covering of the chief apostle is not to be done. When the service is over, it is over.* We believe everything is done decently and in order and leads to fewer problems *after your ministry leaves town;* (2) pulling other persons away from the service to give them a special prophecy and collecting money from them and not letting us know of the transaction by reporting these personal monies (given to you) for such prophecies are not to be done.
- *No fake and ungodly prophecies:* Please keep your prophetic action *pure* and on target. Do *not* ask people questions and then try to prophecy out of what you hear from them. If you have a word, give it. If you don't, move on.
- *No showboating* and *excessively rude or bizarre behavior. No cursing* of any kind will be accepted. The pulpit is not a place for play or unnecessary jesting, joking, or carrying on. Please behave in Jesus's name. Or you will be asked to sit down.
- *Collecting of persons' personal information:* If there is a name or number you need, please let us know. We will make sure you receive it as you have requested. Do not collect personal information from conference attendees.
- *Disrespecting of our leaders,* staff, apostle, and bishop: No disrespect of any kind will be tolerated at the Harvest.

- *Calling persons and having them go by your hotel room* (for any reason): This will not be accepted and leads to trouble every time.

You are here to minister. *This is not a place to have ungodly behavior;* please note that any of the items mentioned above (if noticed) *will cause* your services to us to be cancelled.

* We reserve *the right to cancel* any service at any time for ungodly behavior. Please adhere to the Gospel lifestyle and preaching and *true* prophetic actions, and we will have a joyous time in Jesus!

Eighth Example of Administrative Protocol

Media Ministry and Book Table

Media ministry and service tapings:

All services at GHCC are subject to taping at the discretion of the leadership and staff. Taping that is done and provided at GHCC is the *sole property of GHCC Production* and shall remain as such with all rights and privileges, waiving all speaker rights to profits or proceeds because it is our house and our equipment. We reserve the right to keep the master or/and the first copy. *We will upon request grant you a copy of taped materials to be used as you wish* (if we can provide one to you). *You, as well, may tape your messages and services and have the right to all copies you produce. We request one courtesy copy from you, as well, from all taped services.*

Media book table sales:

First, all products must be counted by our senior minister before book or tape table can be set up.

All merchandise sold within Greater Harvest Services during your stay with us will be tallied up at the end of the night. A *20 percent table—and sale-fee donation* will be requested, and it will become a gift to our building fund ministry.

The senior minister will count again (your products) with you as the table is closed, deduct any items missing, and the 20 *percent* for these sold items (proceeds) will be donated in *cash* for all products sold.

Example	$100 =	$20 donation
	$200 =	$40 donation
	$500 =	$100 donation
	$1,000 =	$200 donation

Please promote your items well, and we will also promote during the service for you; also remember to close book table if you have no one to watch it for you. You will be assessed for all items not recounted at the end of the night. *Or you may pay a $150 vending fee per night and keep all proceeds.*

You may ship items early and provide reshipping packaging and labels. Please speak to Chief Apostle for this information. We will not be responsible for missing or incomplete items. Nor will we open boxes until you are present to confirm order.

We hope this helps you in your media and book table endeavors.

Ninth Example of Administrative Protocol

Flights and Transportation and Accommodation:

Flights: Due to the security issues, *some airline flights may request you to book the flight directly with them.* If this is the case and you book your flight, *we will reimburse you for one round-trip ticket* at an average cost of a normal carrier fee, based on flights price of cheap tickets/ Spirit/JetBlue or other similar reasonable flights.

Please let us agree on cost before purchasing ticket. If you exceed our expected budget for ticket, *we will only reimburse you to our limit.*

Cars: Please keep all gas receipts. *We will reimburse for gas expenditures (not car rentals or rental insurance for your vehicle)* up to the sum of your local ticket for airfare or other transportation, *whichever of the two is the lesser* (airfare or train fare).

Trains: 100 *percent* reimbursement

Hotel Arrangements

Please remember we are inviting you, the gift of God inside of you; if you need others to assist you in your gifts, you must host them and *pay for their expenses to assist you in your* ***Kingdom*** *goals.*

We pay for your room *for you to be in* and have a *peaceful night*; please make sure that *any other (nonspouse or children) guest* should secure a *separate room* for their sleeping needs. Also, please have available your credit card at the time of check in for incidentals and ID purposes. If your card is charged because of a hotel noncash policy or your later arrival, we will reimburse your charges before your stay with us has ended.

Overnight guest: Please be mindful that we will only use God's funds wisely. We will pay for (one) *king-size suite room* for you (you must arrive by 2:00 p.m. for check-in). We do not wish to pay for unused space or time.

If you cannot arrive by that time please let us know. Do not let us pay for a room that you do not occupy. *On your arrival,* we will go to the hotel and meet you and pay in cash for your stay. *You* must provide a credit card for incidentals; we do not pay for any incidentals. Thank you for your ***Kingdom*** consideration and cooperation in these matters.

Information for your guest

Guest (of Speakers)
(This includes all persons who you may invite to travel)

Hello, my beautiful colaborers of the Gospel. I am personally writing this page to you because of "*prophetic unrest*" in this area. We all love to travel and have a ***Kingdom*** good time. However, this "good time" often costs the other ministry; you may travel to extra and unnecessary money.

We at Greater Harvest Christian Center, Archbishop James Rice and I, *invited you to be our guest* and cannot stress this joy enough. However, *the people you invite with you are your guests. And we do not expect to take care of their needs* and expenses in no way, shape, or form.

This is as *blunt as we can put it.* We are saying it this way because of years of going around the bush and our guests not understanding this. We want you to bring as many people as you choose but not to our hurt or extra expense.

- *We do not* expect to feed "family members" who are locals and who decide to "join us for dinner."
- *We do not* expect to feed your armor bearers or traveling *drivers.*
- *We do not* expect to pay for your room and have other people (than your spouse) *taking advantage of our paying* for your accommodation.
- *We do not expect to always have to entertain your guest when we choose to entertain you for lunch or dinner or sightseeing adventures. We really want to spend time with you.* And *speak as "general to general,"* one to another, without "privates" involving themselves.
- Especially, *we do not want to have our personal, private conversations repeated by your guest to our staff.*

As always, this is a touchy subject. *But if we remember who we invited, some of these* light issues will be solved with understanding on both our parts.

In short, make sure your travelers can and do take care of their own financial needs, including giving in the offering, daily expenses, and a "personal room."

____

Thank you for your consideration,
Chief Apostle Rice, your host

Ninth Example of Ministry Protocol

For Emergencies and Cancellations:

Let's face it and be real; those things that come up in life we call emergencies *short of personal and immediate family death are* really *not an emergency.*

As we go in this life, things happen and occurrences will come. *Please be able and willing to complete your assignment as you have taken it as a vow* to our ministry.

Plan ahead for others who may travel with you *to be able to find other ways home in case of their emergency situations.* Let them know you cannot leave because of an emergency in their lives, because you are on assignment.

Other persons—"sick children, ministry issues, or other issues" that may truly come up and may need to be handled by them do not make it an emergency; as far as we are concerned, we have an obligation to the people of the house and to those invited to minister to them. This does not matter how many or how few; we take a covenant and should keep it until the end—period.

When *you agreed to minister for us for a period of time, and we expect you to fulfill your commitment,* never should or will a "suspended child, a sick niece, a hit puppy" become a reason to break a covenant for ministry service.

> Because of this, our policy is firm; *if you refuse to complete your assignment for any reason* (other than [verifiable] immediate family death), *you will not be paid* for any part of your services, in any form, or for travel expenses or for days of service already rendered. You will get ZERO from us because of the inconveniences it will cause and has caused to our ministry. *Please be advised of this before you come or invite others to go with you.*

If you are having issues before you arrive that may cause you not to complete your service, please let us know in advance, and we will try to reschedule you (as we all may have challenges at some point or another).

We must also address and let it be known **that *if we have to ask you to leave* for inappropriate behavior (addressed in this handbook) or otherwise noted, you will be *paid for the services you have rendered up to date* and nothing else.**

You do not have the right to cancel our services, **meetings, conferences for any reason** *(e.g., attendance, money, or people).*

You are our guest. If "*God speaks*" to any of us to cancel, *it will probably be us, first.* Please keep this in mind and do a great job for Jesus and us.

Tenth Example of Ministry Protocol

For Emergencies and Cancellations:

Prophetic Liberties:

- Please *do not receive personal numbers of guests/members of the conference.* (If you need a number of a guest, *please request* it from the apostle or bishop.)
- Please, no cursing in the pulpit in any form.
- Please do not overstep your prophetic boundaries.
- Please do not "question persons" **when prophesying**! If you have a word, by all means give it. However, please *do not* "*ask a question*" to persons and then attempt to make it a prophecy.
- If you have a word of **"rebuke for an elder" or above (especially the bishop or apostle), you must** hold the word and release it in a private setting. Our leaders *will not be rebuked in public; any attempt to do so or to throw off on our leaders will lead to an immediate interruption and ending of your service.*
- You will not display ungodly antics in the pulpit.
- *Please instruct your armor bearers to "give" in the service and be attentive*; they will stay in their places at all times and will be "givers" to the service (financially and to your personal care). It is hard to *ask others* to believe in your ministry and give when the *people you bring do not give themselves.*
- If you have "*issues*" *with women* ministers, **please don't come and don't throw off on women or men of the Gospel for any reason.**
- *Turn your cell phone off before service.*

DO NOT ANSWER YOUR CELL PHONE IN CHURCH FOR ANY REASON!

FINANCIAL POLICIES AND EXPECTATIONS

- Be *on time to all services* as agreed at your arrival time.
- Expect to give *God no less than your best,* regardless of who is in service.
- If you are going for the "*numbers*" *of people* in service who may or may not attend, this assignment may not be right for you. We purpose to move in quality, not quantity, and believe God sends whom he wants to attend any given service—maybe God sends three, maybe three thousand, maybe thirty thousand, but we minister to five just

the same as we do with five thousand. We cannot guarantee you funds or people. But we *will guarantee you that we will be fair.*

Normally our split is 50/50 after expenses.

This 50/50 split is based on attendance, your guest givings as well as ours, and the actual prophetic expenses. Travel, hotel, food, and advertising are considered expenses and will be deducted before the split either daily, weekly.

Remember, it is also based on **you** raising the offering or calling for the offering and your effort or influence with the giving of the people. (A workman is worthy of his hire and double honor for those who labor well.)

Offerings NOT taken by you will not be divided on this basis and will remain totally in-house.

Checks felt to be of no value will not be counted into the tally UNTIL CLEARED! Having said this, 50 percent of checks will be counted as delayed or denied funds and will not included in the tally (credit card payments will be released with approval),and will follow the same count policy.

All offerings will be counted by two parties or more; you or your staff person are welcome to attend this counting or your personal designee. However, monies will be given directly only to you!

If there are any changes to our standard policy, we will inform you otherwise this is our policy concerning the offering.

Do not give others money or promise them any money from us just because they approach you with a "hard-luck story." We did not or do not send anyone to you to request money. Please refer all these persons back to us. Thank you.

Eleventh Example of Administrative Protocol

Verifications and Confirmations of hotel and rooms

Your room has been scheduled at the hotel ____________________

____

Confirmation #: ____________________________________
Type of room requested for your stay: ________________
Hotel location:
Hotel phone number:
Our phone number: 954-603-7729 or Emergency # 954-483-8617
Conference locations: ______________________________

____

Estimated time of your arrival has been agreed upon as _________.

We will pay for your room for _____ days (the days you are scheduled to minister only). These days are __________, the actual conference dates are __________, ending on__________.

Please arrive at check-in (on) time. All early arrivals (persons choosing to go in prior to their service times) to attend the conference as a supporting guest, persons *staying over for additional days that you are not schedule to minister on, as well as late checkout times, will be your totally to pay for, especially at your own request (if not preapproved by the administration staff).* These times and stays *will be your total responsibility.* You, as our guest, *are covered for the night (s) that you actually preach on. These nights and these nights alone will be our responsibility; all other nights will be your total responsibility.*

Please note that any and all incidental coverage will also be your responsibility.

Unauthorized restaurant charges are also your responsibility.

Please have a credit card ready at check-in to cover these items.

Thank you for your gracious service.

Twelfth Example of Administrative Protocol

For Booking our Apostle and Bishop:

Personal booking information for our Bishop and *Apostle is* ***Simple***

When booking us for travel, we will abide by these same principles, unless otherwise instructed by you, our host. We welcome return invitations and hope to forge a lasting Christian relationship and ***Kingdom*** connection.

Please contact us *at 954-603-7729* for booking information. You may book *Archbishop James Rice or Chief Apostle J. G. Rice for separate venues or together as a team to go and minister for you* to conduct conferences, revivals, workshops, seminars, retreats, empowerment camps, and/or other events.

Finally, again welcome to the Harvest. If there is anything not addressed or clear in this guidebook, you may feel free to contact our office at 954-603-7729.

Also visit the following:

http://www.greaterharvestworldwide.com/
or
jrrj57@yahoo.com

We look forward to having you serve here with us in our upcoming conference. And the pleasure is truly ours.

Anything addressed in this section is from our *ministerial experience and no reflection on your integrity or personal ministry standards. Please do not take it as an insult but as clear communications to our ministry needs, for in all our getting we seek understanding and good fellowship.*

In fact, we hope it is a blessing to you. Many of these excerpts are taken out of my book *Prophetic Protocol—Serving God's Admirals and Generals of the Gospel.*

If you desire a copy, contact me. *The book will be released in March 2012.*

We are here to help you in your "prophetic connection." If you need us, please feel free to contact us to host/or minister in your next conference or event. What you make happen for others, God will do for you, so let's make it happen in Jesus's name!

Do not tell persons *to join or leave this ministry.* This is out of order, and it is the order of the *house leadership* to do.

- Finally, be aware that our leaders, staff, and members *have reviewed* this handbook as well and will entreat you as such. *If you are out of order or ask them to do anything out of order, they will not comply with you* and will immediately notify their shepherds of the incident at hand. Do not think them rude; they are obeying the order of the house and should be respected for their *loyalty.*

Again, thank you as you travel across this globe. May God continue to walk and talk with you in Jesus's name. Shalom, shalom.

About Our Author

Author and Chief Apostle Dr. J. G. Rice

Contributor Bishop James R. Rice II

Dr. J. GraceLyn Rice CEO's Ministries include the following:

Judah Praise Ministry and *Women of Worship Power Team*
InterGlobal Association of Christian Churches Worldwide (Inc.)
Greater Harvest Christian Center Churches Worldwide
Rice Ministries International and
InterGlobal Marketing Ministries and Services
Circle '59—A World against Domestic and Mental Abuse (AWADAMA)
Circle of Power—A Ministry of Financial Increase and Investments for the Future

Chief Apostle Dr. J. G. Rice is the founding pastor of the Greater Harvest Christian Center Churches Worldwide (Inc.), which was founded in the year 1992. After Dr. Whiting-Rice served in the evangelism field for eight years and as a local minister for four years, she was consecrated in the year 2004 as a chief apostle in the city of Columbia, South Carolina, where she served most of her junior and senior ministerial services. Chief Apostle Rice is the elected and appointed (2009-2015) chiefapostle to the InterGlobal Association of Christian Churches Worldwide and works daily to ensure global unity and pastoral networking to the fivefold ministry and to the body of Christ. Chief Apostle also serves as CEO of Rice Ministries International. *This dynamic woman of the Cross* is a noted soloist, psalmist, and sought-after revivalist with the gift of taking the body of Christ through exhortation and worship directly into the throne room of God.

Through keynote conferences, seminars, teachings, and preaching, Apostle says she is always a pastor because of her love for God's people. *Apostle J. G. (Whiting) Rice is determined to speak a spirit of perfection into the hearts of the doers of God's Word.* God has graced Dr. Rice with a "shepherd's spirit" and has anointed her to be a *true spiritual general* in the army of God. She is gifted to speak clearly and frankly, giving directions on growth, stability, and excellence. *Dr. Rice believes that God has given us all the measure "to prosper and be in good health even as our souls prosper." She is a known mother of the Gospel and believes in the prophetic revelation in a rhema-enduring and practical delivery.*

Educational Overview

Educated in the public schools of South Carolina, she graduated from Dreher High School in 1981 and later returned to school and received an AA in criminal justice (Midlands Tech, 1989). She received her undergraduate degree from USC in 1995 in biblical studies, her master's from International Overcoming School of

Religion in physiotherapy/business administration in 1999, and a doctorate of divinity from the International School of Religion (Virginia, 2000).

Dr. Rice is also a certified Christian Council-World Council of Global Education (2001), a member of the SC Association of Nonprofit (2000,) and a certified HUD housing counselor (2005). She also attended the Billy Graham School of Evangelism (in 1994). She is a registered property manager in the state of South Carolina (1989), a certified hospice volunteer (1994), and a certified youth mentor trainer (1999). Dr. Rice also was the director for disaster relief (1999-2009). She is a well-rounded person spiritually, educationally, communally, and socially.

Younger Years

Born to Mr. and Mrs. Calvin Moore (James Hudson and Rosa Lee Lott) and raised in Columbia, South Carolina (Cayce for church), she is truly a Southern girl who loves to cook and eat the good things of God. She was raised in a Baptist faith church in Cayce. Her parents were involved in midweek Bible study and prayer meeting, which taught her not to be moved by the crowds. ("Just do what the Lord has for you to do," which is what her aunt would say when no one else but they, her family, showed up for many nights of church prayer meeting.)

She grew up in the BTW and YPA meetings and was gifted in devotional services, which taught her to stand alone and "sing loud." "Close your eyes if you have to, little girl. You can do it 'cause you got it in you," said her deacon. Deacon Owens taught her to love to "raise the hymns." He was her first Christian mentor in the singing ministry. Her deacon taught her boldness and to sing strong when others laughed at her.

Apostle always loved the older people. She says, "They have a lot to leave behind. It might as well be left with me."

She was raised in a faithful Baptist church until she moved to her own. Then she started attending the Holiness Church, where God filled her with the Holy Spirit under the ministry of Pastor Allen D. Williams, Full Gospel Ministry (Columbia, South Carolina). She was trained in the young years of ministry there at Full Gospel in prayer, ushering, choir (youth choir) directorship, and spiritual obedience. There she grew and learned who God was; she was taught to study God's Word. She stayed with Full Gospel for three years until the call of God got so strong that she had to leave to move forward in her journey. She began to work with Pastor Brown as a choir director, and God began to develop her as a minister. It was here she did her first official pulpit sermons.

Ministry years

She was first licensed in 1984 under Spirit and Truth Ministries (as a missionary evangelist) and ordained as a minister in 1988 under Pastor Alma Joe Brown (West Columbia, South Carolina). From 1984-88, she served as a community evangelist/lay pastor meeting in Greenview Gym (many, many souls were saved). In 1988, she was called into the pastorate under the voice of Apostle Wayne Clapp of Greenville, North Carolina, who also laid hands on her and sent her forth. Later, a conclave of fivefold ministers under the director of Apostle Clapp (who served as her set apostle until 1998) laid hands on her at the opening of Greater Harvest Christian Center in June 1992. She was then declared a prophet and began to work in the prophetic openly. Apostle served faithfully (as a pastor until the year 2000). Then she temporarily went into the AME Assembly, where she also holds a license for ministry from the AME Church (2000). Under Pastor Ronald Bradsford in the AME Church, she also served as a community evangelist, women's minister in the prophetic, psalmist, and a prayer leader in the church and in the evangelistic fields. During this time, God lay upon her heart to help other churches establish praise-and-worship teams, which she has continued to do year after year. After much prayer, Greater Harvest Christian Center was reopened in June 2000 under the leadership of Bishop Rice and herself. *During this time, God blessed the union of Archbishop James Rice and Dr. J. G. Rice, who were united in marriage in December 2000.*

In the year 2003, God called Apostle to the apostolic ministry after serving as a prophet, conference revivalist, pastor, evangelist, and a ministry coach and "birther" of many others in the ministry, finally.

She accepted her call to the nation as an apostle under the conclave of apostles, in June 2004, led by Chief Apostle Johnnie L. Clark of Rehoboth United Assemblies, Columbia, South Carolina, and assisted by Apostle Wayne Clapp (Intergrowth Ministries, Greensboro, North Carolina) and a host conclave of apostles, bishops pastors, elders, ministers, prophets and other fivefold gifts, lay ministers, member friends, and loved ones. Apostle J. G. Rice was consecrated, anointed, dressed and robed, and given her apostolic swords, keys, bells, and staff. She was also enthroned into the office and seated in a wonderful service held on the campus of Columbia International University in their auditorium. After a twenty-four-hour prayer and watch service, this woman of God was charged to the office of the *apostle.*

In the year 2009 *she was elected and seated to the office of chief apostle* by the InterGlobal Association of Christian Churches Worldwide in the South Florida district to serve the association interglobally. Humbled by all this, you will still find Chief Apostle at the helm of praise and worship and intercessory prayer, leading others in their deliverance and often ministering on the daily prayer line. *She is a humble woman of power* and teaching, with a prophetic preaching voice that will encourage you and push you into your ***Kingdom*** destinies. Chief Apostle is full of love of God, and it shows. Her favorite scripture is *"I am just the voice of one crying in the wilderness, prepare ye the way of the Lord."*

Chief Apostle Rice, under the covenant of Lift Him Up Ministries Inc. and Greater Harvest Rice Ministries International-Global, and InterGlobal, she reigns, administrates, authors, directs, and governs several (over twenty) combined yet separate ministry works *that she has birthed, founded, or formed,* including Those Preaching Women, USA Clergy Association, Joshua Generation National Youth Ministry, Sisterhood Alive! Support Ministry, Wilderness Voice Newsletter, her personal praise team, Touch of Glory, Nehemiah Family Services, Nothing But the Praise Annual Celebration, and the Annual Conference and Celebration Team as well as the National Phenomenal Woman (P-31) Conference, and Circle 59.

She has been presented on several television stations, including Atlanta Live, Dove Broadcasting, and TBN affiliates. She has hosted her own local daily TV show (*Heart to Heart*). *She has been featured on many radio shows* including Christian (daily shows and weekly shows), gospel regain shows, and other radio talk shows. She has had the highest ratings on many of her radio shows on several radio stations and talk shows around the nation. Dr. Rice, *also known as the master prophet,* on (many of her) radio shows (and Bishop Rice as "the Eagle Prophet") is a *proven accurate mouthpiece from the area of God—a true prophet*—and is loved for her candor and clarity of speaking the truth unto growth and perfection.

She is also known as a *motivational speaker extraordinaire.* Dr. Rice's love for people is evident in her words and deeds—serving those in distress and need, forming and operating in several groups dealing with natural disaster. Her heart and education are also turned toward women of domestic violence, and she tries to educate and empower them with the hope that they need to *fly*! Circle 59 is her new group "formed to expose that every sixty seconds, a woman endures some type of domestic violence and that we need to stop it on the *fifty-ninth second,* before the sixty-second mark."

She is the wife of Archbishop James Rice, whom she loves, respects, adores, and knows God sent him to her. She is the biological mother of three gifted, talented, and dedicated-to-God's-***Kingdom*** kids and the spiritual stepmother and godmother, mentor, pastor, coach, and apostle to the nation. Bishop and Apostle, now grandparents of eight, were both born in Columbia, South Carolina, and now live in South Florida. They pastor the South Florida GHCC Church.

Dr. Rice has traveled as an evangelist throughout the United States, *Canada, Bahamas, Jamaica, Africa,* and is slated to travel to minister in *India, Australia, Brazil, China,* and *Alaska* to run revivals for *Jesus.*

She has earned many other degrees and certifications and believes that education does not stop. When you stop learning, then you die; so she is always in classes and schools, teaching what she learns.

She is a life-changing conference speaker, revivalist, workshop host, and an all-around mentor, coach, and covering to the body of Christ. Apostle believes in ***Kingdom*** *living and* ***Kingdom*** *protocol,* and these two things operating in your life will bring a ***Kingdom*** blessing that will manifest here on earth.

This is *a true voice that must be heard* in every nation, every city, every town, every house; every ear must hear what the Spirit has to say through this Teachings, Preaching, Prophetic, Apostolic gift to he Body of Christ. Chief Apostle Dr. J. G. Rice

Her favorite verse comes out of St. John 1:23 . . . she says of herself also, *"I am just the voice of once crying in the wilderness. Prepare the way of the Lord, our King."*

Our chief apostle, Dr. J. G. Rice.

Chief Apostle's Husband
Archbishop James R. Rice II CFO

The son of a preacher man (the late Elder James R. Rice Sr.) and a vibrant preacher woman, Bishop Doris C. Rice. Born a third-generation minister, Bishop Rice has successfully matriculated to become a giant of a man of the Word of God in his own right. Bishop Rice II is the executive director of the Referral Network and cohost of the Circle of Power Conferences.

*He is a true man of God, a television producer, a business administrator, a workshop and conference orator, and a seasoned motivational speaker. He specializes in financial freedom and the ministry of wealth and prosperity. He is the author of several DVD books and teachings. His ministry will enlighten you on proper **Kingdom** finances and overall well-being. Bishop Rice holds a degree in business administration and a doctorate of ministry and is the editor in chief of all production, global, and TV Ministries. The presiding prelate of the Greater Harvest Christian Center Churches Worldwide and second chair to the bishops' conclave in the InterGlobal Association of Christian Churches Worldwide, Bishop Rice is an awesome orator and teacher of God's Word, a fiery preacher, and a top-notch husband, father, and faithful supporter of the Word of the **Kingdom**.*

The Rices believe in the "five-level impact of practical empowerment" that creates balance. Married to the dynamic Chief Apostle Dr. J. G. Rice, their ministry is evident of these teachings, affecting you "physically, mentally, emotionally, spiritually, and financially." These teachings will bless you and your family for years to come. And by all means, don't wait! Join them at their next empowerment conference, revival, summit, or any other life-changing conference.

Other *Kingdom* Teaching and Available Workshops

Booking Information for Dr. J. G. Rice

Call today for more information.
954-603-7729
or e-mail
chiefapostlerice@yahoo.com

Other Products Available

Books (B) Books Tapes (T) Tapes DVD (D) DVD CD (C) CD

(B) *Credit Correction Manual:* Correct your own credit and regain your financial power ($49).

(B) *Getting the Devil out of Your Life:* A manual to help you stay delivered and in touch with eliminating demonic activities in your life ($29.99).

(B) *Burgundy Hair and Purple Lipstick:* A parents' survival guide to raising temperamental children ($29.99).

(D) *Are You Getting Any Better?* A DVD sermon featuring *Dr. Rice*—a passionate message about spiritual growth and improvement ($10.00).

(D) *Becoming Fruitful:* A DVD sermon by Bishop Rice with instructions on how to become the fruitful vine God has commanded you to be. "Are you cut off from the vine, or are you fruitful?" ($10.00)

(D) *Becoming a "Mustard Tree":* God wants us to pass mustard-seed faith and gain the strength to become a mustard tree. You can learn how from this passionate DVD of teaching and preaching by Dr. Rice ($10.00).

To get a complete product list, call 954-603-7729

Kingdom Principles and _Kingdom_ Fruit
Other _Kingdom_ Teachings (Motivated by the _Kingdom_ Living)

Greater Harvest Christian Center
Other _Kingdom_ Principles and _Kingdom_ Fruit

Conference Teachings
Workshops and Seminars
By Dr. J. G. Rice

Kingdom *Principles Brings the Peace of God*

"From Churchdom to Kingdom"

Establishing the Mind-Set of **Kingdom** *Living*

CDs $10.00

Kingdom ***Principles***

Kingdom *law*
Kingdom *principles*
Kingdom *mind-set*
Kingdom *living*
Kingdom *covenant*
Kingdom *prosperity*
Kingdom *"fruit"*
Kingdom *wealth*
Kingdom *riches* and *success giving*
Kingdom *wholeness: spiritually, mentally, emotionally, and financially*
Kingdom *God-o-nomics*
Kingdom *families*
Kingdom *citizens*
Kingdom *kings (Sons)*

Other "***Kingdom***" Teachings and Workshops

CDs (Order Today) $10.00

<u>Kingdom</u> *Fruit Session*
Fruit of the Spirit
Fruit of Righteousness
Fruit of Vision
Fruit of Divine Destiny
Fruit of Increase
Fruit of the Harvest
Fruit of Educational Learning
Fruit of Concepts
Fruit of Prosperity
Fruit of Repentance
Fruit of God's Favor
Fruit of Evangelism
Fruit of "the Yielding" Good Fruit
Fruit of Maximum Impact
Fruit of Wisdom, Knowledge, and Understanding
Fruit of Righteousness
Fruit of Godliness
Fruit of Holiness
Fruit of Happiness

BOOK OVERVIEW

It's All about the ***Kingdom***

Godly Steps and Instructions for Successful ***Kingdom*** Living

(Apostolic, Spiritual, and ***Kingdom*** Protocol for Fivefold Leaders, Ministers, and Laypersons)

Session I (I-III)

This book will refresh you, challenge you, and compel you to become a better ***Kingdom*** citizen.

Dr. Rice puts thirty-eight years of her spiritual journey into teaching apostolic protocol to the ***Kingdom*** of God, providing godly steps and protocol for successful ***Kingdom*** living.

Chief Apostle addresses everything *with* apostolic clarity and directions from financial operation in ministry to fivefold ministry information—directions to the fivefold to child rearing and ***Kingdom*** protocol for the everyday ***Kingdom*** citizen—a must-have "weapon of spiritual warfare" and "spiritual coaching guide" for all ministers, teachers, counselors, and spiritual parents of the ***Kingdom***. This book (session I) has something for everyone, no matter their level in the ***Kingdom***, a must-have guidebook to ***Kingdom*** training and development. *Questions answered*! Directions given and order established. We all need order, spiritual parentage, and godly directions. Apostolic protocol—establishes this order—a must-have ***Kingdom*** training and direction tool.

Use the book to gain tools and godly steps in protocol for successful ***Kingdom*** living.

Learn ***Kingdom*** principles and godly steps:

How to grow in the ***Kingdom*** mind-set.
To spiritually assess your growth.
To turn your plain church lifestyle into a "***Kingdom*** life" in twenty-one days.
To become a true fivefold minister in the apostolic order.
Learn about the spiritual patrols in your life and spiritual-protocol officer.
Learn what it takes to raise your children as ***Kingdom*** citizens with ***Kingdom*** blessings.

Chart your ministry progress. Are you really growing in Christ?
Establish ***Kingdom*** protocol in your life.
Enhance your daily obedience to ***Kingdom*** direction.

Find your place in the ***Kingdom*** and finally gain ***Kingdom*** access to your financial blessings and ***Kingdom*** wealth.

Use the *workbook* section to enhance your personal growth and understanding of ***Kingdom*** order and biblical protocol.

Take yourself to school and enhance your knowledge of ***Kingdom*** order.

What every ***Kingdom*** citizen should know: "a basic ***Kingdom*** constitution."

Two hundred answers every ***Kingdom*** citizen (Christian) should know!

- ✓ Eighty-nine Principles to ***Kingdom*** Success
    - (A practical application section) To help you grow in your walk with Christ and in ***Kingdom*** living.

- ✓ How to be an armor bearer and take on the ***Kingdom*** assignment and the vision of the house.
- ✓ Pastoral insight for inviting others to ministry, protocol of administration, and financial operations.

There is something for everyone in *It's All about the* ***Kingdom***, and we all will be *enriched, trained, and elevated* as we read this book. We can truly say it is *not just a book, but it is a training manual, a reference library, and a practical application guide* that will help us all grow; and we will refer to it over and over for years to come. I eagerly await section 2. I know it will take me into even deeper *apostolic directions and prophetic revelation.*

Many of my questions were answered, and now I know how to do it the right way.

Endorsements

This is a great resource and an eye-opener for me. Even after pastoring for thirty years, I learned more in this book than I had learned in twenty books put together.

Let God bless Chief Apostle Rice as she continues to bless the ***Kingdom*** *citizens with her training information, revelations, knowledge, wisdom, and* ***Kingdom*** *truths.*

Only a real walk with God (the King) can produce this type of fruit. And having this book has caused more fruit in my life and ministry. It is *clear, easy to understand, and easy to follow.*

I am now teaching this book in Bible class for all fivefold ministers, prophets, and leaders. My members have also been requested to read this book because of the personal, practical application, and workshop information section and to teach it in their Sunday-school classes. Wow! What a book!

It's All about the ***Kingdom****:*
Godly Steps and Instructions for Successful ***Kingdom*** *Living*. will open your eyes, heart, and order your steps in Christ as you too
set it in order!

Apostolic, Spiritual, and *Kingdom* Protocol for Fivefold Leaders, Ministers, and Laypersons

Index

D

E

F

G

H

I

J

K

L

S

T

U

W

Made in the USA
Lexington, KY
03 March 2012